Nature and liberty

Nature and liberty

John Zvesper

Routledge
Taylor & Francis Group

LONDON AND NEW YORK

First published 1993
by Routledge
2 Park Square, Milton Park, Abingdon, Oxfordshire OX14 4RN

Simultaneously published in the USA and Canada
by Routledge
711 Third Avenue, New York, NY 10017

First issued in paperback 2015

Routledge is an imprint of the Taylor and Francis Group, an informa business

© 1993 J. Zvesper

Typeset in Bembo by LaserScript Limited, Mitcham, Surrey

British Library Cataloguing in Publication Data

A catalogue record for this book is available from the British Library.

Library of Congress Cataloging-in-Publication Data

Zvesper, John, 1948–
    Nature and liberty / John Zvesper.
    p.   cm.
    Includes bibliographical references and index.
ISBN 0–415–08923–9
    1. Liberty.   2. Libertarianism.   3. Individualism.   4. Collectivism.
    5. Natural law.   I. Title.
JC585.Z86   1993
    323.44—dc20

92–19908
CIP

Cover illustration: *The Round Tower* by G.B. Piranesi courtesy of the
Courtauld Institute Galleries, London
Cover design: Richard Earney

Publisher's Note
The publisher has gone to great lengths to ensure the quality of this reprint
but points out that some imperfections in the original may be apparent

ISBN 13: 978-0-415-75612-9 (pbk)
ISBN 13: 978-0-415-08923-4 (hbk)

Contents

Chapter 1

Introduction

What shall it profit a political regime if it shall gain the whole world, and lose its own soul? The practical prospects for liberal democracy seem to have brightened during the last quarter of the twentieth century. Along with a growing number of liberal democratic regimes, there has been a resurgence of interest in liberal political theory: in classrooms, thinktanks and political conventions liberal democracy is being studied more seriously, while alternative regimes are being subjected to more sceptical scrutiny. However, it is not clear that this greater attention to liberal democracy has yet resulted in greater understanding of it. This failure of liberal thinking to keep pace with the practical advances of liberalism is troubling, because defeat on the battlefield was perhaps always a less deadly danger than the loss of self-understanding. Even if the danger of defeat in battle has passed, that underlying danger remains. (It could even be argued that the external threats to liberal democracy in the twentieth century have been in a way a product of this internal weakness, in so far as those threats have come from illiberal regimes based on critiques of liberalism, regimes and critiques that have prospered in an atmosphere of liberal self-doubts.)

The continuing weaknesses of liberal democratic theory have had important practical consequences. The primary argument of this book is that the root of many of the practical problems in liberal polities is the tendency of liberal politics either to degenerate into a set of beliefs and practices that are extremely individualistic and antipolitical, or to embrace doctrines and policies that are extremely anti-individualistic and community oriented. Modern liberal politics, in theory and in practice, oscillates between individualistic and communitarian extremes. The first part of this book (Chapters 2 to 4) shows how and why liberals have found it difficult to avoid these extremes in important areas of political practice, and the second part (Chapters 5 and 6) shows how and why the same difficulty has afflicted liberal political theory.

Of course, maintaining the proper mixture of individuality and communality, of plurality and unity, of private and public, is a classic problem of politics, visible long before modern liberal politics appeared. The argument that healthy politics requires such a mixture goes back in the records of human thought at least as far as the second book of Aristotle's *Politics*, in which he criticizes Plato's Socrates for seeking too much unity in the regime described in the *Republic*. However, my argument is that this problem of properly mixing plurality and unity has been particularly difficult for modern liberal politics, for two reasons. The first reason is that the basic liberal doctrine of the separation of state and society has been misunderstood and misapplied. The second and more fundamental reason is that modern liberalism has developed a bad case of *physiphobia* – an unreasonable fear of nature as a guide to human life and politics. Both of these reasons will be explored and explained by means of concrete examples in the following chapters. Here, by way of introduction, I describe them briefly and abstractly.

STATE AND SOCIETY

One of the classic liberal political strategies, going back as far as the beginnings of modern liberalism in the seventeenth century, is to try to reduce the scope of politics, by separating state and society. Doctrinaire pursuit of this strategy can easily lead to a simplistic liberalism, in which facile formulas replace continuing thinking about the ends of political action. This individualistic, libertarian tendency is evident not only in the dogmatic positions of some conservative liberals on the question of the proper relations between polity and economy, but also in the equally simplistic positions of some progressive liberals on matters of religion, morality, ethnicity, family and sex. The temptation to make absolute either economic freedom or cultural freedom (or both) seems a natural development of the liberal strategy of separating the public sphere and the private sphere. But to give in to this temptation is to ignore the intricacy of liberal politics, which, properly appreciated, does not permit such political indifference. Building an impenetrable 'wall of separation' between state and economy, or between state and society, is not only (as critics of liberalism charge) hopelessly unrealistic but also (as liberals themselves too often forget) quite wrongheaded. The liberal separation of public and private is not absolute. It is an attempt to ensure that both public goods and private goods are cultivated, in their separate but related places. It is a means to this end, not an end in itself, and (like any means) it cannot be applied without attention to circumstances and consequences. In order to draw the line – and to bridge the gap – between public and private, liberal politics demands delicate economic and moral judgement, not indifference. The libertarian tendency generally underrates the potential of liberalism, asks too little from politics and seeks too little political unity, deferring too much to human individuality. It does this very often because it overestimates the danger of conflict in a world in which politics has not been neutralized by separating it from controversial questions.

An opposite, communalistic or social unitarian tendency tries to avoid the occasion for conflict not by keeping the contenders separate, but by abolishing their differences. This tendency asks too much from politics and seeks too much political unity, deferring too little to human individuality. This tendency can be inspired by a reaction against the libertarian tendency, but it can also be a rebellion against the earth-bound, bourgeois aspect of liberal politics even in its more sensible forms. Even if liberalism avoids economic and moral indifference, it may seem economically and morally unambitious, too easily satisfied with the imperfections of justice that are entailed by private property and family, or too unaspiring because of its cultivation of the virtues of peace and private prosperity rather than those of fraternity and grandeur. Some conservatives reject liberalism because of this pedestrian morality. Social unitarian liberals share the conservative conviction that liberals aim too low, but instead of rejecting liberalism they try to redefine it, to make moral personality and 'self' development rather than peace and prosperity the goals of liberal politics. From the liberal point of view – as opposed to the libertarian one – the trouble with this tendency is not that it is moralistic, but that its morality is weak and its politics illiberal. By trying to make freedom and autonomy the whole substance rather than the conditions of morality, it moralizes without wishing or being able to say much about what moral humans might do with themselves. This would be bad enough if it were restricted to the private sphere. But by bringing this apparently aspiring but empty and illusory goal to the centre of politics, it must also risk causing serious political disappointments, discouraging liberals and drawing them away from politics.

LIBERAL PHYSIPHOBIA

These two extreme tendencies of individualism and communalism may be intrinsic to liberal politics, because of difficulties and inevitable oversimplifications of the liberal strategy of separating state and society, to distinguish political from economic and cultural power. However, there is a second reason why liberal politics now finds it difficult to mix plurality and unity, which explains why the twin tendencies of hyperindividualism and hypercommunalism are more pronounced in our day. That reason is the fact that both in practice and in theory liberals now generally refuse to base their politics on natural standards. The greatest change in modern liberal thinking between its troubled but confident beginnings in the seventeenth century and its less confident and more confused state in the twentieth century is its abandonment of nature as a source of ethical and political guidance. Modern liberals suffer from an advanced case of *physiphobia*, an unreasonable fear of nature. The question of natural standards for liberal politics has almost everywhere become a closed question. In this book I try to help reopen it, and to suggest that liberal politics must pay attention to what human beings are naturally like, and how, therefore, it is naturally right for them to treat themselves and each other. This question of natural right is not a question that needs to be raised directly in every political context, but to rule it out is disastrous, for that destroys the basis of liberal politics. Liberals do not need a theory of natural right that prescribes in detail actions or virtues for anyone and everyone in all circumstances; but neither do they need an antinatural liberal theory that rules out judgements of what is by nature right, based on insights into what is by nature human.

It is principally this great change in modern liberal thinking – its abandonment of nature – that accounts for the greater susceptibility of later liberalism to communalistic and individualistic extremes. If we neglect human nature, we are more apt to succumb to temptations to think of ourselves as totally encumbered creatures of communities, or as totally free, unencumbered, individual selves. When stated so baldly, this seems so obvious that you may well ask why it ever occurred to anyone that liberal politics should be cut free from natural standards, so I am also concerned to explain why the abandonment of nature appeared necessary or prudent. However necessary or prudent this move has appeared to be, I try to show how, sooner or later, it has undermined the kind of thinking that enables liberals to resist their self-destructive extreme tendencies.

Liberals today typically tend to adopt one of two views: either that nature is a wholly negative standard or that it is an altogether dispensable standard for political life. The first view accords with the libertarian tendency: if it is true that nature provides only negative standards (things to be avoided – chiefly death), once the opponents of this view (chiefly religions) are driven from the field, it is difficult to avoid the conclusion that government is only a necessary evil, so the less of it the better. The second view shares with the first the belief that nature offers only negative standards, and goes on to conclude that therefore nature offers no real standards for human life. This leads to the communalistic tendency: if nature provides no standards, social life must be a free construction by humans themselves – an intersubjective, wholly conventional project, which may be more or less rational, but may not strictly speaking appeal to trans-social, natural standards. Our modern dogmatic scepticism – our denial of the possibility of knowing anything significant about the natural human form and ends – thus leads to a manic depressive liberalism: at one extreme, a libertarianism that denies the claims of human communities on individuals; at the other, an empty but nevertheless demanding moral absolutism, denying claims of individual human beings on their communities. At the first extreme we find facts without values; at the second, values without facts.

A revealing recapitulation of this modern liberal dilemma can be found in Francis Fukuyama's recent reflections on *The End of History and the Last Man*. In this fascinating work, Fukuyama begins by acknowledging the power of economic liberalism in the modern world, but he urges his readers to accept a psychologically broader explanation and justification for modern liberal democracy, by moving beyond the standard liberalism based on a negative, economistic, Lockean viewpoint, to embrace a Hegelian liberalism that takes into account the importance of the trans-economic, psychic ('thymotic') satisfactions that human beings seek in their 'struggle for recognition'. Fukuyama argues plausibly that liberal democracy is psychologically better grounded if it is understood to provide scope for 'rational recognition' (as well as for the odd bit of irrational spiritedness). But he also admits that this Hegelian defence of liberal politics remains open to a nihilistic, Nietzschean inter-pretation, because that defence is based on a historicist understanding of humans as rational and free but essentially antinatural beings:

'Hegel . . . believed that in his most essential characteristics man was *undetermined* and therefore free to create his own nature'.[1] Fukuyama agrees with Hegel: 'human nature' is at most 'a structure within which man's self-creation occurs'.[2] 'The distinction between human and non-human is based', therefore, 'on the radical disjunction between the realm of nature and the realm of freedom'.[3] It follows that the legitimacy of the state rests not on nature but on 'a public debate in which the citizens of the state agree amongst one another on the explicit terms under which they will live together'.[4] Political life is founded on agreement, not on truth: convention, not nature. Fukuyama is no moral extremist; nevertheless, in his presentation of the course of modernity, we are offered two extreme alternative understandings of human beings: we are (in the standard Lockean account) naturally defined but individualistic, apolitical beings, or (in the allegedly more satisfactory Hegelian account) we are essentially unnatural and communally defined creatures. This is not a very promising basis for understanding or defending liberal democracy. In the end, Fukuyama himself points out that liberal democracy understood in this way remains endangered by the fact that 'modern thought has arrived at an impasse, unable to come to a consensus on what constitutes man and his specific dignity, and consequently unable to define the rights of man'.[5] My principal argument in this book is that understanding and defending liberal democracy requires an understanding of human beings that neither demotes us to the individualistic 'economic men' of negative liberalism nor promotes us to the community-defined inhabitants of a pure 'realm of freedom'. What we need is an understanding of nature that allows us to be part of the natural world in spite of our being 'undetermined'.

METHODS AND AIMS

The practical problems examined in this book to illustrate the symptoms of the disease of antinaturalistic liberal theory are drawn from American experience, because it is still possible to see in the United States the image of liberal democracy, with its characteristic virtues and vices. Many observers complain that the American ideological spectrum is very narrow, but this fact helps explain why American political experience is full of articulate explorations of the characteristic problems of modern liberal politics. It could also be argued that the USA, with all its advantages (including its foundation of classic liberal ideas), must surely be able to get it right, otherwise there is no hope for liberal democracy elsewhere. One need not think that the United States has reached 'the end of history' in order to accept that American experience has much to say to modern liberal democrats.

The problems selected for examination – ethnicity, sex and bureaucracy – frequently appear in current political and sociological literature, but they are the hard cases, in that they have been less thoroughly treated than certain other areas – such as religion or political economy – by the thinkers who laid the foundations of modern liberalism during the seventeenth, eighteenth and nineteenth centuries. Nevertheless, the thoughts of these older liberals offer much that is relevant to these problems, because their *physiphobia*, where it exists, is less advanced. When they do address these problems, their resources are greater, because they have not jettisoned nature. When they do not address them, their strategies and tactics on other questions are still helpfully suggestive. So the genre history of political thought often appears in the following pages, even in the more practical sections. However, it is not the kind of history that will be accepted as such by those who are persuaded that it is unreasonable to expect to learn anything useful from intelligent writers who had the misfortune to live before us. My interest in old writers is based not on the authority of the old, but on the authority of the very old: nature itself.

Our world has grown a little weary of systems that offer us perfect salvation. Constructing such a system is not the intention of this book. A genuine reconsideration of natural right might well heighten our sense of the difficulties of the human condition. For example, if we do come to appreciate more fully the fact that there is natural support for both individuality and communality, we should be better able to resist any temptation to neglect either of these human needs, but there is no guarantee that the possibility of tragic conflicts between them will thereby disappear. An appeal to the authority of nature is less an attempt to stop debate about important questions than to restart it. It would be surprising if any reader agreed with every practical conclusion reached in the discussions of policy and institutional problems in the chapters that follow. My ambition is both smaller and larger: I hope that some readers will become more sympathetic to the strategy of thinking about such problems with a greater awareness of the relevance of the question of natural standards.

Chapter 2

Unity and plurality in ethnic politics

Most countries are multiethnic, and ethnic divisions have disturbed the politics of all kinds of regime. However, although the problems of ethnic conflict are not uniquely liberal democratic problems, there are features of liberal democracy that can make ethnic and racial differences greater obstacles to justice. Democracies defer to popular opinion, which includes ethnic and racial prejudice. Liberal regimes also lack techniques of enforcement more readily available to others: for example, in the bad old days before *glasnost*, when the Soviet Army put down race riots, Soviet subjects did not always hear about the incident. The general problem is that liberal democracies, to be true to themselves, have to work on the often contradictory principles of justice to all citizens *and* of popular consent. Are there any countervailing features of liberal democracies that can compensate for this handicap? This is part of the more general question: what is the proper place of ethnicity in the politics of liberal democracies? Should liberals regard ethnicity as good, bad or indifferent? How and how much should ethnic groups be recognized by liberal political institutions?

Reflections on American political experience can help answer these questions. Although the United States of America has never been as innocent of socio-economic class conflict as some portraits of that country have suggested, American ethnic and racial divisions have undeniably been a more immovable object in the path of the forces working towards a sense of the common good and towards justice for individual citizens. That is one reason why American experience has been regarded as a source of useful lessons for other liberal democracies' attempts to solve the problems associated with ethnic and racial politics.

However, in some ways the USA is not a typical liberal democracy. Its ethnic composition is the most diverse in the world. Unlike most liberal democracies, the United States is a settler society. Unlike other settler societies (such as Canada, New Zealand and Australia), it has a revolutionary tradition and political creed that have helped to cut the ties to the mother countries and to establish a kind of super-nationality that looks back and up to the 'founding fathers' of the country not as ethnic fathers but as ethical founders. These untypical characteristics make it doubtful that the American example could be followed in every particular by other countries. But it would be too pessimistic to conclude that modern statecraft remains as constrained as the statecraft of the ancient world to take the ethnic composition of a given country as one of those materials that one just has to accept. In the ancient world (as depicted, for example, in Aristotle's *Politics*), the ethnic characteristics of a country's population were seen as one of those brute facts – comparable to the geography of the country – with which lawgivers were at the mercy of fortune and could accomplish little with the art of politics.[1] In the modern world, ethnic groups are still forces to be reckoned with, especially when supra-ethnic political creeds break down: witness (among the legion of recent examples) the disintegration of the Soviet Union, where ethnic separatism helped to call into question the 'Union' itself. Nevertheless, such political creeds, when they are strong, can make ethnic politics more malleable. Liberalism is one of those creeds, so the USA's very exceptionalism in being based so exclusively on a liberal political creed makes it a good testing ground for a liberal scheme of ethnicity. In the United States, the twin liberal democratic principles of justice *and* popular consent can work in harmony, as long as public opinion remains true to the liberal democratic creed.

This is not to assert that the United States has always adopted the wisest ethnic policies. On the contrary, American failings are as palpable and as instructive here as American successes. Both in responses to 'the immigrant problem' in the nineteenth and early twentieth centuries, and in efforts to cope with ethnic and racial discrimination in more recent decades, American thinking and policy have very often veered towards two opposing extremes, demanding either too much political unity, or requiring too much political plurality. These extreme tendencies have arisen out of misinterpretations of the American political creed, and out of forgetfulness of the demands of the most fundamental principle of that creed: the natural equality of human beings. The most important lesson of American experience is the necessity of remembering and correctly understanding that principle. Failure to cultivate this natural humanistic basis of liberal politics has led to two opposite extremes, whereby liberals tend either to lack awareness of the proper limits to ethnic claims, or to lack awareness of the legitimacy of those claims. Here as elsewhere in liberal politics, the balance between plurality and unity requires awareness of the natural basis of political liberty.

THE DECLINE OF LIBERALISM IN RECENT AMERICAN ETHNIC POLITICS

Multilingualism

In the 1970s and 1980s it became routine for Democratic candidates for the Presidential nomination to speak – in American English, of course – in favour of increased federal support for what is somewhat misleadingly called 'bilingual education'. The Bilingual Education Act (a 1968 amendment to the Elementary and Secondary Education Act – an amendment which was itself amended and strengthened in 1974) has made it feasible for American public schools, in response to pressure from ethnic groups and federal officials, to establish programmes of bilingual and bicultural education, and not merely (as in the past) as marginal solutions to local and sometimes temporary problems, but as long-term commitments to cultural pluralism. Much of the bilingual educational effort has been directed less at easing the transition of immigrants' children into the English-speaking culture than at maintaining their non-English-speaking cultures.[2]

The administrators who originally interpreted the Bilingual Education Act in a way that favoured a commitment to cultural pluralism cited in their support a 1974 Supreme Court decision, *Lau v. Nichols*.[3] But this decision did not even require bilingual instruction, it simply required the San Francisco Unified School District to extend its programme of supplemental English language instruction to all of its non-English-speaking students. (Some of these students had been receiving this help; parents of others wanted it for their children too.) In fact, the Court quoted in its opinion the relevant guidelines of the (then) Department of Health, Education and Welfare, which suggested supplemental English rather than long-term bilingual education as the appropriate 'affirmative step', since the latter would risk establishing 'an educational dead end or permanent track'. Thus the law itself, even as interpreted by the courts, does not demand the bicultural policies that the Department of Health, Education and Welfare and its successor, the Department of Education, along with numerous state education officials, have encouraged schools to adopt. Republican proposals – accepted by Congress (controlled by the Democrats) in 1988 – to make more of the federal funds in this programme available for alternative teaching methods, such as intensive English classes, would appear to be wiser than the Democratic candidates' indiscriminate calls for more funds. (Of course, better still might be more money, as well as more sensible spending of it.) But such liberalization of bilingual education still confronts strong legal and political opposition in several states, and more than 90 per cent of the funding comes from state and local sources.[4]

The testimony of those Americans who have experienced the private loss entailed in movement away from their native language shows that the loss is great, but that this is partly because it is bound up with the inevitably painful movement out of childhood and the intimacy of the family that we all experience. In any case there is public gain to set against it. As Richard (né Ricardo) Rodriguez has pointed out, everyone loses, to a greater or lesser degree, their 'family language', so it is fruitless to cling to 'a skein of words, as though it were the source of . . . family ties'. Although 'one suffers a diminished sense of *private* individuality by becoming assimilated into public society, such assimilation makes possible the achievement of *public* individuality'.[5]

The ethnic separatist sentiments connected with the 'bilingualism' of recent decades have helped make Americans greet the large and increasingly non-European immigration of recent years with a more than usually ambivalent welcome. Immigration in the decade 1981–90 surpassed the previous record total of 8.7 million, set in 1901–10, and these people have emigrated mainly from Asia and Latin America. In 1965 (when the immigration quota system was liberalized, and when European immigration still accounted for 50 per cent of the total), a Gallup poll found only 33 per cent of the adult population in favour of decreasing the numbers of immigrants. In June 1986 – ironically, just as Americans were preparing to celebrate the centennial of the statue of 'Liberty Enlightening the World' (she who beckons immigrants to the United States) – a similar *New York Times* and *CBS News* poll found 49 per cent (among both Democrats and Republicans) favouring such a decrease. As usual, there are economic rivalries and resentments involved here, but there are also serious questions about assimilation *versus* separatism. There are fears that the flocking–dispersion–interspersion pattern of previous immigration will not recur so easily and frequently.

What seems to be most troubling to American citizens is not the non-European flavour of the new immigration (immigrants from different European regions and countries have also found each other intolerable) so much as the fact that these immigrants are perceived to be less inclined (although they are probably not) – and often are less encouraged – to assimilate to the extent of learning and using the American English language, contributing their accents and variations to that tongue. In the November 1986 elections, a measure to make English the official language of the state (Proposition 63) was approved by voters in California; eighteen other states have now adopted similar measures. Just before the 1986 elections, it was reported that leaders of Hispanic– and Asian–American organizations and the American Civil Liberties Union were saying that Proposition 63 'would encourage bigotry, divisiveness and resentment' towards ethnic minorities.[6] This argument underrated American public opinion, which is not that ready to become harshly nativist. After all, the renewed public doubts about immigration merely resulted, in October 1986, after a decade of Congressional consideration, in enactment of a law that made some efforts to reduce the amount of illegal immigration (which some estimates put as high as the legal total), and actually offered amnesty to millions of aliens illegally resident since January 1982.

Nor is the new public concern for linguistic unity simply a harsh nativist position. It is a response to the fact that the predominance of one foreign language (Spanish) among the new immigrants has encouraged its continued usage and the threat of long-term linguistic dualism or Spanish monolingualism in certain areas. The public reaction has retreated when its measures have been found inconvenient; for example, in Miami, Florida, in 1984, a 1980 law restricting the official use of Spanish and Creole was revised when it was seen that restriction of public employees to the English language was interfering with the provision of such services as medical care and with such profitable industries as tourism. (It had been forbidden for signs at the zoo to identify animals in any language except English!) The legislatures of two-thirds of the states have refused to adopt English as their official language. The actual effects of laws like Proposition 63 – whatever the anti-immigrant views of some of their proponents – will probably be mainly symbolic, although one may hope that they will encourage the states who adopt them to give more attention to teaching English to the children of immigrants. It seems probable that opponents of such laws have mistaken the source and the manifestation of 'divisiveness and resentment', which have followed – and will no doubt continue to follow – the sentiments and policies that fail to see any evil in the continued cultural seclusion of some of the new immigrants and their children. Perhaps proponents of multilingualism should cast a glance at the comparable policy in South Africa, where official boards were set up to maintain the purity of tribal languages, to prevent the natural development and fusion of languages and to make detribalization less likely.

There is a strong educational case to be made for genuinely bilingual education, at least to a limited extent, and with English included. In Florida, one can also see effective economic pressures working towards bilingual abilities: ambitious Spanish-speaking businesspeople and professionals often want to (and do) learn English, just as their English-speaking counterparts feel the need to acquire Spanish-speaking ability. But such pressures and ambitions are not felt by the majority, even in Florida. Bilingual ability is likely to remain a goal that relatively few citizens will pursue. Even generously endowed private international schools have found that bilingual courses are too demanding for many students, and that they make in-depth learning of subjects other than language more difficult for almost all. (One such school, in Geneva, recently discontinued a bilingual programme – half of the teaching in English, half in French – having found that the children 'were becoming rootless international types with deficient references in both languages'.) Perhaps that is one reason why the parents of American children with low levels of English-speaking ability often favour instruction for their children in English even over a mixture of English and their family language. Even some teachers in bilingual programmes have been known to send their own children to private schools, so they can learn English more rapidly.[7]

Of course, the point about many of those currently attracted to bilingual*ism* is that they are not deeply committed to producing bilingual *ability* even for a few. Bilingualism is for them an 'ism': a moral cause. They *are* deeply – righteously – committed to the right of everyone to be educated in a foreign language, and this commitment makes them less attentive to (and sometimes even openly opposed to) the desirability of teaching American citizens their common language and culture as well. The rallying purpose of the 'bilingual' movement has been the protection of the self-esteem of students whose family language is not English, by respecting and cultivating their different languages and cultures. This purpose is said to be geared up to lifting the overall educational achievement of these students, by raising their self-esteem.

But students' self-esteem — and what is more, their human self-respect — can be more solidly enhanced by teaching them the language skills that they need to thrive in the United States, and even by exposing them to the human as well as to the ethnic cultures of the United States. This liberal educational philosophy is in some ways more ambitious than the 'bilingual' philosophy, and it can be troubling and painful — for teachers as well as for students — but it need not involve the admittedly humiliating experience suffered by many earlier immigrants, of being thrown into the deep end, to sink or swim. What it must involve is learning. There is disturbing evidence that students in bilingual programmes are not actually being well educated even in mathematics, to say nothing of social and literary subjects, and not to mention English. (Partly in consequence, American business corporations have been forced to set up their own programmes to teach English to their employees.) However, this evidence does not disturb proponents of bilingual education. They ignore it or play it down, because it goes against the grain of their moral commitment to a cultural pluralism that sees little or no need for a common American language and culture. The United States' liberal culture appears to them not as it is, a profoundly human-centred culture, but as one ethnic culture among many, and one that is suffering from an ethnocentric hubris that only a strong dose of cultural pluralism can cure.

Affirmative discrimination

Comparable to multilingualism in its illiberal assumptions and effects is the widespread acceptance of ethnic classifications for the purpose of 'affirmative discrimination', as distinguished from the softer forms of 'affirmative action' that seek merely to ensure that equal opportunities are available and more generally publicized. The harder form, 'affirmative' or 'positive discrimination', originated in administrative interpretations of statutes and in executive orders, not in Congressional actions, and it is not accepted by public opinion, but it is well established in public law and quasi-public practices of employers and educational institutions.[8] In fact, some of the main beneficiaries of affirmative discrimination are the public and private 'equal opportunity' bureaucracies that are needed to maintain the appearance that something 'affirmative' is being done about racial discrimination. Leaders of business and labour organizations do not generally oppose affirmative discrimination. Leaders of both of the two major parties have either promoted or acquiesced in it. It has settled in as a part of the political landscape. It is unlikely, therefore, that affirmative discrimination will depart as quietly as it has arrived. The policy has been challenged in the courts, and there have been a series of Supreme Court cases, the first being the *Bakke* case in 1978.[9] The cases continue, because the justices are so divided that the Court collectively has been unable either to decide the issue on the principle of equal individual rights that is embedded in the constitution, or openly to abandon that constitutional principle in favour of the pluralistic principle of group rights. In 1989 (in *Richmond v. Croson*)[10] five of the nine justices finally applied the 'strict scrutiny' demanded by legal precedent to a governmental racial classification that was part of an affirmative action programme (the city of Richmond's construction contract scheme favouring 'minority business enterprises'). But the Court was obviously still highly fragmented; endorsement of the 'opinion of the Court' was cobbled together from various groupings of the justices, and five other opinions were written (three mainly concurring, two dissenting). So it was not surprising that in 1990 the Court – once again sharply divided, though not so fragmented – refused to apply strict scrutiny to a racial classification, in a case challenging the Federal Communications Commission's programme favouring certain minorities in the allocation of radio and television broad-casting licences, for the sake of broadcast diversity (*Metro Broadcasting v. FCC*).[11] (It remains to be seen whether the recent replacement of Justices Brennan and Marshall by Justices Souter and Thomas will clarify the Court's position.)

Although affirmative discrimination policy is essentially too ethnically pluralistic, it makes some rather feeble and unrealistic gestures in the direction of ethnic assimilation or integration. It is important to see that the policy makes these gestures, and why the gestures fail to amount to anything substantial. The assumptions of affirmative discrimination policies challenge inevitable and even perfectly acceptable cultural differences and experiences among ethnic groups, such as those that make it hard to find Italian-Americans in the banking business, or Jewish-Americans in the construction industry, or anyone but Korean-Americans in the New York City fruit and vegetable trade. As Justice O'Connor has noted (beginning in her dissenting opinion in one of the 1986 decisions in which the Supreme Court slowed down the Reagan Justice Department's already rather forlorn campaign against racial quotas), quota systems make the completely unrealistic assumption 'that individuals of each race will gravitate with mathematical exactitude to each employer or union absent unlawful discrimination'. This assumption turns what might in some cases be 'a sensible rule of thumb into an unjustified conclusion about the precise extent to which past discrimination has lingering effects, or into an unjustified prediction about what would happen in the future in the absence of continuing discrimination'.[12] This abstract rigidity can lead to the denial of those most in need of such services as public housing, since these needs are not evenly distributed among ethnic groups. And experience has shown that quotas can easily become ceilings rather than floors in 'minority' hiring programmes. More crucially, as Michael Walzer has pointed out, even if it is judged that ethnicity is worth making some public efforts to preserve, a quota system is not a good way to do so, since in practice it 'serves to enhance the wealth of individuals, not necessarily the resources of the ethnic community'.[13] (And after all, why should ethnic 'minority' graduates of professional schools be consigned to work in 'their' communities, rather than in the mainstream of their professions?) Affirmative discrimination can thus be ineffective and even counterproductive. Therefore, if affirmative discrimination is thought of as the logical culmination of the long American war for desegregation, it becomes plausible to dismiss the fruits of victory in that war – as some of the warriors themselves now do – as a 'sham' and a 'con job' (the recent epithets from James Meredith, the hero of the battle to desegregate the University of Mississippi in 1962).[14]

The weakness of affirmative discrimination as a means of desegregation stems from the appeasement mentality that produces and maintains the policy. Affirmative discrimination tries to buy peace by offering a phoney solution in place of a slower and harder but necessary attack on the real problem. Expensive judgements on behalf of real victims of discrimination might help concentrate the minds of racially discriminating employers. The provision of good education for everyone from the earliest stages, or even remedial education and preparation for vocational or professional examinations at a later stage for those who need it, would be slower and would appear more expensive than pushing a few ethnic 'minority' applicants through the educational and employment systems, but that would also be more generally effective in ending 'the procession of teenagers who leave ghetto high schools disadvantaged, badly taught, unable to find decent jobs'[15] – and less unjust to 'non-minority' individuals, into the bargain. It is remarkable how openly the cheapness and ease of affirmative discrimination are counted among its advantages. (Here is another parallel with the debate over bilingualism: it is argued that such measures as Proposition 63 might cost governmental time, trouble and money, by requiring an increase in the costs of teaching English.)[16] This argument was read into the legal record of the Supreme Court in Justice Blackmun's revealing concurring opinion in the *Weber* case in 1979. This was the case in which the Court upheld the legality of Kaiser Aluminum's quota for blacks in its craft training programme. Blackmun argued that Kaiser's quota programme was 'reasonable' because it was a way of escaping much greater liability to actual victims of its (and its steelworkers union's) actual discriminatory practices: 'The company is able to avoid identifying victims of past discrimination, and so avoids claims for backpay'.[17] It is equally remarkable how often the reduction of racial tension is offered as a justification for affirmative discrimination.[18] As with other kinds of appeasement, one has to ask: peace at what price, and for how long? In 1896, the need for 'the preservation of the public peace and good order' was the rationale used by the majority of the Supreme Court to justify 'separate but equal' facilities for blacks and whites (in *Plessy v. Ferguson*).[19] Affirmative discrimination, the new 'separate but equal' doctrine, has stored up an abundance of resentment among its real and imagined victims. Will they in turn demand 'affirmative discrimination' by way of compensation – or, more likely, demand an end both to affirmative action, even of the softer and more justified sort, and to harder efforts to reduce and to punish discrimination? As recent Supreme Court cases have demonstrated, harder economic times quickly reveal the short life of the peace bought by affirmative discrimination. As Justice O'Connor argued in another 1986 case, it becomes impossible, for public employers in particular, to avoid being 'trapped between the competing hazards of liability to minorities if affirmative action *is not* taken to remedy apparent employment discrimination and liability to non-minorities if affirmative action *is* taken'.[20] The problem of racial prejudice in liberal democracies cannot be solved by short cuts that try to substitute a false equality and easier consciences for conscientious efforts to reach real equality. Precisely if progress in reducing racism had been as poor as the proponents of affirmative discrimination say, it would be foolish to follow Ronald Dworkin's advice to aim totally to reform 'the racial consciousness' of American society by means that are not 'racially neutral',[21] for non-'neutral' methods would inevitably be dominated by the racist majority.

Because of this need to promote justice without trying to bypass public opinion and political consent, the more pernicious aspect of affirmative discrimination is not its rather flabby and ill-conceived promotion of integration, but the tendency that it shares with bicultural education actually to undermine the integrating effects of liberal culture. Its pluralistic tendency runs deeper than its unifying tendency. Justice Rehnquist's dissenting opinion in the *Weber* case justly observed: 'There is perhaps no device more destructive to the notion of equality than the *numerus clausus* – the quota. Whether described as "benign discrimination" or "affirmative action", the racial quota is nonetheless a creator of castes'.[22] Affirmative discrimination programmes compel citizens to seek equal legal treatment as members of groups. The quota mentality reflects and magnifies a loss of faith in the strength of liberal individualism and in the need for American citizenship and the American regime as guardians of the rights of association. It also forgets the importance for liberty of the dynamism of group politics – the necessity for coalition-building, and for the coalescing and re-coalescing of groups, which depends in turn on the underlying power of individuals as such, rather than merely as permanent members of one or another group. Both the ethnic revival of the 1970s and the black power movement to which it was in part a response forgot their dependence on the idea of natural human equality. Ethnic coalitions and balancing acts have played an important role in American party organization, and ethnic group loyalties continue to influence electoral alignments. However, the attempt to institutionalize ethnic coalitions in recent party reforms that substitute quotas for political power and judgement has only hastened the decline of the party system. This in turn has fed the fires of ethnic rivalry for the benefits now dispensed by the bureaucracy rather than the party. Ethnic groups separately dependent on the state compete in isolation, and coalitions and compromises become less frequent, just as with the new single-minded 'special interest' groups in the new American political 'issue networks' classically described by Hugh Heclo, in which '[t]rade-offs or combinations . . . represent a kind of impurity' that these groups find repellant.[23] In a dynamic coalition politics, ethnic minorities suffering injustice can become members of majority coalitions that attack that injustice, as black Americans and the Democratic party found to their mutual advantage – and to the common good – in the early 1960s. The ethnically balanced ticket was originally a tool of a coalition of ethnic groups against a dominant group. For example, Mike Royko's biography of Mayor Daley of Chicago tells us how in the early days of the Chicago Democratic party machine, 'Cermak had the gall to challenge the traditional South Side Irish domination of the Democratic party. More than gall, he had the sense to count up all the Irish votes, then he counted all the Italians, Jews, Germans, Poles, and Bohemians . . . . He organized a city-wide saloon keepers' league . . . he couldn't be stopped'.[24] And of course, that was not the end of Irish-American power in Chicago. When such dynamic ethnic coalitions are replaced by balkanized, rigidly institutionalized ethnic politics, in which certain minorities are always regarded as 'discrete and insular' and therefore in need of special treatment, individual groups can easily find themselves neglected, in spite of their more insistent rhetoric, as black Americans found in the 1970s and 1980s. 'Insular' groups can be treated as permanent wards of a party, a bureaucracy or a court, who owe their just treatment to these guardians or 'virtual representatives' and to their continued isolation from the majoritarian political process, rather than to their participation in that process.[25] (We shall see in Chapter 5 that this group atomism of the world of affirmative discrimination is identical in its causes and effects to the group atomism in the popular liberal political theory of John Rawls.)

Recognition of the objective truth of the equality of individual human beings, and therefore of the justice of treating them equally and respecting their rights, is the necessary basis for a truly liberal group politics. This was all too obscurely and fleetingly observed in the Supreme Court in 1978, in a footnote to Justice Stevens' partly concurring, partly dissenting opinion in the *Bakke* case. In this unpromising site – would that it were studied as much as the all too frequently revisited footnote in the case that established the 'discrete and insular minority' rhetoric – we find a reference to the basic justice of the Civil Rights Act of 1964, as an Act built on 'the principle of *individual* equality, without regard to race or religion', a principle 'on which there could be a "meeting of the minds" among all races and a common national purpose'.[26] The just and effective means of achieving the harmony and political community of ethnic groups is the pursuit of justice to individuals.

The American judiciary has been inclined to accept the argument (which, again, we shall see being advanced by contemporary Rawlsian liberal theory) that there is no stigma produced by 'benign discrimination', and therefore little if any injustice to 'non-minority' victims of affirmative discrimination. The courts assume, as one commentator bluntly puts it, that 'if all blacks are by definition victims by virtue of their membership in a victim class, then all whites are incapable of being victims by virtue of their being members of an oppressing class'.[27] In a way, this reasoning actually increases the injury of affirmative discrimination, because the victims are being told that they have not been unjustly treated. In the 1980s this argument began to fall a little flat, when layoffs rather than hirings, promotions or admissions became the issue. It is bad enough for an applicant for a place, a job, or a promotion to know or to suspect that he or she has been unsuccessful because of a preference given to someone less qualified, on the basis of a third party's (perhaps the same institution's or employer's) former unjust treatment of a fourth party. (In the words of one recent non-minority victim in Cleveland, 'if the city discriminated against anybody, fine, they should pay an indemnity. But they say, "Gee, we were guilty of discrimination all these years, now we'll get this guy over here to pay [the] penalty"'.)[28] It would be very cold comfort indeed for 'non-minority' firefighters or school teachers to be told, as they would be told by some members of the Supreme Court (including Justice Stevens) that their loss of employment as a consequence of an 'affirmative' protection of 'minority' employment was 'not based on any lack of respect for their race, or on blind habit and stereotype'.[29] Not even a plurality of the Court have yet been able to bring themselves to dish out such 'benign' treatment. In these recent cases, the Court, trying to overcome its now customary fragmented state, has preferred to fudge the issue. But in the truth that comes in Justice Stevens' footnotes, '[t]he fact that the issue arises in a layoff context, rather than a hiring context, has no bearing on the equal protection issue'.[30] Reliance on the diffuseness of the injury to applicants as opposed to actual employees, trainees or students is merely another sign of the underhandedness of affirmative discrimination. However much the current strategy of distinguishing between diffuse and concentrated injuries to 'non-minorities' may 'narrow tailor' the Court's judgements to what seems currently tolerable or conducive to judicial comity, it offers no principled resolution of the issue. As Justice Powell noted in the *Bakke* case, 'The Equal Protection Clause is not framed in terms of "stigma". Certainly the word has no clearly defined constitutional meaning. It reflects a subjective judgement that is standardless', and this subjectivity cannot replace the protection of objective natural rights of individuals as the necessary 'absolute' ground for a consistent interpretation of the meaning of the constitution's guarantee of 'equal protection of the laws'.[31]

Justice Kennedy's dissenting opinion in the 1990 *Metro Broadcasting* case recognizes that the judiciary's preoccupation with subjective stigma is another throwback to the opinion of the majority in *Plessy v. Ferguson*. The majority in that infamous case argued that 'the enforced separation of the two races' did not stamp 'the colored race with a badge of inferiority'.[32] In fact, the Court has never abandoned this subjectivity. When the reversal of the *Plessy* decision finally came with the landmark *Brown* decision in 1954, the Court retained the subjective reasoning of that decision, by finding 'separate but equal' facilities unequal because racial segregation 'generates a feeling' or 'a sense of inferiority' in blacks.[33] The 'color blind' constitution of Justice Harlan's dissent in *Plessy* was not recognized by the *Brown* opinion. In view of the use made of the concept of stigma in affirmative discrimination cases since the 1970s, it is clear that the *Brown* 'reversal' of *Plessy* actually gave new life to the doctrine of separate but equal,[34] which lives on in the theory and practice of affirmative discrimination.

Justice Powell's opinion in the *Bakke* case also briefly noted the other major problem with subjective stigma and the attendant focus on group membership rather than rights of individuals: 'preferential programs may only reinforce common stereotypes holding that certain groups are unable to achieve success without special protection based on a factor having no relationship to individual worth'.[35] Reverse stigma inevitably grows with reverse discrimination. Because those 'helped' by affirmative discrimination are often those least in need of it, this is particularly unfair. The insidious growth of reverse stigma is illustrated by a recent exchange in the *Washington Post* between the President of Harvard University and a black teacher at that university. President Derek Bok wrote in

defence of affirmative discrimination (as long as its 'unfairness' is
'diffuse'), and explicitly disagreed with Professor Glenn Loury's
argument that it 'stigmatizes those it purports to aid' – although, he
patronizingly added, Professor Loury 'speaks with daunting
credibility as a black who grew up on the South Side of Chicago'.[36]
In his reply, as devastating as it was restrained, Professor Loury
pointed out that his 'credibility' might just be derived not from that
experience so much as from his experience in 'a highly competitive,
technically demanding profession'. It was only after accepting a
tenured professorship in Harvard's economics department – 'a professorship extended on the condition that [he] accept responsibilities
in the Afro-American studies department as well, and one offered
despite the views of some in the economics department that [he] was
not quite ready for such a distinguished position – that [he] began to
learn firsthand what being an "affirmative action appointment" can
mean'.[37] Richard Rodriguez also recounts the harm and the pain of
having 'benefited' from affirmative discrimination. Having become a
'minority student' at Berkeley, he then became a critic of the policy
of affirmative discrimination: 'Someone told me this: a senior faculty
member in the English department at Berkeley smirked when my
name came up in a conversation. Someone at the sherry party had
wondered if the Professor had seen my latest article on affirmative
action. The Professor replied with arch politeness, "And what does
Mr. Rodriguez have to complain about?"'.[38] Reverse stigma makes
it more, not less difficult for non-black Americans to repay black
ones for the injuries done to them in the best coin – namely, in
Howard Brotz's phrase, 'by making it possible for them to seek
qualifications with dignity'.[39]

The basic problem with affirmative discrimination is not that it
introduces and tolerates such absurdities and injustices. Focusing
only on the policy's injustice to individuals can foster a merely
libertarian reaction. We need to focus rather on the (related) damage
to the liberal community, caused by the factionalizing effects of the
policy. There are probably cases where the blunt weapon of
affirmative discrimination is necessary. But, especially if it is to be
used, it is important to recognize how much it goes against the grain
of liberal democracy. The reason it involves so much absurdity and
injustice is that, like multilingualism, it pays too little attention to the
necessity of political unity in the liberal state, a unity that can be
founded properly only on the objective natural rights, not on the
shifting and difficult-to-determine subjective feelings, of individual

human beings. If and when the USA veers too much in the direction of political unity, and it becomes desirable to adopt toward ethnic cultures a policy of *encourager-faire*, rather than the more traditional policy of *laissez-faire*, there are ways to bolster ethnic organizations that fall short of the absolute ethnic pluralism that is the ideal of many multilingualists and affirmative discriminators. Walzer has suggested 'tax exemptions and rebates, subsidies, matching grants, certificate plans, and so on'.[40] Only such means as these should be permitted. (These means should also try to avoid the confusion of ethnic distinctions with racial distinctions, the latter of which are always invidious.) In politics – particularly in liberal democratic politics – it matters very much *why* a policy is undertaken. The justifications for policies need to be compatible with the regime's self-understanding. Otherwise the self-contradictions mount up, and the regime crumbles.

For the moment, Americans seem to have less need of cultivating their ethnic cultures than they have of recultivating their liberal, American culture. Contrary to what many observers have said, it is not the power of the 'mechanical and standardising'[41] liberal state and the 'emergence of "rational" universal values'[42] that has encouraged the retreat to ethnicity so much as the opposite: loss of standards by the liberal state and decline in the understanding of rational values. Liberals have been too ready to follow Friedrich Nietzsche's critique of these liberal values and his concomitant praise for the depths of peoples or nations, *versus* the superficial state, that 'coldest of all cold monsters'.[43] In the United States, as in the rest of the world, the extreme ethnic conflicts of the twentieth century have risen within the vacuums created by the failure or the withdrawal of universalistic, or at least multiethnic, political systems.[44] While avoiding 'nativist' nonsense, perhaps it would be useful to acknowledge the truth of the common sense (and etymologically accurate[45]) association of the word 'ethnic' with the foreign, in need of 'naturalization', instead of assuming that ethnicity is natural for everyone.

AMERICAN RESPONSES TO 'THE IMMIGRANT PROBLEM'

Confused and one-sided ethnic policies are not new in American history. However, whereas the one-sidedly pluralistic extreme has dominated recent ethnic policy making, we can see in official and intellectual responses to immigration in the late nineteenth and early twentieth centuries both a similar pluralistic extreme and a sometimes more dominant unifying extreme.

Less than 2 per cent of the present American population descends from the native Amerindians, or from Hispanic residents of the present territory of the United States who were there before that territory was enlarged to include lands into which Hispanic immigrants have come. The American population is also 'racially' diverse. For these reasons, the ethnic problem in the United States has typically not taken the form of 'the nationality problem' (as it was called in Europe) but rather the form of 'the immigrant problem' and 'the Negro problem' (as they were originally called in the United States). Both of these problems have been experienced to some extent by former imperial powers in Europe since the Second World War. But they have received different kinds of response there. They have been more typically 'American dilemmas' (in Gunnar Myrdal's classic phrase) because of the United States' demanding liberal creed, which has played a much greater role in defining American 'nationality' than any creed has played in defining British, French and German nationality. This creed has been a source both of problems and solutions in American politics.

The very success of that creed in some areas of policy made success in ethnic and racial policy more difficult. As Alexis de Tocqueville remarked in the 1830s, the very liberty on which Anglo-Americans could justifiably pride themselves easily became a source of ethnic pride and prejudice, which made liberal ethnic relations more difficult to accept. The pride that Anglo-Americans could take in achieving a solution to the problem of religious liberty in the eighteenth century thus made for a more trying time with ethnic liberty in the nineteenth and twentieth centuries. (An explanation of the greater trouble that ethnic relations have occasioned in the predominantly Protestant USA as opposed to the Catholic Latin American republics might start here.)

'The Negro problem', which of course has been experienced by many besides those who gave it its name, is the problem of racial prejudice. Racial prejudice is a strange and highly irrational thing. This is because, while ethnicity, whether defined in terms of genetic pools or of cultures, is something real, race is not. Racial prejudice consists of two irrational mental steps. Firstly, certain rather unreliable but easily visible ethnic markers (such as height or skin colour) are mistaken for signs of ethnic difference; then the misjudgement is made that this difference amounts to or is identical to an inferiority of species. Visible looks are mistaken for the invisible looks that constitute the human species. Matter is mistaken for form.

This problem of racial prejudice has been thoroughly mixed with ethnic politics ('the immigrant problem') in American history, and ultimately both must be considered together. But it seems worth beginning by distinguishing the two. 'The immigrant problem' seems to be more able to claim to be seriously based on true cultural differences (which may or may not coincide with racial markers), and it has not always been seen in terms of ethnic superiority and inferiority. False perceptions of racial difference – that is, all perceptions of morally relevant racial difference among members of the human race – may be a more intractable problem than perceptions of ethnic difference. Solving the problem of racism might require a coincidence of wisdom and consent, of justice and opinion, which it would be foolish to expect. The race problem is deeper because it is more irrational than the ethnic problem. But if ethnic consciousness makes more sense than racial consciousness, then perhaps more sense can be made out of it. The 'immigrant problem' may relate more seriously and rationally – if less burdensomely – to the question of the practicability of a liberal scheme of ethnic politics. It may make sense to start with 'the immigrant problem' rather than with 'the Negro problem', in order to view both problems in the light of the liberal scheme.

Arthur Mann's study of *The One and the Many* in American national identity has reminded us of the amazing liberality of United States immigration policy, at least from its beginning in 1790 with 'the most liberal naturalization law then in existence', up to the nationally restrictive legislation of the 1920s (repealed in 1965). 'The United States', he writes, 'was the first country to decide, as a matter of national policy, that it would be an immigrant-receiving country'. Even the racially discriminatory line in that policy (only 'free white persons' – no blacks, and, from 1882 onwards, no yellows – were to be admitted) was very difficult for officials and courts to define, and it was simply ignored in many cases even before that discrimination was at last completely outlawed in 1952. Moreover, naturalization rules meant that becoming an American citizen was a voluntary procedure, in contrast to the practice of other countries, and was also unique in requiring evidence of attachment to the republican principles of the constitution. The openness of immigration policy, the exceptions to and ultimate abandonment of its racial exclusions, and the unusual voluntary and ideological criteria of naturalization owed much to what Mann calls 'the burden of a national identity deriving from the Enlightenment's universal values'.[46] Americanization was and is a process directed primarily at heads and hearts, not at material considerations such as bodily ancestry. (Accordingly, the most durable ethnic traits among Americanized ethnic groups have been material traits such as culinary arts.) Of course, in classic American immigration and naturalization policy we can see the force of self-interest as well as that of liberal ideals. Immigrants were welcomed as assistants – often on the lowest rungs of the economic ladder – in the economic development of the country, and they were cynically used as lubrication for the urban political machines. Still, they could not have been so welcome if they had been perceived – as they were perceived by many later on – as a threat to liberty. Thomas Jefferson, in his *Notes on Virginia* (in 1784), wondered whether it would not be better to rely on a home-grown population rather than 'the importation of foreigners', many of whom would bring with them 'the maxims of absolute monarchies', but he concluded not that immigration or naturalization should be restricted but only that 'extraordinary encouragements' should not be offered: 'If they come of themselves, they are entitled to all the rights of citizenship'.[47] As Mann notes, in the first century of independence, only a 'nativist' minority thought there was a contradiction between a unifying, indivisible liberal citizenship and a high degree of cultural plurality.[48]

Although United States citizens at the time of their Declaration of Independence in 1776 already consisted of a number of nationalities ('Europe, and not England, is the parent country of America', noted Thomas Paine)[49], the eighteenth-century liberal creed and its liberal immigration policy created the immigrant problem as it was perceived in the later nineteenth and the twentieth centuries. But the liberal truths so well articulated in the eighteenth century were in later times less often accepted as sources of a solution to the problem. Americans were tempted by more fashionable doctrines. The racial pride of Anglo-Saxonism pursued the extreme of ethnic unity as a requirement of liberal democracy. The intellectual pride of what was called cultural pluralism pursued the opposite extreme, ethnic plurality, as a bulwark of liberty and civilization. Both sides detracted from the possibility of understanding and conforming to a more moderate liberal scheme – in spite of the fact that without the assumption of such a scheme by people like Jefferson in the founding generation, the problem would hardly have existed in the first place.

Assimilationism, amalgamationism and ethnic pluralism

Strong doubts that common liberal citizenship can coexist with a plurality of ethnic cultures led many Americans to treat immigrants either as candidates for assimilation to an absorptive Anglo-Saxon model, or as ingredients in a melting pot which would produce a newly amalgamated race of Americans. 'Nativism' (forgetful of the real natives) and Anglo-Saxon supremacism were great forces behind the nationally restrictive immigration legislation in force from 1924 to 1965. The image of the melting pot was embraced by many opponents of Anglo-Saxon supremacism. Yet both schools of thought made the same mistakes: they exaggerated the breadth of unanimity required in a liberal polity, and they gave far too much weight to genes as determinants of culture. Even if cultural homogeneity is desired, genetic engineering may not be the most effective way to produce it. Ethnic intermarriage can be regarded more properly as a product than as a prerequisite of liberal politics.

Opposite doubts to those entertained by these ethnic unifiers were also expressed in this period of American history, and while they had less impact on policy then, they have had a second and more influential life in our times. Ethnic pluralism has generally been a more intellectually seductive liberal heresy than the doctrines calling for ethnic unity, whether amalgamationist or assimilationist.

Early cultural and ethnic pluralists argued that the best liberal state would be one that included several national cultures, and that the fate of ethnic minorities within such a state would provide a test of a state's liberality. American proponents of assimilation and amalgamation had gone to one extreme; American cultural pluralists went to the other. The case for cultural pluralism was for many a defence of immigrants' ways of life against an unreasonable pressure towards assimilation and amalgamation. In so far as cultural pluralism countered the brutalities of 'Americanization' programmes[50] and the 'nativist' assumption of superiority, it was useful. But it had its own and possibly more dangerous excesses – which perhaps were more emphatically expressed because cultural plurality seemed to be losing the political battles to the anti-immigrant forces.

The father of cultural pluralism was a professor of philosophy, Horace Kallen. Kallen's study of *Culture and Democracy in the United*

States (published in 1924) laid down the principle of cultural pluralism as 'not one man one vote, but one temperament, one point of view, one vote'.[51] He called for and predicted the coming of a 'democracy of nationalities'[52], a 'commonwealth of national cultures'.[53] He was persuaded that political democracy would become a mere 'anarchy of association'[54] if it were allowed to transform genetically fixed ethnic groups into flexible, voluntaristic ethnic organizations. He thought American intellectual culture needed a firm basis in its various ethnic cultures.

Kallen acknowledged that science and industry were the forces to be reckoned with in American society, but proposed that 'Against the architectonic and regimentation of the latter, the logical oneness of the former, the deep-lying cultural diversities of the ethnic groups are the strongest shield, the chief defense'.[55] The monotony of industrial culture was Kallen's chief worry. This concern was also voiced by Kallen's contemporary, Randolph Bourne, who condemned the 'tame flabbiness' of 'rudimentary' American culture, with its 'cheap newspaper, the "movies", the popular song, the ubiquitous automobile'.[56] It has been echoed in our day by writers such as Michael Novak, who denigrate the United States' 'superculture', merely 'commercial in its purposes and its utility': both this 'superculture' and American 'mass culture' are for Novak 'ersatz culture, a sort of false consciousness, insofar as they arise from no particular culture but are constructed for broad communication'.[57]

Unlike Kallen, Bourne added to his suspicion about the lowbrow qualities of the actual American culture a vision of what that culture could be. He saw an opportunity for Americans to avoid nationalistic conflicts of the European variety (the Great War had just shown the depths to which these could sink), and to create a cosmopolitan culture, embodying 'all who have anything life-enhancing to offer to the spirit'.[58] That is what a liberal scheme of ethnicity would have to do: to allow and perhaps even to encourage ethnic cultures, but to encourage a more cosmopolitan, human culture as well. But many ethnic pluralists tend to make the illiberal assumption that the differences among humans are more important than what they have in common. Their concern for the health of ethnic cultures can blind them to the necessity and dignity of liberal culture. Liberal culture and politics may well be convicted of failing to satisfy deeply felt needs of the human soul. But (like interest group pluralism) ethnic group pluralism too soon loses sight of the need for and needs of common, political life. Liberal politics, even if it is seen as allowing and encouraging the salvation of souls only in the private sphere, needs a powerful politico-economic life to maintain the peace and prosperity of that sphere, as well as to ensure security from foreign threats. If one can (like Kallen and Novak) expect rich, particular ethnic cultures to operate in harmony with each other, is it not reasonable to expect them to operate in harmony with a relatively undemanding liberal culture?

Ethnic pluralism assumes – incorrectly – that what Arend Lijphart has called 'consociational democracy' can be a normal democratic arrangement. Consociational democracy incorporates citizens not as individuals but as members of groups. (Belgium and Switzerland are typical examples.) But Lijphart himself has pointed out that this arrangement assumes rare and often fragile conditions, and can be regarded as a phase of development that fades with success, by the resolution and depoliticization of 'segmental divergences' and the creation of 'sufficient mutual trust . . . to render itself superfluous', as in Austria and the Netherlands.[59] Consociational democracy, where it works at all (and its failures are numerous – Lebanon, Nigeria, perhaps Canada) is more of a widely appreciated convenience (as in Switzerland) or a solution of last resort (as in Belgium) than a liberal democratic success story.[60] In the USA, Amerindians have often been treated in law as a group, with their group rights and obligations taking priority over their rights and obligations as individual citizens. It is debatable whether this has been the fairest policy for this unfortunate group; it seems clear that it would be not a success but a failure of liberal democracy in the United States if other groups were to be treated in this fashion.

Ethnic pluralism not only demands an unnecessarily tricky political system, it also makes unrealistic demands on individuals, by expecting them to be loyal members of one or another ethnic group. It forgets that the melting pot does happen. Kallen spoke of the 'primary and indissoluble character' of 'the familial community with its elaboration in the qualities of nationality'; if melting occurred, he thought, it merely added to ethnic diversity: 'Biologically, life does not unify; biologically, life diversifies'.[61] But even if genetic amalgamation cannot be expected to unify the country, it does make the boundaries of ethnic groups impossible to establish. Unlike Soviet subjects, American citizens are not expected to have and required to declare an unalterable ethnic affiliation. Before 1980, many if not most Americans even declined to identify themselves in

census returns by ethnic 'origin or descent'.[62] The subjective and
objective fluidity of ethnic identification in the United States means
that Kallen's 'democracy of nationalities' was as impractical when he
first proposed it as it was fifty years later, when, as part of the
American ethnic revival of the 1970s, Congressman Roman Pucinski
invoked not indeed Horace Kallen but the Soviet model to support
his bill for the Ethnic Heritage Studies Programs. Extreme cultural
pluralism is particularly hard on those Americans (including many
black ones) whose ethnic cultures have not been preserved or have
even been systematically eradicated.[63]

The formal unity of human nature

In practice, Kallen's cultural pluralism overlooked fluidity; in its
theory, it overlooked the unchanging. Kallen's proposal explicitly –
and those of his successors explicitly or implicitly – depend on the
philosophical contention that 'Nature is naturally pluralistic'; even
human nature is 'a true plurality'.[64] In this view, democracy should
not be thought of as a system based on fixed ideals, the finalities of a
dead humanism: 'only the dead can be immortal and changeless and
fixed in their natures. What lives and has a future is labile and fluid.
For it, there are no finalities, whether of rule or being'.[65] Democracy
must be a continuous process of adjustment between old and new:
and this process is guided not by the false light of trans-historical
'Laws of Nature and of Nature's God' (to quote the central American
founding document, the Declaration of Independence), but by a
true, progressive humanism which works on ever-changing
circumstances to create freedom and fellowship by producing 'the
doctrine and discipline proper to the race and generation it
expresses'.[66]

Cultural pluralists such as Kallen shared with the assimilators and
amalgamators whom they opposed, the notion that genes determine
culture, and this materialism led them to the historicist view that
human culture is always particular, never universal. The obsession
with genetics is not shared by many current ethnic pluralists, but it is
significant that all of the American responses to the immigrant
problem have been susceptible to being afflicted by this obsession. At
the bottom of the fascination with genetic determination is that more
common modern intellectual disease (which can be traced back to
Thomas Hobbes), the preoccupation with origins rather than ends,
with material rather than formal and final causes. Thus preoccupied,

we can easily overlook the moral and intellectual similarities that grow on top of the material, genetic differences among humans. Losing sight of the unity of the human species – the 'idea' of the human being – and concentrating instead on the material differences of individual members of that species, we then tend to adopt something like Hobbes' view that conflict among human individuals and groups rather than cooperation is the natural state of affairs, and that ethnic cultures can never really cooperate as human beings.[67]

The human species – like other animal species – has to be defined primarily as a *form* of life, not in terms of the *matter* of which it is made. The word 'species' comes from the Latin translation of the Greek word *eidos*, which means the form, shape or 'looks' of a thing. These 'looks' are immaterial, and therefore, somewhat paradoxically, invisible to the 'naked eye'. (Modern biologists have searched for a materially based definition of species, but in vain; fundamental disagreements and confusions are the most prominent result of this search.[68]) Species are visible to the mind's eye, not the body's on its own, because they consist of forms, not of matter. Thus the human apprehension of species is somewhat mysterious, but it happens.

Defining humanity in terms of ethnic (or individual) gene pools leads to forgetfulness that culture can mean cultivation of the human, and that assimilation can be assimilation to humanity. Of course, some assimilation to English culture has occurred in the United States, as has a great deal of genetic mixture. (The 1980 Census – which pursued questions of ethnic background much more determinedly than previous ones – showed that almost all of the major ethnic groups now have at least half of their members reporting mixed ethnicity.[69]) But English – American English – has provided the medium more than the substance of communication, and genetic mixture and the accompanying atrophy of ethnic cultures has been a natural (though not a necessary) result rather than a necessary condition of liberty.

TOWARDS A LIBERAL ETHNIC POLITICS

However natural and central questions about ethnic policy may seem to us today, ethnicity was not a theme of the classical modern liberal political philosophy of the seventeenth and eighteenth centuries. Superficial critics of liberalism might offer to explain this omission by pointing to the unfortunate preponderance of individualism in that philosophy. How can one expect liberals to give due attention to ethnic groups, when, because of their preoccupation with individuals, they give so little attention to political groups of any kind? But such explanations are inadequate. Individualism has not been as dear to liberalism as many critics and some supporters of liberalism believe. We must remember that the original modern liberal theme, in the seventeenth century, was not individuals but religion (and therefore groups of co-religionists); that there have always been liberal thinkers and politicians who have made a significant place in their regimes for social groups such as churches, families, educational institutions and civic associations; and that some classical liberal political thought – especially that of political economists – is more obviously about economic interest groups than about individuals. The proper relationships between government and various groups within the political community, especially religious and economic groups, have been major themes of liberal writings. Liberal legislation on religious and economic issues today can benefit from the study of such writings. But liberal political literature has not dealt equally thoroughly and precisely with the relationship between politics and ethnicity. There is nothing equivalent to Benedict Spinoza, John Locke and Thomas Jefferson on religious toleration, or Locke, Adam Smith and James Madison on political economy, addressed to the problem of ethnicity. Even when liberal democrats faced the elements of this problem, it seemed to them somewhat beside the point. For example, Alexis de Tocqueville treated his 'considerations concerning the present state and probable future of the three races that inhabit the territory of the United States' as topics that were 'tangents' to his subject, 'being American, but not democratic'.[70] In *The Federalist*, John Jay somewhat inaccurately assumes 'one united people . . . descended from the same ancestors, ...very similar in manners and customs'[71]; other numbers of *The Federalist* tell us much about economic and religious diversity, but little or nothing about the diversity of ethnicity, considered separately from religion. This silence of liberal philosophers may help explain why ethnicity has proved to be such a problem in liberal politics. Confusion and uncertainty about the proper role of ethnicity that stem from the silence of these liberal lawgivers may have exacerbated ethnic problems when they cropped up in liberal regimes.

Nineteenth-century liberal responses to nationalism

In spite of their relative silence on ethnicity, liberal thinkers in the middle of the nineteenth century did find it necessary to come to terms with a rather extreme version of ethnic politics, in the shape of nationalism. Nationalism is the thesis one nation, one state; the view that each nationality should have its own independent state. Politics should reflect the natural development of human beings in separate linguistic (and racial and cultural) groups; in other words, politics should not try to reshape these groups in the image of anything beyond these naturally given units of humanity. The rather romantic character of nationalism should make it immediately suspect to liberals, even to liberal democrats, because liberalism does not suppose that (reverting to the Declaration of Independence) when a people 'assume among the Powers of the earth, the separate and equal station to which the Laws of Nature and of Nature's God entitle them', they are merely enforcing cultural boundaries. Liberal peoples make themselves 'separate and equal' not by naturally, gradually developing a distinctive national culture in a necessary and unique historical process, but by freely, possibly suddenly, agreeing 'to institute new Government, laying its foundation on such principles, and organizing its powers in such form, as to them shall seem most likely to effect their Safety and Happiness'. The end of liberal politics is not the particular right to linguistico-cultural integrity, but the universal right to pursue safety and happiness. This right is based on the nature of human beings, it is not to be justified on historically given facts. (The historicism – the denial of trans-historical, universal human standards – that we have seen in cultural pluralism is also apparent in nationalism.) Ethnic cultures are if anything means rather than ends of liberalism.

This was essentially the reaction of liberals to nineteenth-century nationalism. But this reaction took two main directions, and these have been the directions taken by liberals ever since, for it is possible to agree that ethnicity is only a means to liberty and to disagree as to how the means and end are to be related, and as to whether it is better for the means to be unitary or plural. In the writings of two Englishmen, John Stuart Mill and Lord Acton, we can see the elements of a liberal scheme of ethnic politics – elements that were to appear in a distorted fashion in the extreme American reactions to 'the immigrant problem' that have been analysed above.

A forerunner of the American doctrines of ethnic unity can be found in a chapter on 'Nationality' in Mill's *Considerations on Representative Government*. Mill admitted that 'Where the sentiment of nationality exists in any force, there is a *prima facie* case for uniting all the members of the nationality under the same government, and a government to themselves apart'.[72] But for Mill the purpose of this concession to nationalism was not national purity or the survival of all national cultures – some of which, he did not hesitate to say, were less civilized than others. Cultural homogeneity had a purpose beyond itself. 'Among a people without fellow-feeling, especially if they read and speak different languages, the united public opinion, necessary to the working of representative government, cannot exist'.[73] Especially at the beginnings of free government, prudence suggested that the attempt to unite 'different nationalities of anything like equivalent strength under the same government' be avoided, because this played into the hands of the established despotic government, who could effectively resist popular liberal movements by 'keeping up and envenoming' the antipathies of the different nationalities comprising the people.[74] But these were prudential considerations, not matters of principle. Mill saw no harm, and possible benefit ('gain to civilisation'), in 'the admixture of nationalities, and the blending of their attributes and peculiarities in a common union'.[75] He thought Bretons and Basques benefited from their French nationality, just as the Welsh, Scottish Highlanders, and even, at least recently, the Irish benefited from their British nationality. Far better for a member of such a group 'to be brought into the current of the ideas and feelings of a highly civilised and cultivated people . . . than to sulk on his own rocks, the half-savage relic of past times, revolving in his own little mental orbit'.[76] At the same time, each composite nationality was itself more enriched by inheriting 'the special aptitudes and excellences of all its progenitors, protected by the admixture from being exaggerated into the neighbouring vices'.[77] Nationalities were not inviolate, but they were an important consideration for liberal statesmen.

Mill's response to nationalism could be mistaken for agreement with it, since he argued that national unity was necessary for a viable liberal politics: 'Free institutions are next to impossible in a country made up of different nationalities'.[78] Prudence suggested the encouragement of one national culture per country, at least for political purposes. At the time Mill was writing (1861), nationalism seemed to work towards the enlargement and unification of states more than, as in later years, the reverse. Far more obviously critical of nationalism, and more sensitive to the double-edged blade of the nationalistic sword, were the reflections of Lord Acton's essay on 'Nationality', published in 1862.[79] Just as Mill's thoughts can be seen as a moderate precursor of the American case for ethnic unity, Acton's anticipate American ethnic pluralism.

Acton was not as concerned as American pluralists were to be about the dehumanizing character of homogenizing industrial culture. He was more worried about the overbearing state. Acton quoted Mill as a representative of the liberalism which too readily acquiesced in the thesis one nation, one state (although, as we have seen, Mill really argued for the reverse: one state, one nation, for the sake of political unity rather than for national integrity). Acton's own thoughts led him towards a more pluralistic conclusion: one state, many nations. He reminds us that ethnic solidarity can be a greater problem for liberals than ethnic difference.[80] He saw in nationalism a serious threat to liberty and democracy. The application of this 'French' 'theory of unity' to a country

> overrules the rights and wishes of the inhabitants, absorbing their divergent interests in a fictitious unity; sacrifices their several inclinations and duties to the higher claim of nationality, and crushes all natural rights and all established liberties for the purpose of vindicating itself . . . . In supporting the claims of national unity, governments must be subverted in whose title there is no flaw, and whose policy is beneficent and equitable, and subjects must be compelled to transfer their allegiance to an authority for which they have no attachment, and which may be practically a foreign domination.[81]

Acton counterpoised this with a 'theory of liberty', the 'English' theory,

> which represents nationality as an essential, but not a supreme element in determining the forms of the State. It is distinguished from the other, because it tends to diversity and not to uniformity, to harmony and not to unity; because it aims not at an arbitrary change, but at careful respect for the existing conditions of political life, and because it obeys the laws and results of history, not the aspirations of an ideal future . . . . The presence of different nations under the same sovereignty is similar in its effects to the independence of the Church in the State. It provides

against the servility which flourishes under the shadow of a single
authority, by balancing interests, multiplying associations, and
giving to the subject the restraint and support of a combined
opinion . . . . Liberty provokes diversity, and diversity preserves
liberty by supplying the means of organisation . . . . That
intolerance of social freedom which is natural to absolutism is sure
to find a corrective in the national diversities, which no other
force could so efficiently provide. The co-existence of several
nations under the same State is a test, as well as the best security
of its freedom. It is also one of the chief instruments of
civilisation; and, as such, it is in the natural and providential order,
and indicates a state of greater advancement than the national
unity which is the ideal of modern liberalism.[82]

Acton predicted that the course of the 'absurd and . . . criminal'
theory of nationality would 'be marked with material as well as moral
ruin',[83] but he hoped that the utopian quality of the theory – the
physical impossibility of conforming to the rule one nation, one state
– would mean that one beneficial practical result of asserting the
claims of nationalities would be, ironically, to contribute to 'the
liberty of different nationalities as members of one sovereign
community', which the theory of nationality itself condemns. No
future government would be able to ignore national claims; in this
way, the theory, although in itself 'a retrograde step in history',[84]
could contribute unintentionally to historical progress. Part of this
progress would be the growing recognition by liberals of the
disadvantages of the simple parliamentary system of government, and
of the advantages of the institutional safeguards against centralization
provided by such devices as federalism and localism.

Liberal unity and ethnic plurality

Mill's *Considerations* argue for unity, Acton's essay argues for
diversity. Both arguments were addressed to an extreme fusion of
ethnicity and politics, but neither response was extreme, and a
common middle ground seems visible. After all, both writers were
able to praise the ethnic arrangements of certain countries – although
Mill praised the amalgamation, and Acton the multiplicity. Mill's
point is that a degree of common culture is necessary for the
operation of liberal democratic institutions. One can agree with that
and still agree with Acton that a degree of cultural diversity can

constitute a useful barrier to tyranny and a source of civil vitality through the commingling of different nationalities in what he called (anticipating the 'melting pot' image) 'the cauldron of the State'. What is needed to combine the requirements of both insights is the liberal separation of state and society, which assumes that politics is not all there is to life, and that citizens who find security and a degree of identity and friendship in their common citizenship can also find a fuller friendship in their separate social lives. The desire to promote both common civic loyalties and ethnic cultural (i.e. subcultural) loyalties can be coherent if neither set of loyalties is absolutized, and if both are recognized as worthy of human devotions. In particular, in the USA today, it has to be emphasized that such a system requires a sufficient degree of common culture to act as a political *lingua franca* in the sphere of citizenship and politics proper, so citizens can understand each other and associate with each other for political purposes. W.E.B. DuBois, pondering relations between black and white citizens in post-Civil War America, had something like this in mind when he argued that 'national' or 'race ideals' might 'strive together . . . as well, perhaps even better, than in isolation', so long as there is 'substantial agreement' on 'political ideals' and language, and 'a satisfactory adjustment of economic life'.[85]

The ideal liberal formula, then, would seem to be one state, one nationality and many subnationalities. Here, liberals could follow Plato's advice, with suitable modifications. In the *Laws*, Plato suggests that the basis for the best practicable regime is provided in a multiethnic colony, where the mixture of groups may cause conflicts but nevertheless facilitates the introduction of the best laws, equally new to every group.[86] Liberals expect less but still significant benefit from the multiplicity of ethnic groups; they hope to introduce not the absolutely best regime, but merely a good polity, in which there is public acknowledgement that none of the groups' regimes is good enough to govern the rest. Not rivalry to rule, but mutual tolerance, perhaps punctuated by deflating ethnic jokes, is the liberal formula for inter-ethnic relations. Ethnic favouritism or discrimination, like nepotism, will inevitably occur in private as long as the family and that greatly extended family, the ethnic group, are not abolished, but if the degree of justice that is possible in liberal polities is to be achieved and sustained, such considerations must not be allowed to attain the status of public law. Justice Harlan summed it up in his famous dissenting opinion in *Plessy v. Ferguson*. That opinion is most famous for its statement that the constitution is 'color blind'; but

Harlan also stated that 'pride of race' can be expressed 'under appropriate circumstances, when the rights of others . . . are not to be affected'.[87]

In the liberal scheme, the separate cultures or subcultures not only must be kept essentially private, they must also not be allowed to lead citizens to act against the necessary common culture and the common interest of the whole country. Liberal policy on ethnicity here parallels that on religion, and it has to reserve the right to be equally tough. As John Locke pointed out in his *Letter Concerning Toleration*,[88] religious toleration has certain limits; those sects should not be tolerated who teach 'opinions contrary to human society', who fail to preach tolerance of others, or whose sectarian loyalties lead them to favour foreigners over fellow citizens. (Locke's fourth category of intolerables is public non-believers, but ethnicity does not seem to be on a par with religion in this respect, for public absence of ethnicity does not detract from one's ability to fulfill the duties of liberal citizenship.)

The liberal scheme is not unproblematic. As Locke indicates, the public power needs to make tactical incursions into the private realm in order to maintain its strategic withdrawal from that realm. There can be no impenetrable 'wall of separation' between state and society. So there is always the difficulty of judging which incursions are justified, and a need for prudence in those who make that judgement. Locke says 'it is easy to understand to what end the legislative power ought to be directed',[89] but the means to that end are clearly more contestable. Some of the most moving cases in American constitutional law have dealt with just this question. Consider one classic case, that of *Wisconsin v. Yoder* (1972)[90]: should children of the Amish be legally compelled to attend school beyond the age of 14 (up to the standard leaving age of 16), even though that attendance would endanger the free exercise of the Amish religion, by keeping the children exposed to values and beliefs at odds with that religion, and by taking them away from the informal, more vocational schooling that the Amish themselves want their children to have at this age? In fact, the Supreme Court did not find this a very hard case to decide: the only partly dissenting opinion agreed with the rest of the Court that the Amish should win the case, but argued that the religious views of the children, rather than those of the parents, should be decisive. Nevertheless, this case raised some hard questions about the relationship between mainstream culture and serious but – to the mainstream – eccentric cultures. One of the reasons that the case was relatively easy to decide was that the USA does have space for such eccentricities. The film of the case, *Witness* (produced in 1985), shows the deep contrast between the ways of the Amish and American ways. The all-American hero (played by Harrison Ford) and the Amish heroine (played by Kelly McGillis) have to go their separate ways in the end; little productive interplay between the two ways seems possible. This is not the best of all possible worlds for a liberal scheme of ethnicity to aim at. The film also makes it clear that the reason for this lack of creative interchange lies mainly in the Amish ways, not the American ones. The Amish call outsiders 'the English': politically as well as technologically they remain in pre-Revolutionary America, in the days before the ideas articulated in the Declaration of Independence started creating American super-nationality.

There is also the question whether the fulfillment of the duties of liberal citizenship can be expected from humans whose souls are primarily attached to and cultivated in private associations rather than public, political activities. This Rousseauian objection to the liberal scheme applies, of course, to other activities in addition to ethnic ones. One good response is that such associations and activities need not be wholly private. (We shall see in Chapter 5 that this point is too often overlooked by contemporary liberal theory.) However, the strength of liberalism in its depoliticization of soul-fulfilling pursuits can also be its weakness. How, for instance, can citizens be expected to develop sufficient loyalty to a country that they would risk their lives for it, if their citizenship in that country is based on a thin, minimal political culture that relegates to the plural social sphere such things as education, religion and ethnicity? Perhaps this question is harder to answer when considering things other than ethnicity. The liberal decoupling of politics and ethnicity may prove to be one of the least troublesome liberal decouplings. Acton argued that patriotism was in fact more natural to the political state than to the nation. He suggested (anticipating twentieth-century sociobiology) that the nation, like the family from which it is extended, preserves itself more by selfish physical instinct than by moral obligation. 'The great sign of true patriotism, the development of selfishness into sacrifice, is the product of political life'.[91] However, Acton also pointed out that nationality in the modern world 'was no longer what it had been to the ancient world,... a result of merely physical and material causes, – but a moral and political being'.[92] The transition from the material

and physical to the moral and political had been accomplished by
modern nationalities themselves. Modern nationalism is an
expression of the Kantian philosophy of moral self-determination
and freedom.[93] Acton may have been right to contend that nations
could not have developed their moral sense without the assistance of
the state. But the fact remains that they have developed it, and it is
difficult to deny that in practice modern national and ethnic groups
have been at least as successful as liberal states in eliciting moral
self-sacrifice. So the viability of the liberal scheme remains
problematic. If it works, it will be not because there is no problem
in the relationship of private and public, but because thoughtful
efforts are made to cope with that problem.

In American politics, perhaps the most penetrating statement of
the elements and aims of the liberal scheme of ethnicity and
citizenship is still to be found in the reflections of Abraham Lincoln.
In 1858, in the course of his debates with Stephen Douglas about the
future of slavery in the United States, Lincoln noticed some of the
uses of the American celebration of the anniversary of the
Declaration of Independence:

> We are now a mighty nation, we are thirty – or about thirty
> millions of people, and we own and inhabit about one-fifteenth
> part of the dry land of the whole earth. We run our memory back
> over the pages of history for about eighty-two years and we
> discover that we were then a very small people in point of
> numbers, vastly inferior to what we are now, with a vastly less
> extent of country, – with vastly less of everything we deem
> desirable among men, – we look upon the change as exceedingly
> advantageous to us and to our posterity, and we fix upon
> something that happened away back, as in some way or other
> being connected with this rise of prosperity. We find a race of
> men living in that day whom we claim as our fathers and
> grandfathers; they were iron men, they fought for the principle
> that they were contending for; and we understand that by what
> they then did it has followed that the degree of prosperity that we
> now enjoy has come to us. We hold this annual celebration to
> remind ourselves of all the good done in this process of time of
> how it was done and who did it, and how we are historically
> connected with it; and we go from these meetings in better humor
> with ourselves – we feel more attached the one to the other, and
> more firmly bound to the country we inhabit. In every way we

are better men in the age, and race, and country in which we live for these celebrations. But after we have done all this we have not yet reached the whole. There is something else connected with it. We have besides these men – descended by blood from our ancestors – among us perhaps half our people who are not descendants at all of these men, they are men who have come from Europe – German, Irish, French and Scandinavian – men that have come from Europe themselves, or whose ancestors have come hither and settled here, finding themselves our equals in all things. If they look back through this history to trace their connection with those days by blood, they find they have none, they cannot carry themselves back into that glorious epoch and make themselves feel that they are part of us, but when they look through that old Declaration of Independence they find that those old men say that 'We hold these truths to be self-evident, that all men are created equal', and then they feel that that moral sentiment taught in that day evidences their relation to those men, that it is the father of all moral principle in them, and that they have a right to claim it as though they were blood of the blood, and flesh of the flesh of the men who wrote that Declaration, and so they are. That is the electric cord in that Declaration that links the hearts of patriotic and liberty-loving men together, that will link those patriotic hearts as long as the love of freedom exists in the minds of men throughout the world.[94]

If Lincoln is right, the cause of equal freedom itself can inspire a sufficiently deep liberal patriotism – a loyalty not to ethnic patriarchs, but to what he called that 'father of all moral principle', the self-evident truth of human equality. The liberal scheme requires establishment of and loyalty to the liberal creed. Of course, the establishment of such a creed can coexist with monumental practical denials of its truth. Hypocrisy on a large scale can be maintained, as in the case of American slavery, which, to some abolitionists, even to such a moderate one as Frederick Douglass, made American celebration of the Declaration of Independence look like 'mere bombast, fraud, deception, impiety, hypocrisy – a thin veil to cover up crimes which would disgrace a nation of savages'.[95] But the creed seems necessary, even though it is not sufficient. The best basis of a liberal scheme of ethnicity, a scheme that gives due weight to both plurality and unity, is public recognition of the idea that human beings are in a politically crucial sense naturally equal. Yet, as we shall see in Chapter 5, liberal thinking has been progressively abandoning this idea.

A common language on its own can produce some degree of ethnic harmony (as the example of French linguistico-cultural imperialism shows). But there will be limits to the liberality of such a multiethnic community if the common language is not used for liberal thought and speech. After all, the multiplicity of ethnic groups on its own is neither necessary nor sufficient for liberal democracy. In fact, the idea of a multiethnic polity – although one lacking a liberal basis – can be traced in modern political thought to an illiberal source, Niccolo Machiavelli. In his *Discourses*, Machiavelli showed how the greatness of Rome depended on the policy of admitting the ethnics – the 'nations' – into Roman citizenship.[96] This policy, when it was successful, did not defer to the ethnic cultures so much as it reinforced the Roman understanding of political life, which was universal in the sense that ethnic differences were seen to be less important than the natural differences between humans of whatever nationality. In Machiavelli's modern project – his new 'Rome' – humans would unite for the aggrandizement of Romans – or humans in general, opposed to the world – rather than for particular ethnic regimes, opposed to each other. But in Machiavelli's scheme, they would unite in a cynically undemocratic manner, with an enterprising class of 'princes' making the running and an apolitical class of 'peoples' merely responding. Lincoln's reflections put equality and its ethical and political implications back into Machiavelli's modern universalism, and thereby produce a vision of a unified multiethnic polity that is more viable because it is more liberal.

CONCLUSION

The leading arguments in favour of the current American policies of multilingualism and affirmative discrimination have wrongly assumed not only that a choice between ethnic melting pot and ethnic pluralism is necessary, but also that pluralism should be preferred. Elements of consociational democracy have thus crept into American liberal democracy. Such elements may at times be necessary or helpful, but it is insane to choose to inflict them on a regime that can attain – or retain – higher standards. In fact, if Americans had to choose between ethnic unity and plurality – between melting pot and cultural pluralism, or (less extremely) between Mill and Acton – they would be wise to go for the former. Ethnic groups cannot survive without the country, but the country could probably survive without ethnic groups. While the ethnic revolt of the 1960s and 1970s can be seen (as it has by some commentators[97]) as a return to a healthy emphasis on local participation and decentralization, there are other bodies between the American state and the individual that can provide the protection that Acton sought in ethnic groups, as there are other sources of cultural vitality. Perhaps the relative silence of classical liberalism on the role of ethnicity is in this way comprehensible; ethnicity is more dispensable than the family or religion or liberal education. The liberal scheme assumes that this choice is unnecessary. Liberalism should not imitate Marxism-Leninism, which assumes that ethnic activities, like religions, will eventually be discarded as (in Karl Marx's phrase) 'snake-skins cast off by history', and supports ethnicity only as a tactic in the strategy for abolishing it.[98] Liberal universalism, in contrast to Marxist universalism, attempts not to eradicate particular ethnic and religious attachments, but merely to keep them in their place. Liberal democracy can gain much from ethnic cultures, especially if these encourage family life and the virtues nurtured by families (the topic of the following chapter). Ethnic diversity can also assist economic diversity, an indispensable tool in the liberal political workshop. However, liberals should be able to live without 'unmeltable' ethnicity if they have to. It would probably be utopian and anti-democratic to aim at this result, but if it should arrive or threaten to arrive, it should not cause undue alarm.

Even if a more soundly liberal approach comes to be taken in American ethnic policy, it will be worth remembering the history of the less sane policies that have been examined in this chapter, as bad ideas whose times came, and might come again. One of the reasons for this continuing vulnerability of American liberal democracy to such bad ideas is that the basic notions of liberal democracy are currently so badly understood, not only by public officials in charge of ethnic policies, but also by the educators in charge of teaching political science and political philosophy. American thinking and policy on ethnic affairs have been badly served by contemporary liberal political theory, the shortcomings of which will be explored in Chapter 5. The thoughts and policies that are too preoccupied with the desirability of ethnic heterogeneity or pluralism have their counterpart in the current theoretical tendency towards a libertarian extreme that finds it difficult to rise above individualism and pluralism to support political community. The opposite thoughts and policies, those that are fascinated by the need for ethnic homogeneity – 'amalgamation' or 'assimilation' – have their counterpart in an opposing current theoretical tendency, towards excessive social community, for the sake of human cooperation. Or, more often, merely for the sake of *social* cooperation, regardless of how *human* the social activity happens to be, for, as we shall see, contemporary communitarians base their political theory on appreciation of human nature no more than do contemporary libertarians. The neglect or misunderstanding of human nature that we have seen in past and current ethnic policies can only be encouraged by the dominant schools of liberal political theory.

Before we look more deeply into the failings of current political theory (in Chapters 5 and 6), we consider two further areas of political practice in which serious problems arise partly because of those failings.

Chapter 3

Sexual difference and human equality

The argument of this book is an old-fashioned liberal argument that if we want to secure and to improve liberal policies and institutions, then we have to respect the nature of the human species more carefully than we generally do. But what sex is a member of that species? This question is often posed by critics of liberalism in order to suggest that the liberal focus on a supposedly universal human nature is hopelessly wrong. We have to admit that this question is more troubling for liberal politics than the parallel question, also posed by the critics, what ethnicity is a human being? This is because although (as the previous chapter argued) liberals can contemplate the disappearance of ethnic divisions, they cannot adopt this philosophical attitude to sexual divisions. They can sometimes see ethnic differences disappearing, and yet remain calm; they can do neither of these things in the case of sexual differences. It is not just that sex is fun, it is also that sex is useful for human beings and human societies, so its disappearance would be troubling. In any case, because it is both biologically and sociologically more firmly rooted than ethnicity, it shows few signs of disappearing. (In spite of several decades of expressions of doubt about the naturalness of sexual differences, it still would sound much stranger to talk of our ethnic natures, than it is to talk of our sexual natures.) Sex seems here to stay, so liberals have to make the best of it.

Just as with the problem of ethnicity, we can discern two extreme reactions to the problem of sexual difference, one longing too exclusively for human and political unity, the other too content with human and political plurality. As we shall see, both of these reactions are for various reasons quite tempting, but they are avoidable, and liberals should try to avoid them. The first of these reactions is a simplistically liberal feminism, tending towards a sex-blind humanism. Within this school of thought, the contention is that in politics, sexual differences are more harmful than helpful, and that they can and should disappear from the political world. In this view, the desirable goals of political unity and human cooperation could be much more perfectly achieved if sexual differences among the cooperating individuals were to become less evident, or at least less important. The second and opposite reaction is a more radical feminism, involving a humanity-blind sexism that denies the human homogeneity behind sexual heterogeneity, and argues that the standards of rationality and human nature to which liberals appeal are in fact rather badly disguised weapons of sexual politics, weapons that serve the patriarchal ambitions of males. The first reaction is too preoccupied with the need for unity and homogeneity, and tends to overlook humans' sexual natures; the second is too preoccupied with sexual differences and tends to overlook the human nature that is shared by men and women.

Unfortunately, one cannot simply combine these opposing reactions, or play them off against one another, and thereby hope to produce a wiser and more moderate way of thinking about sex and politics, because neither of these reactions holds onto and builds upon the strength that one might expect to accompany its respective weakness. As we shall see, the liberal feminists who play down *sexual* nature also water down or simply reject the moral and political relevance of *human* nature. And the radical reaction, which even more emphatically rejects *human* nature as any sort of moral or political standard, in fact builds not upon *sexual natures* but, more precisely, on *gender roles*: not biological sexual natures, but historically determined, socially created 'gender' roles are, for the radical feminist, what make the liberal feminist hope for sex-blind politics unrealistic. It is less accurate to call radical feminism 'sexist' than it is to call it 'genderist', if we are true to its self-understanding. (As in the case of ethnicity, the unity-oriented extreme thus shares with current 'communitarian' political theory the historicist view that human community, in the things that really count in making us human, is based purely on human conventions, not on nature.)

If we accept one of the arguments of this chapter, that sexual difference is more natural than ethnic difference, and that a sex-free society would be more doubtfully human than an ethnicity-free society, then, in contrast to our conclusions about the problem of ethnicity, we shall find that the more deeply-rooted problem of sexual difference cannot be so confidently approached with a tilt (however hypothetical) towards the unity extreme (liberal feminism and humanism), against the plurality extreme (radical feminism and genderism). However, as with ethnicity, the intellectually more tempting extreme lies at the plurality pole, where we find principled neglect of the human nature that men and women have in common. This is the intellectually more tempting extreme because it (like ethnic cultural pluralism) presents itself as the less abstract, less formal, less sociologically naïve view – also, perhaps, because it often seems to be the more demanding, uncompromising, politically engaged view. Therefore it should be helpful to begin thinking about these matters by appreciating the strength of the case that one can make on the other side, in favour of a liberal feminism. To make a strong case for liberal feminism, we shall need to put human nature more clearly into the picture than many liberal feminists allow, and we shall need to be particularly wary of the defects of an atomistic, community-destroying individualism that has too often been mistaken for the essence of liberalism, and has too often made liberalism more vulnerable than it need be to radical and communitarian critiques.

THE ENDS AND LIMITS OF LIBERAL FEMINISM

In *The Left Hand of Darkness*, a work of science fiction by Ursula Le Guin, we find a society of androgynous humans living on a planet called Gethen. Gethenians live behind a veil of sexual ignorance: when they have sexual intercourse, they do not know until the culminant phase whether they will be acting as male or female. Apart from four days each month during the twenty childbearing years, they are neither male nor female: sexuality does not pervade social life. This seems to be a welcome improvement on terrestrial nature in at least one respect: everyone shares sexual burdens and privileges pretty equally, and there is not one group always in danger of being identified with household responsibilities. One possible drawback is also made clear: no one 'is quite so free as a free male elsewhere'.[1] However, the reason for this is that Gethenians retain a sexist division of labour: the female-for-the-time-being is the one who stays at home for at least the brief period that meeting an infant's demands is incompatible with other employment, so eventually practically all citizens combine homemaking with their other careers.

We earthlings have found it even harder than Gethenians to separate economic division of labour from the sexual division.

Radical feminists complain that some of the pressures of liberal industrialism have pushed both women and men to accept a family division of labour that is even more rigidly sexist than the traditional one. Even as technological advances have loosened the economic and biological ties of women to family life, the emotional role of women in families has grown. As economic progress has introduced a greater distinction between home and workplace, and the extended family has become much more uncommon, atomized families have come to depend more on their isolated women for their emotional binding.[2] This complaint may be a little romantic, but it is true that the economic progress required by liberalism is not necessarily an unmixed blessing for the cause of equal opportunity of the sexes. The liberal recipe of private households plus intense economic development can be a recipe for heightening rather than for reducing gender differentiation.

The missing ingredient in this recipe is feminism: the abolition of legal disabilities and occupational barriers to women (as urged by some nineteenth-century liberals such as J. S. Mill), and (going beyond Mill) the dissolution of the connection between childbearing and childcare. The argument that the health of the private family requires the woman to retreat from any demanding occupation outside the home rests on the observation that in general there is seldom a substitute for her: Mill asserted that 'nobody else takes' care 'of the children and the household' if she does not. This argument was questioned in Mill's day, and has been subject to massive doubts in ours. Mill himself was already careful to specify that this was something to be regulated by opinion rather than by law, and that 'the utmost latitude ought to exist for the adaptation of general rules to individual suitabilities'. He was prepared to excuse married women from childcare and household management (assuming 'due provision' could be made for any necessary substitutes) in the case of women with 'faculties exceptionally adapted to any other pursuit'.[3] Treating married women's liberation from the household as a permitted exception to a general rule may sound weak, but was shockingly feminist to many of Mill's contemporaries: he still had to defend himself against charges that he underrated the domestic virtues of women, and that his proposals threatened the survival of the family.

Since Mill's time, the opinion and practice of some liberal democracies has begun to transform his exception and excuse into the neutral expectation desired by most feminists today. In 1986 a

Roper poll found 51 per cent of women in the United States preferring employment outside the home (compared to 46 per cent in 1980 and 35 per cent in 1974).[4] In 1987 Louis Harris reported 63 per cent of American women saying they wanted to combine marriage, a career and children (compared to 52 per cent in 1977); the number looking forward to 'marrying, having children and no career' dropped in that period from 38 per cent to 26 per cent.[5] Another recent Roper survey has shown that American public opinion supports openness to both sexes in most occupations (the exceptions were construction worker, with only 44 per cent in support, and firefighter, with only 40 per cent).[6] By the mid-1980s, women comprised nearly half of the paid work force, and slightly over half of the professional work force (6.9 million out of 13.8 million, with recent gains in medicine, law, engineering and other traditionally more male-dominated professions now added to the large dominance of women in education and nursing).[7] In 1985 a woman was elected president of the National Cattlemen's Association. An ongoing survey of the attitudes of first-year American college students shows much larger moves among females than among males in the shift towards saying that one of their 'very important' goals in attending college is 'to be very well-off financially'.[8] As E. M. Forster noticed nearly a century ago, in the heart of woman

> there are springing up strange desires. She too is enamoured of heavy winds, and vast panoramas, and green expanses of the sea. She has marked the kingdom of the world, how full it is of wealth, and beauty, and war – a radiant crust, built around the central fires, spinning towards the receding heavens. Men, declaring that she inspires them to it, move joyfully over the surface, having the most delightful meetings with other men, happy, not because they are masculine, but because they are alive. Before the show breaks up she would like to drop the august title of the Eternal Woman, and go there as her transitory self.[9]

Not all of the immediate results of the more dispersed feminization of the professions are unqualifiedly good. For example, releasing intelligent and educated women from the track that led many of them into school teaching as the only suitable profession has pushed down the percentage of intelligent school teachers.[10] But in the longer term, such extension of equal opportunities can be expected generally to improve on what Plato's Athenian Stranger (in the *Laws*) long ago referred to as the 'mindless' arrangement whereby keeping women at home makes a country 'half of what it might be'.[11] As Mill contended, humanity can ill afford 'to dispense with one-half of what nature proffers' in the way of 'individual talent available for the conduct of human affairs'.[12] The goals of liberal feminism are political as well as individual: liberal feminism tries to facilitate contributions of all talented humans to the common good, as well as to remove social and political barriers to the human rights and human development of individual women.

Among the female extradomiciliary workers in the United States are nearly half of mothers with children less than 1 year old (up from 24 per cent in 1970)[13], and more than half of those with children aged between 3 and 5.[14] Many of these women have only part-time or part-year jobs. (A survey in 1984 found only 27 per cent of children under 18 with full-time, full-year employed mothers, another 37 per cent with mothers employed only part time or part year.[15]) But there is growing pressure to accommodate the (currently) conflicting demands of childcare and paid employment. Although trade unions have been reluctant to help women manage motherhood and jobs[16], the number of employed women has reached the point at which they and their male colleagues (many with employed wives) are more willing to assert their parental obligations against the rigidities of practices and expectations in their work places, helping to make the recognition of workers' family responsibilities the mark of a good employer – *and* often thereby increasing productivity too.[17] Still, if (for good reasons) the family remains monogamous and if (for economic reasons) the length of the working day is not halved, in some cases neutrality on the question of who minds the home can have a hard implication: if women are to be liberated, some men's liberties may have to be curtailed, to the extent of them becoming not quite 'so free as a free male' is accustomed to being. The premise of Mill's 'general rule' was the unwillingness or inability of men to be good homemakers. For the general rule to be abolished without damage to family life, more men may have to be persuaded to undertake more childcare and household management, and to be educated in such a way that they are prepared to do so. In fact there is evidence that American men – including those whose wives have no paid employment – are taking on more domestic responsibilities (although hardly their fair share, at least in the case of men whose wives have full-time jobs).[18] Attitudes towards this are apparently changing rapidly; for example, in a 1970

survey, 58 per cent of men and 68 per cent of women said they
would have less respect for a man who decided to stay at home and
take care of his children while his wife went out to work; in 1986,
only 23 per cent of men and 27 per cent of women voiced that
opinion.[19] More generally, sociological studies have shown that the
idea that American men are *psychologically* more dependent on their
jobs than on their families for their happiness is false. It may be, as
one researcher has concluded, that their 'high degree of psychological involvement in their families provides a foundation for
enlarging men's performance of housework and childcare'.[20]

It is sometimes difficult for liberal feminists to make the case for
more male homemaking, because it sounds too much like an
argument against liberty, although it can be presented (as Betty
Friedan does) as a case for men's liberation from lives as 'passive
robots of the corporation'.[21] But it is the logical liberal position,
however harsh it may sound. True, families should ideally be a realm
where loving friendship, not justice, presides, but we can respect that
ideal even while noticing that tyranny can well begin at home. Some
radical feminists, less convinced that childcare is humanly limiting
(even if household management is), are perhaps able more easily to
persuade the men, but have less incentive to do so, because they look
less to the private family as the proper moral nursery for children.
(Radicals are also less attached to economic growth, or at least to the
economic division of labour that liberals assume is necessary for
economic growth.)

Part of the harshness of the logic of liberal feminism is caused by
the fact that even if both men and women mother, there can still be
economic pressure for partners to specialize. The disappearance of
gender differentiation could leave untouched the division of labour
and attendant cultural differences between those who mother and
those who do not. Going back to Le Guin's story about Gethen, one
could ask, why should rational androgynous partners not agree that
one of them shall do the mothering and the other continue working
as before, no matter which of them gets pregnant? Why should even
temporary females always be the ones who do the mothering? Why
should one partner not be quite as 'free as a free male elsewhere'? An
established division of labour between the two adult partners could
claim at least one advantage over the more interchangeable
partnership imagined by Le Guin: a partner who specializes in work
in the home could be better at it, while the partner whose work
outside the home is not for some decades always potentially and

occasionally actually interrupted could retain the freedom and competitiveness not enjoyed by any Gethenians. However, such economic calculations as these become less harsh and even altogether less relevant as the number of children per family decreases and household management becomes less time-consuming. And the economics of childcare tips more in favour of communal arrangements of some sort, as family size decreases.

It would be wrong to conclude from these limits and problems of liberal feminism that even the complete achievement of its goals would be pointless. But it is fair to conclude both that this achievement would not entirely remove the kinds of cultural division currently connected with the existence of private households, and that – in spite of this somewhat limited effect – the success of liberal feminism depends less on formal legislation than on great changes in informal social attitudes and education, which are likely only gradually to counteract the inertia of traditional attitudes and opinions. This is an area of policy in which even the activist American judiciary of recent decades have been most active simply in bringing the law into line with accumulating social changes.

INDIVIDUALISM AND FAMILIES

We noted in the preceding chapter that the charge that liberal political thinking is historically and sociologically naïve in its concentration on classless, raceless, sexless, parentless, childless individuals is inaccurate, because the most sensible liberals have not at all ignored the past and continuing political importance of these and other social characteristics. Understanding individual human beings rather than families or other groups as the elements of political society does not imply that politics can dispense with such groups, and in fact liberal political thinkers in general have tried to encourage the flourishing of many kinds of subpolitical groups, for the sake of human happiness and for security from overbearing political power. However, from its origins in the seventeenth and eighteenth centuries, liberals have – and have quite rightly – insisted on the importance of the actions, responsibilities and rights of individual human beings, as opposed to the prerogatives of churches, ethnic groups and families, all with their internal and often very illiberal hierarchies. And as we have seen, the permeability and dynamism of liberal interest group politics and ethnic group politics depend on that underlying individualism. So individualism brings both moral bite and political life to liberalism. It brings considerable analytic power as well, for it is not wholly inaccurate to see individuals as the basic elements of society; realistically (as analysts – both advocates and opponents – of tyranny have often remarked), if individuals do not feel secured by the social fabric, that fabric may very well not long cohere. But for liberals the main attraction of individualism is its moral force, its power of revealing the injustice and unhappiness that individual human beings suffer under illiberal social and political regimes.

The moral attraction of individualism – as distinguished from its purely analytical attraction – seems particularly clear in the case of the liberal analysis of family life. However plausible it may be to understand religious, class and ethnic groups as products of individual calculation and action, this approach seems much sillier when applied to babies, and perhaps to family life in general. Here the individualistic assumption of human independence and rationality is stretched to breaking point. Nevertheless, liberals have good reason to cling to a moderate individualism, even when thinking about sex and family life. Modern individualism, from its origins in the political philosophies of Thomas Hobbes and John Locke, was optimistic, but not thoughtless. As Joyce Appleby has remarked, 'Locke and Hobbes had not forgotten their childhoods. Rather they had the prescience to realize that one's childhood was becoming less important – from a political point of view – than one's autonomy as an adult'.[22] In other words, liberals' abstraction from family life and reinterpretation of family life in terms of this abstraction – in terms of individuals – were part of their optimism about economic and social progress.

Women stood to gain – or at least to be affected – more than men by this progress. Even feminists who reject the argument that women have any biological fitness to do the mothering needed in a society admit (as one of them writes) that 'Originally, and in contemporary gathering and hunting societies, the sexual division of labor in which women mother was necessary for group reproduction, for demographic and economic reasons'.[23] A primitive 'state of nature' is the wrong place to see sexual equality flourish. But with technological progress, the sexual division of labour can be diminished. As Roger Masters has argued, 'although the introduction of industrialized technology *increases* the differentiation between male and female roles, . . . [a]s industrialization progresses, the growth in social wealth and security permits increasing equality between men and women'.[24] And liberalism, its admirers and its critics agree, has been an engine of technological progress. One of the effects of this progress is that in modern times women have become much less disadvantaged in contributing in diverse ways to a community's material prosperity and security, and much more indiscriminately involved in warfare, modern economic life having become somewhat tamed, and modern warfare having become more technological and rather less tamed. Modern economics and politics are more cerebral, therefore less constrained by bodily sexual differences and more reflective of mental human equality.[25] Improved birth control, increased life expectancy and declining infant mortality have made it possible for childbearing to impinge less on women's lives. No doubt it is premature to announce (with Susan Okin) that 'We have reached a point in technological and economic development at which it should be possible to do away with sex roles entirely, except for the isolated case of woman's freely chosen exercise of her procreative capacity'.[26] Will love ever be quite so rationally organized? But it is clear that modern technology has made men's and women's common human nature more politically relevant. It is not necessary to support radical modernity's resentment of nature and its attempt to liberate us from our bodily sexual natures in order to support a greater realization of our common bodily and psychic human nature.

Why, then, should liberals today abandon their original optimism and individualism? The argument that they should usually rests at least in part on the assumption that the preservation of family life requires the preservation of traditional notions of male and female contributions and burdens within families. But liberal individualism (even, as we shall see, its early versions in the writings of Hobbes and Locke) concurs with feminism in the rejection of this assumption.

To see the moral and analytical strength of liberal individualism when dealing with sex and families, it is helpful to contrast the brutalizing, egoistic individualism of Hobbes with the more humane and more genuinely liberal individualism of Locke. In Hobbes' analysis matrimonial relations are reduced to an example of 'dominion established by natural force', and children's relations with their parents are so harsh and calculating that Hobbes has trouble distinguishing the rights and duties of children from those of servants. He understands the family as an inevitably abortive attempt by individuals to gain the security that only the Leviathan state can in the end provide. Strong family ties are obstacles to, rather than part of, healthy politics. Hobbes' unrelentingly individualistic re-interpretation of the family undermines it, by making it less attractive to individuals, and more subject to manipulation by the state.[27]

The extreme response to this extreme, atomistic individualism is best expressed by Jean-Jacques Rousseau's romantic elevation of family life. Rousseau's solution to the problem of social atomism is not the Hobbesian state but the loving family. In Rousseau's analysis, sexual love replaces the fear of death as the decisive political motive. Rousseau accepted the Hobbesian view that reason – essentially the calculation of the individual motivated by fear – undermines familial and political loyalties. But instead of following Hobbes to the conclusion that the family should be reinforced – in effect replaced – by individual subordination to the state, Rousseau tried to refound family and political loyalties on the ground of sexual passion, a stronger and more reliable motive than fear and individualistic calculation. As Allan Bloom has summarized Rousseau's teaching, in the enlightened modern world, 'the love between man and woman must be preserved and encouraged, for it is the politically undangerous fanaticism that ennobles human beings and can, by way of the family, even strengthen the political order'; consequently both sexual liberation and liberal feminism (treating men and women the same) 'must be combated in order to avoid the demystification of love'.[28]

But does Rousseau (and Bloom too, for that matter, in his recent pen portrait of the decline and fall of modernity[29]) not assume a too Hobbesian version of modern liberalism? Are humans really as naturally unpolitical as the individualistic Hobbes and the communitarian Rousseau both make them out to be? Is liberal citizenship chimerical? Chronologically and logically between the two extremes represented by Hobbes and Rousseau is the more moderate individualism of John Locke. Because of this moderate position, and because of the widespread misunderstanding of that position, it is worth considering Locke's thinking at some length. (Locke is among those many political thinkers who have recently been unmasked by feminists, to reveal the sexism lurking in their thinking, but Locke, for one, has often been treated more roughly than he deserves.)

Locke steers a course between patriarchalism (as represented by one of the most obvious targets of his political treatises, the writings of Sir Robert Filmer) and an illiberal, Hobbesian, atomistic individualism. He supports a political system in which the moral virtues needed for healthy public life are cultivated in private families. He interprets this liberal morality and family life as products of individualism rightly understood. Locke – contrary to the feminist view that makes him a crypto-patriarchalist[30] – accepts the Hobbesian premise that individuals (not families) are the basic units of political life, but he avoids the Hobbesian tendency to allow this recognition of the power of individualism to destroy the prospect of a physically and morally robust family life independent from the state. Locke establishes a more tenable liberal position, by explaining family life in a way that does not make it appear as an obsolete forerunner of the state, which can be allowed to run down as soon as the state is secure. For Hobbes, the successful state replaces the unsuccessful family. For Locke, successful families reduce the role of the state, thereby making it easier for the state to succeed as well. Locke protects politics and the family from each other, by explaining each in its own terms, as quite separate, although complementary associations. He retreats a little from the radical individualism of Hobbes, and thus addresses the question raised by the illiberal features of Hobbes' thinking, the question as to whether liberals can moderate their individualism without diminishing the physical security that Hobbes argues is possible only by a thorough individualism that reduces the power of associations (such as the family) that come between individuals and the state.

If Locke's argument is correct, such moderation will not diminish but will augment the liberal end of security. His argument for the separation of family and state is part of his argument for limited government and the separation of church and state. He accepts the Hobbesian political goal of individual security: humans, 'by the consent of every individual', join a political community 'for their comfortable, safe, and peaceable living one amongst another, in the secure Enjoyment of their Properties, and a greater Security against any that are not of it'.[31] But Locke's thinking is to Hobbes' what Aristotle's is to Plato's: the cautious, moderate, prudent version of a powerful but too revolutionary (or at least too paradoxical) political philosophy. Like Aristotle, Locke criticizes those who destroy political and family life by lessening the distinction between them. But he does not return to the Aristotelian view that political society is an extension of family and village life. He agrees with Hobbes on the individualistic basis of political life. But the problem with Hobbesian individualism is that politics and family life become too inimical to each other. Locke makes them less so, not by returning to Aristotle – nor by anticipating today's 'new right' fusion of family and politics – but by firmly separating family and political life, just as he separates church and state, so that each can flourish in its own sphere.

Locke is particularly interested in separating the power of education from the political power entrusted to government. Educational freedom is needed to disarm government, which remains strong but less totalitarian. Locke's concern resembles that of John Stuart Mill, who would qualify his call for state-supported education with the insistence that government not be given a monopoly on education. Locke's advice to educate children at home rather than in schools may seem irrelevant to twentieth-century liberal societies, where formal education within the home is very rare, and where the majority of pupils (in the USA, 7/8 of them) attend state schools. But Locke's point is still germane. In the first place, he emphasizes the importance of instilling good moral and intellectual habits during the pre-school years. In the second place, he is less concerned with intellectual than with moral education, and this (in spite of competition from schools, mass media and mass entertainment) still very commonly occurs within families. As Nathan Tarcov (in his commentary on Locke) concludes, in our day 'the concentration of population and the improvement of transportation make division of labor between family and school commonplace, but the usual allocation of moral and religious education to the family or its chosen church, and of learning and some aspects of social education to the school, is not far from where Locke's arguments point'.[32]

Locke argues that the appropriate means to liberal ends is not an illiberal Leviathan state dictating religious beliefs, prescribing educational doctrines, dominating families and their property, and otherwise exercising 'Arbitrary Power'. '*Absolute Monarchy* . . . is . . . *inconsistent with Civil Society*', for a human being would 'be in a far worse condition, than in the State of Nature', where he is exposed to the arbitrary power of a large number of individuals, if he were to expose himself instead to the arbitrary power of a government which can absolutely command and unify the force of that same large number of individuals.[33] A similar argument applies to parental authority: children should not be supposed to give '*Absolute Arbitrary Dominion*' to an adult; this would be a dehumanizing betrayal of their birthright of reason. Human beings are equal because they are rational – not (as in Hobbes) merely equally fearful, but equally capable of knowing their natural rights and duties, and asserting their autonomy. Therefore the bonds of parental subjection can only be 'temporary', 'like the Swadling Cloths they are wrapt up in, and supported by, in the weakness of their Infancy. Age and Reason as they grow up, loosen them till at length they drop quite off, and leave a Man at his own free Disposal'. Thereafter he owes his parents not obedience but only honour and 'compliance', and these, Locke adds, only 'more or less' as the 'care, cost and kindness' of their education of him have been more or less. A child becomes free and equal by becoming aware of his rationality, not (as for Hobbes) by a grant of enfranchisement from an adult.[34] Locke admits that children will often find the promise of an inheritance 'no small Tye' on their continued obedience after they reach the age of reason and freedom.[35] This is his explanation of why they often choose not to exercise their reason and freedom in a rebellious manner. It is a way of maintaining the historical and sociological plausibility of the principle that parental dominion rests on consent, and is naturally limited, not absolute. Locke is thus no less individualistic than Hobbes in the basic principles of his reinterpretation of family life. He simply draws more recognizably liberal conclusions from these modern liberal premises. He accepts that political societies hitherto have been for the most part (though not without exception) patriarchalist, but he urges that a more enlightened view will see consent as the only rationally acceptable basis of conjugal and parental relations. Families become more consciously consensual and liberal as their younger members grow up and become more rational, just as the family of humankind progresses in political liberalism as it becomes more experienced and enlightened, and moves from innocent deference to kings to more critical, sceptical and demanding political attitudes.[36]

The parental undertaking to nourish and to educate children is not seen by Locke (as it is by Hobbes) as a right based on adults' ability to kill children. Exercise of that ability – at least when not necessary as part of the executive power of the state of nature[37] – merely shows how brutal a human can be 'when he quits his reason'.[38] There is no equivalent in Locke's thought to the Hobbesian notion that women first had dominion over children, because parental dominion – such as it is – is rightly based not on ability either to nourish or to withhold nourishment from children, but on the ability and the obligation to educate them – an ability and obligation not restricted to females. Locke's rational parents – both men and women – are naturally obliged *'to preserve, nourish, and educate'* children. Why? Parents' natural 'tenderness for their Off-spring' is recognized by Locke, but only as a force that tempers their government of children, not one that inspires them to nourish and to educate them.[39] Why should they want to govern them in the first place? What is the incentive for them to nourish and to educate them?

An adult does benefit from educating children by their later return of filial honour. But Hobbes had already pointed to this as the parental motive, and it seems insufficient on its own, as Hobbes admitted by bringing in the political sovereign to reinforce it. That is the illiberal step that Locke wants to avoid. For Locke, the more rational motive for parents is 'continuing themselves in their Posterity'. However, this desire, in humans more than in certain brutes, is subordinate to their 'first and strongest desire . . . of Self-preservation',[40] and not every human being is compelled by natural law (that is, by reason) to become a parent in the first place.[41] Less immediately but no less rationally, and more decisively, are the generally beneficial effects of increasing the proportion of rational and industrious humans, in opposition to the 'lazy and quarrelsome'.[42] Locke needs the family as a nursery for rational, liberal human beings, and rational, liberal adults benefit from the propogation of others like themselves by the greater security that this provides for their own liberties. Liberal parents' care of children is thus intelligible as a consequence of the parents' divining their own self-interest. Family and society rightly understood are results of individualism rightly understood.

Locke's educational scheme, outlined in *Some Thoughts Concerning Education*, shows how he thought of children being transformed into citizens with a highly-developed social sense. Tarcov points out that the central virtues cultivated by Locke's liberal education include 'civility' and 'humanity'. Locke does not promote 'a mean-spirited, selfish materialism'.[43] Civility requires liberal citizens to seek from others and to be willing to give in return a freely-granted esteem, rather than a slavish, Hobbesian submission. Civility thus rests on a predisposition to esteem others, to the extent that 'esteem, unlike fear, implies not merely a recognition of the power of others but also a recognition of their desire for freedom'.[44] Humanity or 'compassion' is also required by the recognition that others share the 'basic human desire' to be esteemed as a free agent. But Locke sees these altruistic virtues as perfections of rational self-interest, not departures from it in the direction of a Rousseauian socially defined creature motivated by love or sentimental compassion. We saw in the previous chapter that equality of esteem is a central consideration in ethnic policies today, and we shall see in Chapter 5 that it is a large theme in current liberal political theory, but in both places it generally lacks the objective grounding that Locke gives it. Locke thinks of 'humanity' and 'compassion' less in terms of active concern for others than in terms of merely avoiding the unnatural cruelty of taking delight in the suffering of others.[45] Locke's liberal citizens are to be highly social creatures, but only because they learn that sociality is the best policy.

Locke does not assume that children are sufficiently rational to see their duty temporarily to subject themselves to their parental educators. If they were that rational, they would not need to undergo the subjection and education. Since they are not yet rational, they are not truly bound by the law of nature (reason) to this subjection, 'for no Body can be under a Law which is not promulgated to him'. Children's subjection to parental authority is, 'to speak properly', a privilege rather than a duty. Their honouring of their parents is a natural duty, but this duty falls short of subjection, and in any case it is 'stronger on grown than younger children', because it requires rational recognition by the child, and because it is a return for the benefits of nourishment and education, and both the recognition and the benefits will be greater in the case of older children.[46]

How, then, can young children be brought to recognize their privilege and to subject themselves to their educating parents? Locke explains how children's early experience can be artfully arranged so that their natural love of pleasure is transformed into a love of their parents' esteem, a solid basis for filial subjection to parental education.[47] Hobbes would have rejected this basis of parental authority, not only because it leads to a subjection that is insufficiently absolute, but also because it is less humbling than fear, and risks making children too vainglorious.[48] This does seem to be a danger. But Locke wanted to avoid the Hobbesian attempt to stifle human stubbornness, and instead to channel it towards civility and humanity.[49] Locke's acceptance of a measure of human pride is followed up by later liberals such as J.S. Mill and Alexis de Tocqueville, who value the 'intractability' inspired by modern egalitarianism. (We shall see in the following chapters how important this notion remains in liberal thinking today.)

If Locke's education succeeds, it will conserve warmer and more amicable relations between parents and children than Hobbes can justify, at the same time that it leaves individualism intact. Children will be psychologically manipulated by their parents, and be brought by them to value social esteem, but the basis of this manipulation is the children's natural and reasonable individual love of pleasure. This love, if properly cultivated, will eventually flower into rational and industrious activity in adults. Not all adults need to be rational enough to see that social esteem is less an end in itself than it is a means of encouraging industrious activity for the sake of the better security of individuals. It is enough that their concern for esteem be kept on that track by appropriate social and political institutions. Locke sees individualistic ends being served by deeply social means. He does not absolutize individualism.

In this, Locke follows the same strategy that he follows with his other basic policies. Church and state are to be separate, but not absolutely. Executive political power is to be limited, but not without exception. This strategy of harnessing pre-individualistic practices to advance the ends of individualism is the great secret of a plausible and tenable liberalism, which is such a secret to liberals today only because they have lost sight of the subtle intricacy of such schemes as Locke's.

But, we must now ask, where does all this subtlety leave women? As in Hobbes' analysis, Locke holds that '*Conjugal Society* is made by a voluntary Compact between Man and Woman'.[50] Thus (in spite of feminist analysts' statements to the contrary) he *does* 'argue that . . . patriarchal dominion [even] in the family is artificial', not natural.[51] Moreover, Locke's un-Hobbesian distinction of political from family powers means that for him conjugal relations no more than parental ones are based on a contract extracted under duress in some desolate corner of a battlefield in the state of nature. Locke's reasoning (his natural law) again starts from the same premise as Hobbes (that individual security is the primary goal) and reaches very different conclusions. He admits that 'there is . . . a Foundation in Nature' for the historical fact of womens' usual (but not universal) subordination to men in conjugal contracts. It is not wholly clear what this foundation is. It seems to be the passions undergone by women in connection with childbearing: 'In sorrow thou shalt bring forth children'. But perhaps this lack of clarity is not important, because Locke also asserts that women are not obliged to be content with this natural curse on Eve; they are free to 'endeavor to avoid it'.[52] For Locke (as for Hobbes), human conventions do not have to defer to nature, especially when nature is unkind; human civilization is an attempt to escape or at least to keep at bay various 'inconveniences' of the state of nature. Thus, Locke does *not* argue that 'here a natural difference creates a justified domination of one person by another', or that there is 'a natural familial authority' not resting on consent.[53]

In a state of nature, when there is no government to decide any controversy between spouses, if and when controversies arise, differences of ability and strength may give males the rule.[54] But whether in the natural or the political state, conjugal rule is limited to matters concerning the family (including its property); it does not amount to political power (the '*Right* of making Laws with Penalties of Death'[55]), and it leaves to any subordinate spouse his or her own rights and property, just as parental power does to children. These limits may not be well understood in the state of nature (this is one of the reasons it is so important to escape it). Nevertheless, they define the nature of conjugal society. Furthermore, even in the natural state – although perhaps more so when political government provides an arbiter for matrimonial disputes – Locke's last word is that there is no natural necessity for conjugal society to embody any particular form of rule, or any rule at all. Family rule can be held by 'Master or Mistress',[56] perhaps by both, especially in civil society. Locke emphatically does *not* assume, as he has often been accused of assuming, 'that a free and equal female individual will always enter a marriage contract that places her in subjection to her husband' – nor, for that matter, that it is only 'the fathers of families' that 'enter Locke's social contract'.[57] The only natural rule for conjugal society is that it must be arranged in such a way that its ends are served.[58] Its 'chief end' is procreation (of potentially rational, liberal beings), and this would seem to require some degree of 'Communion and Right in one anothers Bodies'.[59] But the other usual details of conjugal contracts that Locke mentions, 'Community of Goods, and the Power over them, mutual Assistance, and Maintenance', along with unspecified 'other things', 'might be varied'. Locke clearly does *not* assume that 'absolute authority over the disposition of property' must be 'vested in the husband alone'.[60] All that is necessary for conjugal society is that children be conceived, born and maintained 'till they could shift for themselves'.[61] The variability of conjugal society is facilitated by the fact that the education of children is included by Locke not within the rights and powers of conjugal society, but in those of the '*Society betwixt Parents and Children*'.[62] The parental duty of educating (and corresponding right of obedience) is alienable: for example, 'a Man may put the Tuition of his Son in other hands; and he that has made his Son an *Apprentice* to another, has discharged him, during that time, of a great part of his Obedience both to himself and to his Mother'.[63] One of the allowable variations of conjugal society is that conjugal contracts need not be permanent, as long as the maintenance and education of any children are secured.[64] Locke even draws our attention to the naturalness of situations 'where one Woman hath more than one Husband at a time', and others where mothers rule over children and live separately from the husbands.[65] He would not allow what some feminists have advocated, in effect the replacement of illiberal patriarchy with illiberal matriarchy, dehumanizing children by treating them as the property of the natural mother, products of her 'unique labor of reproduction'.[66] But he does show awareness of the natural variety of conjugal society. He does not insist on the republican rule, one person, one lover.

However, for economically advanced, liberal civilizations, the natural variety of conjugal society is limited by an important consideration. While the 'increase of Mankind' can result from a variety of domestic arrangements, 'the continuation of the Species in the highest perfection' seems to require 'the distinction of Families, with the Security of the Marriage Bed'.[67] In perfected, liberal civilization, private families are needed to counterbalance political power. Furthermore, parents and children need to be identifiable so that they can carry out their duties. Nancy Levine's recent study of Tibetan polyandry confirms some of Locke's suggestions: she notes that even with strong fraternal ties between brothers (the most usual common husbands in polyandrous marriages), it is important for children and fathers to be bound to each other individually, as well as to the whole family.[68] Yet it is obviously more difficult in polyandry than in monandry for children and fathers to be certain of their natural relationship.

Locke notices that in fact durable unions of one man and one woman are historically most common, because of the long and overlapping periods of dependence of their children. If this overlapping were avoided by contraception, by abortion, or (as one brave feminist has suggested[69]) by women avoiding sexual intercourse until the first born child was off its parents' hands, the 'chief end' of conjugal society would not be well served; it is erroneous to believe that in Locke's thinking, 'no value is attached to reproduction'.[70]

Locke particularly welcomes one effect of the natural fact of long and overlapping periods of child maintenance: it encourages the parents' 'Industry . . . , which uncertain mixture, or easie and frequent Solutions of Conjugal Society would mightily disturb'.[71] (Even those anthropologists like Levine, who emphasize the *cultural* supports to polyandry – especially the ideal of fraternal solidarity – admit that it is a system that is *economically* adaptive where it is established, in undeveloping regions with limited resources and land, where polyandry permits some economic specialization without demanding the proliferation of households.[72]) In Lockean liberalism, industry, an important effect of children's education as well as of conjugal society, is the common human curse that binds individuals of both sexes together in the progressive but continuing escape from natural poverty: 'Nature and the Earth furnished only the almost worthless Materials as in themselves'.[73] Adam's curse is less avoidable than Eve's.

Once again we see how Locke's individualistic end – industry for greater peace and individual security – requires and supports a non-atomistic, pre-individualistic institution, at the same time that it requires a liberal understanding of that institution. This understanding does not permit the abandonment of the private family, for that would combine political and parental (educational) powers, as Hobbes does, and deprive individuals of one of their most important refuges from political tyranny. It favours monogamy, as a support for the family and its property, and as a spur to industry. But it leaves open the possibility of many of the kinds of changes in family relations that have taken place in liberal societies since Locke's time. Locke insists only that conjugal and parental arrangements, whatever their precise form, must serve their end: the production and education of rational, industrious, liberal human beings.

BEYOND INDIVIDUALISM

Locke's thinking shows how liberal and humane an individualistic account of sexual and family relations can be. But even if one accepts the superiority of Locke's account of marriage and the family to that of Hobbes, one may still wonder whether Locke's individualism is not ultimately as corrosive of these forms of human relation as Hobbes'. Lockean liberal citizens need not be as inhuman, perhaps not even as bourgeois, as they are often made out to be. But are they fully human, or even as fully human as it is possible to be within modern liberal regimes? At least in the case of conjugal and parental relations, in spite of the fact that Locke can be rescued from the charges that he was either too simplistically individualistic or hopelessly sexist, there remains something questionable in the individualistic premises that he shares with Hobbes. The basis of Hobbes' individualistic natural right doctrine – the view that the only 'right of nature' is individual self-preservation – is his observation that 'every man . . . shuns . . . death . . . by a certain impulsion of nature, no less than that whereby a stone moves downward'.[74] But this deterministic view seems empirically inaccurate, or at least very incomplete. Even if one adopts the Hobbesian method of compounding with the most powerful human motivations, instead of repressing them or refining them, individualism may be inaccurate. Critics of liberal individualism have often (and rightly) repeated one of Diotima's lessons to Socrates recounted in Plato's *Symposium*: generally, and particularly when in danger, humans, like other animals, instinctively act not for their own self-preservation, but for the preservation of their children, 'in whose behalf they are ready to fight hard battles, even the weakest against the strongest, and to sacrifice their lives'.[75] (Although Locke suggests that humans do not share this characteristic with other animals,[76] there is evidence that they do. Moreover, humans, unlike other animals, care for children of other members of their species.) Besides, can Locke's calculating account of conjugal relations capture the bonds of love and friendship between wives and husbands?

Whatever may be the moral advantages of individualism in combating illiberal hierarchies, family life is not wholly explicable on individualistic grounds. Indeed, one of the main virtues of human sexuality and family life is that they remind us of our lack of total independence as individuals. Human clothing can hide but cannot obliterate the fact that we are in important ways halves, not wholes. Leon Kass, in a remarkable essay, 'Thinking About the Body', reflects on this fragmentary character of human beings: 'In looking . . . at our bodies as sexual beings, we discover how far we are from anything divine. As a sexual being, none of us is complete or whole, either within or without'.[77] In this way, although our sexual natures divide us, they also unite us by making us participate in the shared human nature that distinguishes humans from gods. (This distinction, which seems obvious enough, is often lost sight of in current political theory, but remains an essential ground of healthy, constitutional politics, as we shall see in Chapters 5 and 6.)

The individualistic assertion of equal human freedom and responsibility needs to be complemented and moderated by this acknowledgement of equal human limits and dependence. Having children of one's own – more precisely, of one's and one other's own – is perhaps more an acknowledgement of human limits and mortality than it is a means (an obviously defective means) of transcending them.[78]

There are other virtues of sex that liberals can take on board, and that a too individualistic approach can endanger. To take individualism to a revealing extreme, we can imagine technological advances that would make it possible to continue the human race but to abolish one or the other sex. (It might prove easier to find a permanent substitute for men's less complex procreative contribution than to relieve women of childbearing.) This could be the final solution to the problem of sexual inequality, whether that inequality is partly natural or wholly conventional. But would a common human nature on its own, without the complication of different sexual natures, really be better? Apart from any effects on individuals' somatic and psychic health, what would the absence of the sexual division do to political health? Sexual difference, which can be such an obstacle to liberal justice, can also be seen as a necessity for liberal society. If sexual eros did not move humans to form families, they might well be atoms too inert to combine even for the limited purposes of liberal politics. This is the deeper problem that emerges in *The Left Hand of Darkness*. The name of the planet on which the story is set ('Gethen') means 'Winter', and the planet is very cold. So is the social climate. The lack of sexual attraction and friction in Gethenian society is disorienting and demoralizing for terrestrial humans. The first investigator from Earth warns his successors: 'One is respected and judged only as a human being. It is an appalling experience'.[79]

Sex can break the ice. Does the cold modern state not have an even greater need than previous kinds of polity had for citizens who experience sexual eros? That is the conclusion to which we are driven by Rousseau's criticism and extension of Lockean liberal politics and education, in that wonderful and powerful piece of modern political writing, *Emile* (the publication of which was, according to Immanuel Kant, an event comparable in importance to the French Revolution[80]). Liberals can learn much from Rousseau's criticism, without accepting his sexist conclusions.

Rousseau complains that the liberal social contract, as described by Locke and other writers, cannot overcome the atomistic forces of the state of nature;[81] and this is, crucially, because Locke's educational scheme is one of those that consist of 'useless, pedantic, bloated verbiage about the chimerical duties of children, and we are not told a word about the most important and difficult part of the whole of education' – education in sexual love.[82] Of course, Rousseau's criticism is much too extreme. Locke's liberal education, as we have seen, is not as cold and barren as that. Locke does not go as far as Rousseau in replacing calculation with love, but he does argue that he who calculates wisely will see that love is the best policy, and that the social virtues nurtured by family life are essential for liberal citizenship. Rousseau therefore simply overstates a truth that liberalism can accept: the truth that an atomistic liberalism, emphasizing common human nature and forgetting or suppressing sexual natures, risks making the mistake of assuming that conventional social and political loyalties can flourish in the absence of the natural sentiments of sexual love.

It is not only modern individualists who make this mistake. It was also made by Socrates in Plato's *Republic*. Rousseau intended *Emile* as a modern rival and replacement of the *Republic*; it was to become *the* book on politics and education. In *Emile*, Rousseau's critique of the *Republic* is that it was written 'as though there were no need for a natural base on which to form conventional ties; as though the love of one's nearest were not the principle of the love one owes the state'.[83] Without a sexual eros that unites humans in private, patriotism and political unity would become more difficult, because humans – especially the individualistic humans of the liberal state, who lack the super-Spartan subordination of private to public favoured by Socrates – would approach public life with wholly and narrowly selfish motives, unschooled in the loving friendship of the family and therefore unable to participate in political friendship. Unlike both Plato and Rousseau (in their more radical moments), moderate, Lockean liberals do not try to make the tension between the selfish individual and the community completely disappear, by completely subordinating the private to the public, but they do try to make humanity and citizenship compatible. Sexual eros is the basis of family life, and family life can be the best training ground for learning to share the burdens and the benefits of a liberal community. And as J.S. Mill pointed out, precisely because citizenship, which itself, 'in free countries, is partly a school of society in equality', nevertheless 'fills only a small place in modern life' relative to the family, liberals need to give greater rather than less attention to the kind of moral education taking place within families: 'The family, justly constituted, would be the real school of the virtues of freedom'.[84] There are liberal moral and political advantages to be gained from human sexual difference, so there is reason for liberals not to push their individualism so far that it leads towards the condition in which that difference has disappeared.

An important implication of these reflections on the goodness of eros and families is the profound doubt that we should feel about the prospect of making babies in laboratories instead of in human homes and bodies. As Leon Kass has argued, 'The complete rationalization and depersonalization of procreation (i.e., as in ectogenesis), and its surrender to the demands of the calculating will, would be in itself thoroughly dehumanizing'. Human procreation – in contrast to godlike creation – 'is not simply an activity of our rational wills . . . . It is a more complete human activity precisely because it engages us bodily, erotically, and even spiritually, as well as rationally'. Manufacturing babies with brave-new-world technology would depersonalize and degrade parenthood and could well destroy its tendency to promote caring for others, for posterity, and for human vitality.[85]

Liberals can acknowledge the strength of the case for the political and human benefits of sexual difference without following the next step in Rousseau's argument. This is the step that leads to the conclusion that healthy families need women whose humanity is overwhelmed by their sexuality. This step is fatal to feminism, and unnecessary for liberalism.

Alexis de Tocqueville's portrait of American family life in the 1830s shows how this step of Rousseau's need not be totally anti-feminist. Some American conservatives today point to de Tocque-ville's description of the relations between men and women as an ideal towards which Americans should return. De Tocqueville remarks that, while Americans 'have allowed the social inferiority of women to continue, they have done everything to raise her morally and intellectually to the level of man'. American women do not 'leave the quiet sphere of domestic duties', but in that sphere they are, and are acknowledged as being, equal to men 'in their intelli-gence and in their energy', while remaining womanly in their appearance and manners. This strategy of separate but equal spheres for women and men allows de Tocqueville's Americans to dispense with certain European double standards that Rousseau was happy to perpetuate, and to regard men and women 'as beings of equal worth'. Unlike European women, American women are not 'denied some of the greatest attributes of humanity, and . . . regarded as seductive but incomplete beings', who 'think it a privilege to be able to appear futile, weak, and timid'.[86] However, the strategy that de Tocqueville admires still maintains an Old World-style denial to women of 'some of the greatest attributes of humanity', if social and political activity is as important for humans as de Tocqueville himself seems to believe it is. De Tocqueville's position is less sexist than Rousseau's, but more sexist than liberals need to be today.

In any case, it is too late to turn the clock of women's liberties back to the 1830s. Even if one could explain the parlous state of the American family by pointing to the increased employment of married women outside the household, it is difficult to see how that trend could be reversed. It is also difficult to see why it should be reversed, where the result has been a happy one. It may be cause for concern where women who are working outside the home would prefer not to be doing so; the 51 per cent of American women that recent surveys report preferring having jobs to being housewives is more than in previous years, but less than the percentage of women of working age who actually do have jobs.[87] But this may well be related to the fact that family dysfunctioning is currently associated less with the absence of mothers than with the absence of fathers from the household. The problem is not working mothers but absentee fathers. A declining acceptance (by males more than by females) of both moral responsibility and sexual interdependence may well be the root cause of much current family disorganization. (In an unfinished sequel to *Emile*, we learn that even Emile and Sophie, the perfect couple perfectly educated by Rousseau in the pages of *Emile*, broke up in the end, because of Emile's excessive love of independence.) The proper focus of attention would seem to be on increasing the understanding (especially among men) of human moral interdependence and responsibility, rather than on developing government 'family policy'. As Gilbert Steiner has remarked, 'Government has no mechanism to enforce love, affection, and concern between husband and wife, between parent and child, or between one sibling and another'.[88] Yet neither traditional nor newer styles of family can flourish without such individual moral responsibility and loving friendship.

Besides, one should not exaggerate the death of the American family. The notable changes in family size, living arrangements, and divorce rates in the 1960s and 1970s have been replaced by comparative stability in the 1980s and 1990s. Statistics on lifetime marital patterns show that nearly 90 per cent of all marriages survive. The older marrying age now prevailing is associated with lower divorce rates. (The divorce rate peaked in 1979.) In the 1980s, 71 per cent of the US population lived in households headed by a married couple (down from 84 per cent in the 1950s, but still quite high). Seventy-five per cent of children under 18 lived with both parents (down from 91 per cent). The number of households comprised of the so-called 'traditional' family of a married couple with two or more children and a wife at home has declined to around 7 per cent of the total, but even in the 1950s was no higher than 23 per cent.[89] Some of the effects of the forces undermining family life have been exaggerated, and some of these forces themselves seem to be weakening or spent.

THE CONTINUING RELEVANCE OF SEXUAL NATURES

As part of guarding against their tendency to be too relentlessly individualistic, liberals need to be on guard against a related tendency to be too 'genderist' – a tendency, that is, to dismiss all sexual differences as products of culture and socialization rather than (in part) also of sexual *natures*. Liberal feminists do not need to argue that 'there is no such thing as male and female nature'[90] – an argument that is often imputed to them by radical feminists, many of whom are happier to accept, and often exaggerate, the relevance of sexual differences, although usually less than happy to say that such differences are natural. Liberal feminists do, however, need to come to terms with the persistence of natural limits to sexual equality, at least until new – and questionably desirable – technologies of childbirth and genetic engineering arrive and remove those limits. As we have just seen, the complete liberation of human nature from sexual natures might well prove to be politically more of a problem than a solution. The cloud of sexual difference has a silver lining. But even if it did not, this is one cloud that will not soon roll by. As long as human beings do not shed their sexual natures like snakeskins cast off by historical progress, there will be limits to the lack of sex discrimination in public opinion and policy in liberal societies.

Liberals such as Locke gave feminists the argument that these limits are movable. But that they are totally removable is a further and much greater step, which liberals should decline to take, because they should recognize that a wholly sex-blind polity is neither desirable nor (without dehumanizing technology) possible.

The most obvious limit to liberal feminism's project of supplanting humans' plural sexual natures with an individual human nature is the fact that most women can for some years have children, while men cannot. The political implications of this fact are dramatized in Plato's political dialogues. A utopia (or dystopia) is described in his *Republic*, with rule by philosopher-kings, communism (entailing the abolition of the family) and sexual equality as leading features. But while women are here given equal opportunity and responsibility to participate in political life, they are treated unjustly by being unjustly desexed. As Rousseau remarked, 'Having removed private families from his regime and no longer knowing what to do with women, he found himself forced to make them men'.[91] In the *Republic*, Socrates (however playfully) treats women as if they had no significant talent superior to men's; he ignores their absolute superiority in bearing children.[92] (Arlene Saxonhouse persuasively argues that in the *Republic*, equality of the sexes is as unjust to women as philosopher-kingship is to philosophers; the natural, universal, non-political aspect of females and philosophers is forgotten.)[93] On the other hand, when, in Plato's *Laws*, the Athenian Stranger describes the 'second-best' regime, he qualifies his argument that men should 'practice the same things as women' (as if they differed no more than left and right hands) and recognizes the peculiarly female contribution of childbearing,[94] but this recognition entails treating female humans unjustly in a second sense, for it entails treating them as females rather than as humans, and valuing them primarily for their capacity to bear children, not (as is imagined in the *Republic*) for their other contributions to political economy or warfare. The Athenian moves his Spartan and Cretan interlocutors towards a greater degree of sexual equality than their native regimes allow, but stops far short of Socrates' abstraction from sexual differences. The Athenian thus raises the question pursued by modern liberal feminism: how far this second kind of injustice to women can be removed – which is another way of asking whether the first kind of injustice can become just. How much moral and legal recognition of the differences between men and women is needed in modern conditions? Should such sex discrimination be entirely abolished, given the economic and military equalization of male and female?

While recognizing the important effects on this question of changes brought about by modern technology, we should neither overestimate these changes, nor underestimate the possible advantages of the sexual differences that remain untouched by them. Women and men are still different, a fact that some feminists have avoided, especially those indifferent or opposed to women's childbearing.[95] One thing that has not yet been made technologically obsolete is the womb. So-called 'test-tube babies' are only test-tube conceptions, requiring a female bearer in order to survive. So even if one eagerly looks forward to the day when human birth becomes tidied away to artificial wombs, for the moment it remains imprudent to give women full equal opportunity without reserving the right to take 'affirmative action' to ensure that this opportunity will not be exercised in a way that prevents adequate repopulation.[96] Of course, such action would have to consist of more indirect methods than the recently disbanded Romanian 'birth squads', but it would still be in one sense unjust to women. Population is not a subject on which liberal polities can always adopt a *laissez-faire* policy; prudent political judgement is needed.

The spectre of depopulation may still be a pretty remote contingency on which to base policy. As Mill pointed out over a hundred years ago, it is an argument that is used far too quickly and carelessly in the modern world. Anti-feminists try to justify closing the door on equal opportunities in occupations outside the home with two contradictory arguments: first, 'that the natural vocation of a woman is that of a wife and a mother', and then, that 'if they are free to do anything else . . . there will not be enough of them who will be willing to accept the condition said to be natural to them'.[97] The first argument is an exaggeration of female nature. The second has some substance, but it has not yet proved to be accurate. Mill himself favoured female emancipation in part because it would help prevent *over*population. In countries where Mill's feminist goals have been largely achieved, some subsidies for children have been instituted (family allowances and tax concessions, maternity benefits, publicly-funded education), but there has seemed little reason to revive the kind of concern about depopulation common among political economists before the nineteenth century and (in Europe) in the first half of the twentieth century. At least in rich industrial societies, many women no longer need to choose – as even Mill still thought they did (at least until they no longer had 'the cares of a family') – between having children and pursuing a career outside the home. Because of absent or uncooperative men, low pay and the embryonic or merely conceptual state of child-conscious working arrangements, many women face, as Sylvia Hewlett puts it, only a 'crummy' choice, but it is a choice.[98] They may have children later, but they still have them. In the United States, the median age of women giving birth for the first time rose from 21.8 in 1960 to 23.2 in 1982. (The median age for marrying rose by about the same amount.[99]) But more American women than ever are having at least one child. Motherhood is not going out of fashion (a fact that 'second stage' feminists have been taking into account).[100] On the other hand, there may be some reasons for concern. Modernization does seem to entail almost everywhere a declining fertility rate, perhaps to below replacement level. A Gallup survey in 1986 showed that two is now considered by 59 per cent of adult Americans to be the ideal number of children in a family (up from 54 per cent in 1983 and 46 per cent in 1973).[101] Fertility rates have dropped steadily and drastically since 1957. The Census Bureau projection (based on immigration estimates as well as fertility expectations) is for a continued growth in population. However, even if this projection proves to be accurate, the rate of growth will decline, becoming negative in the middle of the twenty-first century.[102] These statistics are worth watching. In Europe, politicians in the 1970s and 1980s have been confronted by a worrying collapse in the fertility rates in their countries. In the United States, worries are beginning to be expressed about 'the birth dearth'.[103]

It is curious how reluctant are many who favour the political encouragement of birth control to admit their implication that pro-natal policies might also be justified in some circumstances. Perhaps the sensible thing to focus on here is the cultural attitudes towards the value of children. In modern societies, children often confront cultural indifference or hostility as well as economic hardship. Many contemporary anti-women sentiments are really anti-children sentiments – perhaps anti-life sentiments. If those could be changed, not only might more and happier children be raised, it might also be easier to stop the employment marketplace from treating women (as well as men) who care for children as if it were an irrelevant, distracting occupation with no connection and no constructive contribution to their other occupations.

One of the policy implications of the female monopoly on having children is that the widely claimed 'rights of women to their own bodies' are bound to be in some respects less absolute than men's. Even an adamantly 'pro-choice' advocate in the dispute over abortion policy would presumably find it hard to favour public indifference to, for example, a pregnant woman knowingly taking a drug (e.g. thalidomide) that would help her but do great harm to her child. There are also serious questions about allowing fertile women to engage in occupations that involve high risks to foetuses. In 1991 the US Supreme Court reversed a decision by a federal appeals court that had permitted an automobile battery manufacturer (Johnson Controls, Inc., based in Milwaukee) to maintain its policy of barring women not in possession of a doctor's certificate stating they could not have children from hazardous (and higher-paying) jobs that expose workers to lead. Fear of lawsuits from children born with injuries caused by such exposure, as well as a general concern for workers' safety, had prompted the company to institute the policy. In this case, the Supreme Court decided that the company's legal liability was too remote to justify its policy, but this was because the company already complied with federal job-safety standards and warned women about the hazards of lead exposure. It seems that even on fairly individualistic grounds, then, a liberal society cannot treat the capacity to have children as a totally private matter. (This does not begin to settle the dispute over abortion, but it is bound to be one consideration in thinking about that dispute.)

In addition to the female monopoly on gestation (and lactation – although this is a disputed point), males and females naturally differ in several well-studied ways. Many existing gender-conscious manners, policies and laws reflect these natural differences. Perversions of these manners and laws, twisting them from a proper degree of consciousness of sexual difference into unjust denial of common humanity, tax and often defeat the abilities of liberal moralists, policy-makers and jurists. But overturning the manners and abolishing the laws is no solution; as long as the natural facts remain, the liberal solution must be constantly to weed out the perversions and to cultivate the proper reflections.

One of the most observable differences between females and males is average bodily size and strength. The differences are less than among many other species, but they are significant, and even a feminist as dedicated to the nurture (*versus* nature) explanation of sexual differences as Anne Fausto-Sterling admits that there are 'hormonal bases' for these differences, although cultural influences can enlarge or minimize them.[104]

Hormonal actions similar to those producing the absolute difference in the ability to have children and the average differences in size and strength seem to lie behind certain psychological predispositions as well. Here we enter a minefield of scientific controversy so densely laid that we are bound to set off a few explosions. However, only the most fervent nurturists deny that there is any evidence for the natural base of these psychological differences. The mechanisms are still being explored, but there do seem to be sex differences in neural organization (stemming from prenatal, not cultural, developments) and corresponding differences in female and male sensing and thinking. Granting, then, that nature as well as nurture is at work here, the more difficult and interesting question might be whether we are dealing here only with average differences, or whether there are also some absolute differences in this murky area.

Modern scientific studies of child development concur with many parents' observations in suggesting that there are innate differences between the sexes, including not only tendencies matching the traditional (and much disputed) stereotypes of more nurturing and diplomatic females, *versus* more violent and hierarchy-climbing males, but also certain interesting differences in sensory and cognitive capacities (linkable to those stereotypes). Alice Rossi, a sociologist sensitive to the way that 'genes, organisms and environment interpenetrate and mutually determine each other', summarizes some conclusions of the 'growing accumulation of evidence of biological processes that differentiate the sexes':

A profile of gender differences in sensory modalities reads like this: females show greater sensitivity to touch, sound, and odor; and have greater fine motor coordination and finger dexterity . . . women pick up nuances of voice and music more readily . . . . The sense modality in which men show greater acuity than women is vision . . . . At birth, females are four to six weeks more mature neurologically than males, which persists in their earlier acquisition of language, verbal fluency, and memory retention . . . .

Gender differences in social and cognitive skills are also found: females are more sensitive to context, show greater skill in picking up peripheral information, and process information faster; they are more attracted to human faces and respond to nuances of facial expression as they do to nuances of sound. Males are better at object manipulation in space, and rotate objects in their mind, read maps and perform in mazes better, and show a better sense of direction. Males are more rule-bound, less sensitive to situational nuance . . . . Male infants are more attracted to the movement of objects, females to the play of expression on human faces. Girl babies startle to sound more quickly than boy babies and respond to the soothing effect of a human voice, while boys respond to physical contact and movement.

Viewed as a composite profile, there is some predisposition in the female to be responsive to people and sound, an edge in receiving, interpreting, and giving back communication. Males have an edge on finer differentiation of the physical world through better spatial visualization and physical object manipulation. The female combination of sensitivity to sound and face and rapid processing of peripheral information implies a quicker judgment of emotional nuance, a profile that carries a put-down tone when labeled 'female intuition'. It also suggests an easier connection between feelings and their expression in words among women. Spatial perception, good gross motor control, visual acuity, and a more rigid division between emotional and cognitive responsivity combine in a counterpart profile of the male.[105]

One consequence of these kinds of differences between women and men – differences based on some natural distinctions and often reinforced by social practices – is that even the perfection of equal opportunity is likely to leave significant differences in the occupational statistics of the two sexes. Because of the natural basis for sexual difference that is lacking in the case of ethnicity, it is even more unreasonable to expect identical utilization of equal opportunities by men and women than it is to expect even participation in various occupations by different ethnic groups (as discussed in Chapter 2). For example, one can expect there to be more males doing architecture and technical drawing. More disappointingly to some feminists, more women than men would probably still do mothering and homemaking; professional childcaring is also likely to be done by more women than men. In Sweden, where pay differentials between men and women are rather low and childcare provision is high, the percentage of women homemakers is still much greater than that of men.[106] In the Israeli kibbutzim that tried to make

childcare a communal responsibility, it was some of the women –
especially those who had been raised in this communal manner
themselves – who eventually demanded closer contact with their
children.[107]

Even when the two sexes do more of the same things, it is likely
that they will do them differently, partly because of natural
psychological differences. Rossi's summary of sex differences quoted
above is taken from a paper on the changes currently taking place in
parenthood, in which she draws our attention to studies that have
brought out the different styles that men and women bring to
mothering. Research on parenting shows 'gender differences similar
to those that emerge in psychological research: greater empathy,
affiliation, sensitivity to nonverbal cues and social skills in women,
greater emphasis on skill mastery, autonomy, and cognitive
achievement in men'.[108] These differences make men on average
relatively better attuned to older children than to newborn infants;
in

> caring for a nonverbal, fragile infant, women have a head start in
> reading an infant's facial expressions, smoothness of body
> motions, ease in handling a tiny creature with tactile gentleness,
> and soothing through a high, soft, rhythmic use of the voice. By
> contrast, men have greater tendencies to interact with an older
> child, with whom rough-and-tumble physical play, physical
> coordination, and teaching of object manipulation is easier.[109]

Rossi emphasizes that these are 'general tendencies . . . neither biologically immutable nor invariant across individuals or cultures',[110]
but she also rejects those radical feminist theories that deny the fact
that 'men bring their maleness to parenting as women bring their
femaleness',[111] and wrongly allege that gender differences arise out of
no natural sexual differences but simply out of social and cultural
practices. (The above-noted tendency for cultural differences
between mothers and others to persist even when both men and
women mother is likely to be qualified or at any rate complicated by
this fact.)

At the other end of the traditional feminine-to-masculine
spectrum, it can be expected that more men than women would still
be active where greater size, muscular strength and endurance still
matter – such areas as law enforcement, firefighting, and military
combat. (The American public opinion polls cited above, showing
only selective acceptance of women in various occupations, may

reflect these natural expectations, as well as unfounded prejudices.) The issue of women in combat raises several passionately debated issues. In the US military, women are currently barred by law from combat assignments (which can lead to quicker promotion, as well as to injury or death). Of course, with the blurring of front lines in modern wars, women soldiers (who are now about 11 per cent of the total) are likely to suffer heavy casualties in any big conflict, but it is argued that treating women as if they were as expendable as men is not only unchivalrous but also inaccurate. It is also argued that in any case putting women into combat assignments would decrease the effectiveness of combat units, by interfering with the creation of the 'band of brothers' bonding that military strategists have always heavily relied on. On the other hand, critics of that view can cite experience in the Gulf War in 1991, during which some non-sexual intersexual friendships sprang up, American military personnel (even married couples) being bound by a 'no public displays of affection' rule. This suggested to some participants and observers that a less sex-based bonding could become militarily effective. So while it is hard to deny that there is some natural basis to arguments against the total equalization of men and women in combat, it is also hard to deny that the direction of policy may be inexorably towards laying these arguments aside, at least temporarily, to experiment with the fuller equalization of male and female fighting opportunities. The experiment could be costly, but it is bound to be revealing one way or the other.

Especially in human beings, sexual natures are obviously amazingly plastic, and can be shaped and reshaped by social culture. Genetic determinism is absurd. Human biology, the study of human life, is not just the study of genetics; it would perhaps more properly be defined as the study of both human nature and human culture, interacting with each other. But – at least until genetic engineering makes culture triumphant over nature – cultural determinism is equally absurd. Certain important and measureable psychological predispositions do seem to be naturally linked to male and female development. Femininity and masculinity are not merely cultural constructs. What we should make of natural masculinity and femininity is open to debate, but it seems prudent to acknowledge that these things exist in our natures. Then we can try to decide what combinations or alternations of them would be most fully human, and therefore to judge what it would be most suitable to cultivate in any given circumstances. We can also then try to decide which social shapings of natural femininity and masculinity amount to misshaping. (Consider the practices of clitoridectomy and infibulation, surely a misshaping of natural femininity, although clearly a well established cultural interpretation of femininity as well.[112])

From a social and political point of view, as well as from a human point of view, the natural psychological differences between women and men are not at all unflattering to women. Rather the opposite. Measurements of sexual differences by modern science confirm beliefs as old as Aristotle that feminine virtues are if anything more important than masculine virtues for the health of political life, and that in any case the two sets of virtues can and should be complementary. In principle, because natural femininity and masculinity are generally tendencies rather than absolutes, and because humans have a much greater degree of freedom than other animals to nurture these natural tendencies in a variety of different ways, all humans can cultivate both masculine and feminine qualities. The more perfect realization both of human nature and of political life would seem to require the combination of masculine and feminine qualities. In the modern world as in the ancient, it is easy to mistake the warrior virtues for the whole of political (or even of human) virtue. It is one of the oldest and enduring problems of social and political life that the more masculine humans (women as well as men), because of their spirited love of victory, often successfully ignore and suppress the more feminine humans' greater social intelligence. That is one reason why it is so discouraging to see the extent to which women are being compelled to be hypermasculine in order to succeed in the world of work. Not only does this make many women unhappy, it is also economically inefficient. As business management turns out to be more and more a matter of 'human resources management', feminine approaches are actually becoming more and more economically as well as socially valuable. In the world of work, as well as in political life and the family, if humans became somewhat more feminine, everyone could benefit.

Feminine people could also become more masculine. Sexualities are not mutually exclusive categories. Combinations of masculinity and femininity need not be contradictory or incoherent. Observations of humans as well as of other primates have shown that even the supposedly antithetical patterns of 'male' aggression and 'female' cooperation are in practice often found in combination or alternation.[113] Perhaps it is reasonable to suppose that, just as older adult human beings generally display less exclusively masculine or feminine sexuality, older, more advanced, more fully human civilizations can be expected to nurture citizens who can combine some of the desirable characteristics of both sexualities. Women who do not fear autonomy and men who do not fear intimacy can be better citizens and happier human beings. Liberal politics, as we have already seen, does not demand a 'wall of separation' between public and private; neither does it require a wall of psychic separation between masculine and feminine. Maggie Scarf's recent study of *Patterns in Love and Marriage* suggests that happier lives can grow out of a less strict division of psychic labour, when each partner develops powers of feminine intimacy *and* masculine autonomy, rather than projecting these different human needs onto each other in a strictly sexist way.[114] Less divided psyches could be better citizens in a good liberal polity where public and private are distinguished but intermingled.

This case for increasing androgyny – or, to put the more important element first, for gynandry – need not amount to a call for greater human uniformity. The main concern of this book is to underscore the complexity of political unity, to avoid the extremes of uniformity and of plurality. Within a less sexuality-divided society, there can still be room for braves and sirens, as well as for monks and maiden aunts. Nor need this case amount to a call for weaker masculinity and femininity, even in the more gynandrous types who set the tone of society. Less exclusive does not mean less extreme. Does a recipe that calls for two strong ingredients necessarily sacrifice the strong flavours of either? Less sexist need not mean less sexy. The contention that less sexist sex is more superficial sex is parallel to the ethnic pluralist contention – questioned in the preceding chapter – that liberal, human culture is more superficial than strong, ethnic cultures. A humanistic liberalism must be sceptical about such contentions.

JUDICIAL SCRUTINY OF SEX DISCRIMINATION

As with ethnicity, much American public policy on sexual matters is made in the 'private' sector, by employers and educational establishments, and, in the public sector, by unelected administrators and judges. The affirmative discrimination regime put in place to oversee the interests of certain 'protected' ethnic or 'racial' groups has been extended by this policy establishment to women in many cases, where no doubt it is often even less just and effective. However, if sex-blindness is less justifiable than ethnicity-blindness, legal discrimination is more justifiable in this area. This has been recognized – hesitantly – by the American judiciary. American judicial decisions concerning sex equality are less illiberal than feminist rhetoric often makes them seem, partly because they have – sometimes – successfully avoided the simplistic, sex-blind standard that many liberal feminists have advocated.

The feminist catalogue of outrageous US Supreme Court decisions usually begins with the case of Myra Bradwell, decided in 1873.[115] Bradwell, a citizen otherwise qualified for admission to the Illinois bar, was excluded from it by the courts in Illinois, who held that her status as a married woman impaired her ability to make contracts that her clients could enforce against her. This was not a case that challenged the real basis of unjust legal discrimination against women. Illinois' exclusion of married women from the bar (although it was out of step with some other states – which admitted married women without much fuss as early as 1860 – and although it was reversed a year after the Bradwell decision by an Illinois statute that banned non-military occupational sex discrimination) followed logically enough from their defective contractual capacities; these were the root of the problem. The Supreme Court upheld Bradwell's exclusion, but on the relatively narrow ground that 'admission to the bar of a state of a person who possesses the requisite learning and character' is not one of those 'privileges and immunities which belong to a citizen of the United States as such', and which the Fourteenth Amendment prevents states from abridging. The opinion of the Court, noting that many non-citizens were admitted to practice in both state and federal courts, simply argued that if admission to a state bar had any relationship to citizenship, it must be to citizenship of that state, not of the United States. It was only a concurring opinion (written by Justice Bradley) that relied on broader assertions of the 'wide difference in the respective spheres and destinies of men and women', and that argued that it was natural to exclude women from occupations that require 'those energies and responsibilities, and that decision and firmness which are presumed to predominate in the sterner sex'. These sexist pronouncements were a rhetorical gift to feminists, and have been cited in this century by the Supreme Court itself in order to demonstrate the backwardness of nineteenth-century opinion, but they were not the opinion of the Court.

More troubling for the legal establishment of women's equal

rights, although benignly protective in intent, was the Court's opinion in *Muller v. Oregon* (1908).[116] This decision upheld the Oregon statute under which Curt Muller, the owner of a laundry in Portland, had been fined for permitting a female employee to work more than ten hours per day. Muller's appeal to the Court invoked the (now) infamously *laissez-faire Lochner* decision of 1905,[117] which had struck down a New York statute restricting bakery workers to a ten-hour day, the Court deeming this an unreasonable interference with the liberty of the individual to enter into labour contracts. But the Court rejected the analogy, by taking 'judicial cognizance' of the natural inferiority of women 'in the struggle for subsistence', which justified special protective legislation 'to secure a real equality of right'. The Oregon statute was upheld on the ground that a woman's 'physical structure and a proper discharge of her maternal functions – having in view not merely her own health, but the well-being of the race – justify legislation to protect her from the greed as well as the passion of man'. The *Muller* opinion can be (and has been) castigated for its assumption that inherent biological differences between the sexes dictate large and immutable differences in their economic, social and political roles. But (as is less commonly noted) the Court was right to recognize that different legal treatment of men and women can be justified on grounds of their natural differences. The *Muller* decision is troubling not because different treatment is always wrong, but because the different treatment in this case was based on a sexist stereotype that did injustice to both women and men.

Reaction against the *Muller* opinion and its progeny have led many commentators – and some members of the Court[118] – to take the view that any differential treatment of the sexes should be inherently suspect, and subject to 'strict scrutiny' by the courts. It is often remarked that such scrutiny, which is now applied by the courts in cases of race and ethnicity, is 'strict in theory and fatal in fact', always leading to the conclusion that legislative classifications based on these categories are unconstitutional (at least when not a piece of 'affirmative action'). Recognizing that it would be a mistake to place sex on this same ground, and to insist that men and women always be treated identically, the Court has recently developed an 'intermediate' test of the legitimacy of legislative classifications. This test requires that legal 'classifications by gender must serve important governmental objectives and must be substantially related to achievement of those objectives'.[119] As with 'strict scrutiny', the burden of proof that a gender classification is justified rests on the classifier. However, 'intermediate scrutiny' also has some attributes of the 'reasonableness' or 'rational relation' test, which is the one applied to non-suspect legal classifications (and to gender classifications as late as 1971).[120] This is the traditional test that courts have applied to all legislation. It demands only that a legislative classification must be (in the words of a standard opinion) 'reasonable, not arbitrary, and must rest upon some ground of difference having a fair and substantial relation to the object of the legislation, so that all persons similarly circumstanced shall be treated alike'.[121] The 'intermediate test' is more demanding than this, but agrees with it in not presuming that classification as such is tantamount to unconstitutionality. There is not such a strong presumption against the classifier as there is in cases where strict scrutiny is applied. In contrast to the Court's refusal to countenance racial or ethnic classifications (at least when they are 'detrimental'), it continues to acknowledge that 'there are differences between males and females that the Constitution necessarily recognizes'.[122]

Judicial confusion of changeable and misleading social stereotypes with unchanging natural differences can and does still occur, with unjust results for men as well as for women. Sylvia Law's recent survey of sex discrimination decisions demonstrates this. She points, for example, to several cases in which 'the stereotype of the absent, unknown, irresponsible father was simply false', thus making unjust the application of laws favouring unmarried mothers over unmarried fathers in such areas as adoption proceedings.[123] (She is less sensitive to the natural basis of such legal rules, in the greater difficulty of determining paternity as opposed to maternity.) 'Intermediate scrutiny' is not a substitute for thinking. But it is a prudent reflection of, on one hand, the fact that many conventional notions of sexual differences are based on sexist prejudices, and, on the other, the fact that there are natural sexual differences. Adding to the constitution an Equal Rights Amendment like that passed by Congress in 1972 (but not ratified by the states) might well compel the courts to apply strict and fatal scrutiny to gender classifications;[124] if so, such a move would be an illiberal step, supported only by a simplistic liberalism that sees only a thin common human nature and ignores sexual natures, and that sees solutions in simple formulas rather than in formulas that do not dispense with thoughtful judgement.

THE CONTINUING IMPORTANCE OF HUMAN NATURE

The primary temptation that pulls liberal feminism towards an untenable extreme is the temptation explored up to this point in this chapter, the temptation to ignore or to suppress the sexual natures of human beings. That temptation is inherent in the guiding principle of liberal feminism, that women and men are equally human beings. But to rehabilitate liberal feminism, it is also necessary to cure its current weakness in asserting that guiding principle itself. Liberal feminists today are too quick to concede that human nature is, as many radical feminists say, too unreal or too amoral to provide any political guidance.

At least for the female half of mankind, Rousseau anticipated Sigmund Freud by observing that the original liberal idea of human nature was so narrowly rationalistic that it overlooked the kind of passion that determines human conventions. (Rousseau could accurately say that Hobbes and Locke mistakenly assumed that humans could be understood to be moved more by rational aversions than by passionate desires.[125]) Rousseau was content with his observation, because he was content with sexist morals and politics. Liberal moralists and politicians, even if they sensibly concede that sexual differences and desires are natural and politically useful, must reject the idea that common human nature and reason are always overshadowed by sexual nature and passion.

The main difficulty that contemporary liberals have in maintaining this rejection is that they themselves often abandon the idea of human nature and the confidence that the human mind can objectively perceive that and other parts of the natural world. The fundamental limit to contemporary liberal feminism (as with liberalism in other policy areas) is this internal logical weakness, rather than any external challenge. Contemporary feminists find themselves caught up in the powerful intellectual currents of positivism and historicism. Thus the same difficulties that we have seen afflicting liberal policy on ethnicity (and we shall see again in the next chapter, in the case of government and bureaucracy) handicap liberal thinking about sex. These handicaps will not disappear simply because we recognize them, but recognizing them is a necessary first step in removing them. If they can overcome their logical handicaps, thoughtful liberal feminists can benefit from logical strengths not available to their radical colleagues.

The American feminist movements that have exerted themselves since the Second World War were preceded by two previous periods of intense activity: the first, associated with the slavery abolitionists in the 1830s and 1840s, the second, with the progressive reform movements of the years preceding the First World War. The third wave of feminism has enjoyed certain sociological, organizational, and strategic advantages over these predecessors.[126] But it has suffered more than they did from this massive intellectual disadvantage. Many of those feminists who (justifiably) focus our attention on the dark side of the 'sexual revolution' see that darkness more in the male bias of the revolution than in its overemphasis on the sexual side of humanity. If the revolution were less one-sided – if female as well as (or rather than) male sexuality were being liberated – they would be less offended. Their partisanship on behalf of women is not moderated by a well-understood view of a common human nature that can make the battle of the sexes into less than total war. Few feminists today would follow that first manifesto of the American feminist movement, the Seneca Falls Declaration of 1848, and attempt to base their arguments on the 'position . . . to which the laws of nature and of nature's God entitle' women as 'one portion of the family of man', or on 'a self-evident truth growing out of the divinely implanted principles of human nature'.[127] Nature and human nature (to say nothing of God) have become highly suspect notions, subject to 'strict and fatal' intellectual scrutiny. The feminist cause has been tempted to give up the liberal principle of a common human nature, a principle that has served it well and could continue to do so if not jettisoned as outdated propaganda.

In our day, positivism – the denial that careful logic and natural standards are compatible – tends to reduce liberal feminists to what one of them (Janet Radcliffe Richards) has called her book: *The Sceptical Feminist*. This sceptical feminist admirably and helpfully leaps to the defence of reason, but defends reason only as a dry exercise in building logical frameworks with inner consistency, not as an attempt to reach opinions consistent with nature, which cannot 'be taken as any guide at all for distinguishing good from bad'.[128] As we shall see in Chapter 6, the case against natural standards in morality and politics is much weaker than many feminist writers assume. These writers often cite J.S. Mill's early essay 'On Nature' and the equally cautionary remarks that he makes about the *abuse* of that concept in his feminist work, but they generally fail to notice the corresponding *use* that Mill himself made of this concept. For example, in *The Subjection of Women*, he argues that 'freedom is the first and strongest want of human nature', and that *therefore* it is unjust to make women unhappy by making them live 'a life of subjection to the will of others'.[129] Some natural facts imply moral values.

The sceptical attitude of liberal feminists towards the moral and political relevance (and epistemological status) of human nature weakens their cause, and aids and abets radical feminism. Radical feminists are less sceptical or positivist, but they accept neither human nor sexual nature; they are more inclined to historicism, seeing masculine and feminine not as aspects of human nature but as two personality types into which malleable humans happen to have drifted (somewhat inexplicably into a bimodal distribution) in the course of their evolutionary history. In this view, good science is historicist, denying not just (as positivists) the knowability, but even the very reality, of relatively constant natural phenomena (whether facts or values). Nature is too changeable, too chaotic, to provide any guidance to human lives. In Ruth Bleier's formulation, 'Doing good science involves an appreciation of the complexity of all phenomena and the constancy of only the process of change'.[130]

Radical feminist writers do often go on from their observations of different female and male personalities to argue that men and women need to learn to share the characteristics of these personalities, but they avoid arguing that we should (and would thereby) become more human, because they are inclined to think that a common human nature is unreal. The notion of human nature is merely a tool invented to perpetuate male dominance. The whole liberal project is vitiated, they say, because it rests on a peculiarly male way of looking at things.[131] The sceptical feminists may remain liberal, but are logically rather impotent if not wishy-washy. The radical, developmental feminists, although they have been criticized as mere dissectors of the unfair status quo,[132] may be potent enough, but only in so far as they abandon liberal humanism.

Radical feminists follow Rousseau's critique of liberal rationalism and individualism, while resisting (or merely reversing) his sexism (and overlooking or disbelieving his opinion that women would be more powerful than men in his sexist society). Many of them are attracted by Carol Gilligan's brilliant analysis of male and female moral orientations. Gilligan's work (widely disseminated by a book that she published in 1982, *In a Different Voice*[133]) depicts these different orientations as results of socially induced modes of thinking. The men that she listened to tended to resolve moral problems by 'formal and abstract' thinking, her women by 'contextual and narrative' thinking. Men thus emphasize 'rights and rules', hierarchy and separation, achievement and competition, while women emphasize 'responsibility and relationship', network and connection, care and intimacy. Her own method is, in these terms, very feminine; she narrates concrete examples of men and women acting in a social context, and does not make abstractions about the natural context or the natural basis of moral actions. However, one of the leading instances that she narrates tells against her: it reveals a woman defending her morality of obligation and responsibility (as opposed to the male morality of rights and rules) by appealing to her knowledge of 'human nature' and 'the universe'.[134] I am not denying that Gilligan's exploration of the differences between masculine and feminine ways of thinking is subtle and revealing (although it might have been even more revealing if she had also examined the opinions of males who care for children and manage households, and of females who do not, as control groups). What I am suggesting is that her interpretation of her discoveries is weakened by her concentration on the social, contextual (and sexually segregated) generation of morality, and neglect of the natural human basis of morality. She remarks[135] (and I assume this is not merely her feminine way of seeing things) that the male and female orientations that she describes are complementary rather than opposed, but she does not make it clear what the result of a combination of the two orientations would be (or is, if it already exists). If it is a natural human orientation, then we are back with the liberal insight that this is the proper guide to morality, and that social contexts are merely moral contexts, not moral texts. If, as she urges, the woman's point of view has something to add to the liberal ('male') view of humanity, it should be able to do so – in fact it should be better able to do so – if it admits that there is a human nature that is neither male nor female, and that there is a corresponding science that is neither 'inherently masculine' (Ruth Bleier's description of science to date[136]) nor inherently feminine. In recent responses to some critiques of her book, Gilligan has claimed that she was working towards improving our 'thinking about what is of value and what constitutes human development'. This sounds promisingly humanistic. But then we are told that listening to women (whose voice had previously not been attended to by psychologists studying moral development) shows us 'a different way of constituting the idea of the self and the idea of what is moral', a 'care perspective' that 'is neither biologically determined nor unique to women'. This 'constituting the idea' of the self and of morality sounds suspiciously historicist: in the historicist moral theory that Gilligan is extending, the human *self* – unlike a human *psyche*, with natural propensities and constraints – creates itself, owing little or nothing to its nature; it *has* no nature until it 'constitutes' itself. Gilligan clearly follows the historicist law: thou shalt find no *natural* human standards, for, she proclaims, '[t]here are no data independent of theory, no observations not made from a perspective'. The natural, universal *human* perspective is simply not available.[137]

Admittedly, liberal humanism, morality and politics have left themselves open to the charge that they are too abstract, because many liberal doctrines are intentionally abstract and formal. However, liberal principles are neither; they are empirical observations of the natural needs and activities of humans, whether male or female. The abstract ('male') rights and rules preached by liberals are based on a solid empiricism, which may be inaccurate, but is not in itself abstract. It is odd to hear radical feminist complaints about the 'somatophobia' of modern liberalism, when the historical basis of that liberalism is rock solid concern with the preservation and health of the human soma in this world, as opposed to the salvation of the human psyche in the next. Alison Jaggar has recently voiced this complaint as part of her indictment of liberalism as a 'conceptual framework . . . that maintains rigid distinctions between mind and body, reason and emotion, fact and value, and public and private'.[138] This not only exaggerates the rigidity of these distinctions in liberal thinking, it also risks leaving to women only the line: 'Yes, you men are right, we women are closer to the natural and the bodily, and that's what gives us superior insights and morals'. Jaggar doubts that women would have developed 'a political theory that presupposed political solipsism, ignoring human interdependence and especially the long dependence of human young', nor 'a conception of rationality that stressed individual autonomy and contained such a strong element of egoism as the liberal conception'.[139] As is clear from our examination of liberal views on marriage and children, this is a very misleading caricature of liberalism – at least of Lockean liberalism, if not of the less defensible positions adopted by Hobbesianism or by twentieth-century libertarianism (which is equally individualistic). It also assumes that males inevitably err (if only Marx had been a woman . . .); therefore what is needed is a 'total reconceptualization of reality from the standpoint of women'.[140] The ambition and arrogance of this view are nicely brought out by Shere Hite's sympathetic summary: 'Some feminist philosophers', she says (citing Jaggar), 'have been working on questioning the values of the "male" system, analyzing possible alternative world views, trying to think beyond Western philosophy or patriarchal philosophy as we know it, with its parameters so narrowly limited by classical Greek thought and the Judeo-Christian tradition's tightly patriarchal values.'[141] The deepest problem with this view is not its ambition, but the incommunicability of its results, which makes it impossible to know how far its ambitious goals have been reached; Jaggar warns that men will find the new, female science 'more difficult to comprehend than women' will, so 'widespread male acceptance of it will require political as well as theoretical struggle'.[142] Again, as with Gilligan, we are left wondering why and whether female insights as such will be all that superior, and, even if they are, how one can possibly put them to men in such a way that they will understand them. A real and dangerous sexual solipsism threatens to grow out of radical feminists' false alarm at liberal solipsism. If existing scientific truth and reality are (as Ruth Bleier claimed) merely 'male-created' truth and reality, will female-created reality be perceptible by men? *Female-sensitive* scientific studies – as opposed to *female sciences* – are, of course, possible and helpful (as they always have been, however unfashionable the scientific establishment has viewed them). For example, Sarah Hrdy's studies of primates, by dwelling on the behaviour of females that had previously been overlooked, have shown that the females of some species are less obviously but no less impressively aggressive than males. But, as Hrdy herself has recently pointed out, intelligent male scientists have been capable of admitting the male-centeredness of previous primatology that had kept such insights hidden from view.[143] Bad human science, not male science, was the problem; good human science, not female science, was the answer.

Liberals themselves (including liberal men) open the door to the sexual solipsism of radical feminism when they adopt the positivist approach and move away from the conviction that humans can communicate with each other because of their common external reference point in nature. Radicalism enters this door and takes the feminist cause back to what Mill called 'one of the characteristic prejudices' of the nineteenth century: 'to accord to the unreasoning elements in human nature the infallibility which the eighteenth century is supposed to have ascribed to the reasoning elements'.[144]

Somewhat inexplicably, it was men (in particular, Rousseau) rather than women who originated this romantic prejudice. Nevertheless, impugning reason as merely male, and accepting or insisting on the observation that women's values are derived from a superior source, radical feminism inclines to the belief that women are morally superior. As Mill pointed out, this is a belief often used by anti-feminists to maintain the distance between women and the corruption of public life. Of course, many radicals hope to make politics less corrupting, but this requires that they abandon the liberal insight into (in Mill's words) 'the corrupting influence of power',[145] an insight that has been useful in the struggle against the subjection of women to men's power; and that they depart from the liberal conviction that self-interest cannot be completely repressed and had better be anticipated in political institutions and education.

For all its historicism, radical feminism is historically inaccurate, not only in its failure to admit that it is based on a kind of thinking first expressed by men, but also in its unduly pessimistic assessment of the history of and prospects for feminism advanced by thoughtful humans instead of by the harsh and unreliable dialectic of history. Liberal feminists who have marched under the banner of human nature have not had to rely on developmental drift to do their work for them. Liberal feminism has limits, but if it recognizes these without reducing itself to scepticism, it can still attract the support of men and women for whom reason still has its charms.

CONCLUSION

Even more with sexual difference than with ethnic difference, liberal politics needs constant reasonable judgements to avoid the extremes of unity and plurality. As suggested at the beginning of this chapter, in this case, in contrast to the case of ethnicity, we cannot even confidently set our policy course to take us more closely by the extreme that overemphasizes unity at the expense of plurality. We have all the more reason to avoid views that underrate the ability of human reason to help us make the necessary judgements in the light of human nature. Are we thereby merely indulging ourselves with consoling but unproven articles of faith? Is nature a noble lie that we tell ourselves? That question will be addressed more completely in Chapters 5 and 6. Before that, we turn away from policies to look at the troubles of the USA's liberal policy-making institutions.

Chapter 4

Bureaucracy and liberal constitutionalism

When Aristotle argued against the ideal of total political unity, on the grounds that political association requires plurality as well as unity, he was explicitly taking exception to the communistic arrangements proposed by Socrates in Plato's *Republic*. In the modern world too, the most obvious pair of opposite extremes in policy-making arrangements is an extreme degree of central decision-making generally favoured by communist theory and practice (as well as by some reactionary regimes), *versus* an extreme degree of decentralization often favoured by more individualistic political theory and practice. However, we cannot find in this obvious contrast the threads of those *liberal* political extremes that we have followed through the policy areas connected with ethnic and sexual differences. Because of our concern in this book for the *internal* problems of modern liberal democracy, the contrast between the extremes of communism and individualism is less arresting than the contrast between another pair of extremes, related (as we shall see) but not identical to those: namely, the contrast between the public-spirited ideals of 'the administrative state' (known to its enemies as 'bureaucracy'), and the private-spirited ideals of 'interest group liberalism' (known to its defenders as 'pluralism').

One of the characteristic problems of liberal democracies in the nineteenth and twentieth centuries has been taking on board the apparent necessity of bureaucratic administrative arrangements that go against the grain of liberal democratic politics. The liberal recognition of natural human equality, the heart of liberal democratic politics, has marked out the course of constitutional development for liberal democracies in the nineteenth and twentieth centuries. The political equality of humans by nature is the basic reason why human beings need constitutional government. In the modern world, the wider public acknowledgement of human equality has supported the growth of various systems of representative democracy and plural party politics. Political representation and party government have become widely recognized hallmarks of liberal constitutionalism. They are the stuff of the politics that students of liberal democracies study, and that citizens of these regimes live. But an uninvited guest has come to the liberal democratic feast: bureaucracy, whose liberal democratic credentials are highly suspect. The administrative state sits uneasily beside representative democracy. Their constitutional forms seem antithetical to each other, the one emphasizing efficiency and rationality, the other emphasizing attention to government accountability and the demands of popular opinion. The forms of representative democracy are bound to appear more legitimate than those of the administrative state, if natural human equality is the source of legitimacy.

Therefore it is not surprising to find that, two hundred years after the foundation of the American republic, and at least a century after the foundation of the modern federal administrative state, American professors of administrative law are still concerned (as one of them has recently put it) with 'developing a theory of the legitimacy of the administrative process'.[1] This project should keep the professors in business for some time. But it is revealing to see why that project is so ambitious, to see more precisely what it is about bureaucracy that makes it so difficult to integrate it into liberal democracy, and to what extent – and in what fashion – these two antithetical political phenomena might more or less peacefully and prosperously coexist.

The widely commented upon malfunctioning of the American political system today follows in part from an unproductive tension between the ideals of bureaucracy and liberalism, caused by the exaggeration of these ideals into an excessive denigration of private interests by the liberal bureaucrats on the one hand, and a careless denial of public interests by conservative (or mere 'pluralist') liberals on the other. Here, in the case of constitutional forms and policy-making arrangements, we shall find that a liberal middle way is available, perhaps more evidently than in the cases of policy substance that we have examined. But, as in those cases, it is available only if we can narrow this gap between public- mindedness and private-mindedness, between unity-mindedness and plurality-mindedness. Unfortunately, as we shall see in the next chapter, the currently dominant schools of contemporary liberal political theory are busy widening that gap.

CONSTITUTIONALISM AND FORMALISM

As feminist critiques of liberalism often remind us, the constitutional doctrines of liberalism are abstract and formal. The main reason why liberal constitutionalism emphasizes forms and procedures over substance is that liberals, by definition, are reluctant to allow governments to 'legislate morality' (as the sceptical saying goes). For liberals, government itself, bureaucratic or not, is a problem.

To some extent, that is true of pre-liberal constitutionalism as well. As pre-liberal constitutionalists (such as Aristotle) already recognized, the natural equality of humans means that political government is not as natural or at least not as unproblematic as non-political government (such as the government of children by parents), where the equality of the governed and governor is only potential. The equality of human beings is the natural fact that implies the value of constitutional government. Constitutional government is government based, as John Locke puts it, on 'settled standing Rules, indifferent, and the same to all Parties'.[2] The constitutionalist call for the rule of law follows from the fact that humans are by nature free and equal, however much that individual freedom and equality may be obscured by the often more hierarchical relationships within subpolitical groups such as families. Because humans are equal, there is always something merely conventional about political hierarchies. Ancient constitutionalism (articulated most clearly by Aristotle) was also, although more quietly, based on this recognition that political ruling differs from other kinds of ruling because it is rule over those who are 'free and equal'.[3] That fact is what makes political ruling a serious, controversial, problematic business, not a tidy, technocratic exercise.

In modern, liberal constitutionalism, the more emphatic and public assertion of human equality makes government even more problematic. Government is clearly necessary, but it has to be constructed and consented to. Sane liberalism (which will be expounded in more detail in Chapter 6) does not require indifference to the flourishing of human nature: political government can and should serve natural ends, and its form can and should be related to these ends. But in the liberal understanding, there are no citizens within the regime who can legitimately claim to rule by natural or supernatural right, without the consent of the governed. Moreover (as we shall see), prudence dictates that constitutional government in the modern world – a world of large, multinational states with experience of universal religions – be more decidedly reluctant than before to rule by prescribing virtues. This prudent strategic separation of politics from ethics intensifies the problem of government. The variety of solutions proposed for this problem – ranging from the fringes of despotism (looking towards Hobbes' arbitrary Leviathan) to the fringes of anarchism – is a sign of the persistence of the problem. How can one construct legitimate government without recourse to classical notions of ruling? Liberals do not go as far as doubting the continuing need for government. They even acknowledge that policies favourable to certain moral and political virtues are permissable and often – perhaps always – necessary. But they see a question mark behind every government even if it is one that is carefully constructed with a view to its natural ends. This may be a mark of vitality; nevertheless it is of the essence of modern liberal politics and helps explain the possibilities and limits of modern liberal regimes. These regimes must try not to be regimes, in the hard classical sense of arrangements and rules that nurture a particular way of life. The basic natural ends of human beings – life, liberty, even welfare – are much more open-ended. Because the basic ends of liberal government are themselves thus rather formal, it becomes more difficult to determine the proper form and to judge the proper actions of government. Who should govern? (Who would want to govern?) What domestic policies should governments pursue? These questions become difficult matters of prudential judgement, not simply (as in pre-liberal regimes) with an eye to the given circumstances and materials, but more particularly with an eye on the limited and rather formal ends of government. If we sensibly recognize that liberal politics should not always try to be neutral on moral questions, we will see that there is a case against absolutizing this formalistic tendency of liberal politics, but the tendency is undeniably there.

Given this formalism of liberal politics, is the opposition between liberalism and bureaucracy as great as we have supposed? Modern analysts of bureaucracy, classically those of G. W. F. Hegel at the beginning of the nineteenth century and of Max Weber at the beginning of the twentieth century, have found the core of bureaucracy to reside in its formalism and abstract 'rationality'. Is there not therefore much common ground shared by liberalism and bureaucracy? Is liberalism as opposed to bureaucracy as it is often supposed to be? Is the formalism found in liberalism not the very essence of bureaucracy as well?

Weber identified an ideal bureaucracy as the kind of authority typical of the purest kind of modern '*formalist* juristic rationalism'.[4] He followed Hegel's argument that the modern state's appointed and permanent officials have the advantage of detachment from particular interests, and so are in a position to pursue the less subjective and more universalistic ends of the state. In contrast to these dispassionate modern officials, previous ruling classes appear in Hegel's *Philosophy of Right* as colourful but also as personal and as unreliable as knights errant. In Weber's view, the liberal separation of public and private is made practicable by 'the complete depersonalization of administrative management by bureaucracy'.[5] Perhaps Hegel and Weber exaggerate the bureaucratic leanings of liberal governments; however, the rule of law, as opposed to the discretion of public officials, is emphasized by liberal constitutionalism even more than by classical constitutionalism, and this does seem to enhance the position of judicial courts and civil administration, the 'non-political' branches of antipolitical modern liberal governments. Even John Stuart Mill, a strong critic of bureaucracy, stresses the importance in modern representative governments of 'the acquired knowledge and practised intelligence of a specially trained and experienced Few', for 'freedom cannot produce its best effects, and often breaks down altogether, unless means can be found of combining it with trained and skilled administration'. Representation on its own, Mill claimed, is too inclined to push ignorance, inexperience, and 'interested motives' into the machinery of administration.[6]

BUREAUCRATIC HEARTLESSNESS AND LIBERAL SPIRITEDNESS

Given these affinities of liberalism and bureaucracy, what is it about bureaucracy that still makes it suspect to liberals, even more suspect than government in general?

There is, of course, the problem implied by the word 'bureaucracy' itself: bureaucracy means rule by and quite possibly for the officials, as opposed to the officials merely serving the civil authorities. This problem is so widely recognized that there is even a popular BBC television series based on the observation of the impotence of elected officials and Westminster in the face of the Whitehall mandarins.[7] Hegel, Mill and Weber all noticed the problem, and suggested various institutional arrangements – in particular the representative assembly and political parties –

addressed to the problem.[8] Students of western governments for some time now have been warning us of the danger of the gradual collapse of legislative, judicial and executive controls on government, leaving the bureaucracy to 'run on', as an early twentieth-century observer predicted, 'a vast machine without a controlling hand, until (its native defects unchecked) it finally runs out of gear, and some new master steps in to control it'.[9]

But it is not merely a question of the machinery of representative government breaking down, although that is a serious enough matter. The illiberality of bureaucracy runs deeper than that. Bureaucracy's illiberality consists primarily of its heartless psychology and morality. It is the bureaucratic spirit that is so troubling for liberal politics. Even if there were no danger of bureaucracy usurping the roles of the more political branches of government, the illiberal spirit of bureaucracy would remain a threat to liberal democracy. The bureaucrats we will probably always have with us, but even if we did not, the spirit of bureaucracy is infectious and perhaps endemic to liberal politics; it can survive the death of any number of bureaucratic bodies.

The illiberality of the spirit of bureaucracy is an absolutization of its affinities with liberalism. In a word, the spirit of bureaucracy is antispiritedness. Bureaucracy aims to be non-thymotic: the ideals of rational bureaucracy overlook the psychological bridge between private interest and public interest that can be provided by that crucial middle part of the human psyche, *thymos*, the Greek word translatable as 'heart' or 'spiritedness'. *Thymos* moderates between desire and reason, and makes it possible for human reason to influence (not to say completely to control) human desires. In ancient political philosophy and psychology, *thymos* was identified as a troublesome but irrepressible part of the human psyche, and an intrinsic element of politics. The tripartite arrangement of the utopia described in Plato's *Republic* corresponds to this Socratic analysis of the three parts of the human soul: the philosopher-kings are the reasoning rulers, who give orders to the 'guardians', the spirited defenders of the city, who in turn rule over the desiring, money-making class. This arrangement is designed to ensure the internal unity of the city, and to protect the city from foreign domination. Spiritedness and its love of righteous victory are the springs of courageous internal and external political actions. *Thymos* is the essential ingredient of all important political phenomena, contributing the feeling that what is at issue goes beyond selfish interests ('who gets what, when and how') to the rights and wrongs of the matter. Righteous indignation in defence of one's own can lead to defeat and even to loss of life and liberty, but without this somewhat unreasonable human characteristic, which can make self-defence go as far as self-sacrifice, politics will reduce itself to bourgeois calculation and political life will give way to domestic managerial despotism, if not to foreign domination. Not calculating reason, and not raw desires, but courageous, spirited speech and deeds constitute the essence of politics.[10]

Yet that is precisely why political unity can never be as great, nor the rule of reason as strong, as Socrates imagines when he builds his 'city in speech' in the *Republic*. For, as Aristotle explained in his critique of the *Republic*, the spirited guardian class – who, with the deadly perfect logic of Socrates' plan, are deprived of the desires and interests of private property and families – have too little at stake in the community to be expected to obey the reasoning rulers, rather than to strike off on their own political projects[11] (which would undoubtedly be nobly courageous, but would also be cut off from political reason and interest). Spiritedness is politically useful, but on its own, isolated from ruling reason and from interested desiring, it is insufficient and dangerous. More reliable citizens are those whose spiritedness remains firmly rooted in their own interests, even while it leads them to cherish and to defend the public interest.

Modern liberalism often appears to be opposed to this understanding of the central political role of spiritedness. The formalism of liberalism, as we have seen, can make it seem more akin to a cold, impersonal bureaucracy than to hot, spirited politics. But what separates liberal politics and bureaucracy is also prominent in liberalism – at least, it is prominent in the best liberal theory and practice. We saw in the preceding chapter how liberal education accepts a healthy dose of the kind of stubborn pride and 'intractability' that is bound to lead to a much more contentious and spirited political life than would be allowed in a Hobbesian state. Angry, self-righteous assertion of rights and condemnation of wrongs is surely of the essence of liberal politics even in today's allegedly de-politicized world. The sane liberal strategy is not to repress ruling passions and spiritedness but to moderate them. Liberalism opposes legislating morality, but not to the extent of altogether eliminating spiritedness, which is the fuel not only of moralistic politics but also of liberal politics.

Bureaucracy's antithymotic pretensions are much greater than those of liberalism. Hegel notices the 'dispassionate, upright, and polite demeanour' which is customarily presented by civil servants. Their attachment to the 'universal interests, points of view, and activities' of the state is supposed to detach them from 'the stress of family and other personal ties', from 'such passions as hatred, revenge, etc.'.[12] Similarly, Mill's concern about the absorption of all the talents of a country into its governing body are based on his belief that countries need a talented, 'active and ambitious' private sector, because 'the official body are under the constant temptation of sinking into indolent routine, or, if they now and then desert that millhorse round, of rushing into some half-examined crudity which has struck the fancy of some leading member of the corps . . . . The disease which afflicts bureaucratic governments, and which they usually die of, is routine', for 'whatever becomes a routine loses its vital principle'.[13] Weber's obvious distaste (in spite of his 'value-free' posture) for bureaucratic ways comes through in his description of the character of bureaucracy, which

> is the more fully actualized the more bureaucracy 'depersonalizes' itself, i.e., the more completely it succeeds in achieving that condition which is acclaimed as its peculiar virtue, viz., the exclusion of love, hatred, and every purely personal, especially irrational and incalculable, feeling from the execution of official tasks. In the place of the old-type ruler who is moved by sympathy, favor, grace, and gratitude, modern culture requires for its sustaining external apparatus the emotionally detached, and hence rigorously 'professional', expert.[14]

Clearly, the bureaucratic virtue, or public claim to rule, is not so much a political claim, incorporating a spirited judgement of right and wrong, as it is a managerial, technocratic claim. Such claims assume that there is a class of expert rulers, positioned like the guardians in the imaginary regime in the *Republic*, who listen only to the dictates of reason and never to their selfish desires (which they are not admitted to have). This violates the fundamental principle of constitutionalism, which holds that human equality is more politically relevant than the kind of inequality that is implied in such privileged managerial positions. Constitutionalism entails limits to the will of government experts, not in order to hobble government, but for the sake of encouraging reason, rather than will, to prevail (or at least to be heard) in political deliberation; complete deference to the will of governors would imply inequality in a decisive political sense. Liberalism amplifies this ancient and still fundamental constitutional principle, so it should be not more open but if anything more closed than pre-liberal politics to the temptation to replace politics with bureaucracy. (Perhaps Machiavelli was right to see bureaucratic Caesarism as the logical culmination of ancient politics.) Even if bureaucracy does naturally become part of liberal constitutions, it is normally recognized as a subordinate, 'non-political' branch of government.

THE ADMINISTRATIVE STATE AND THE LIBERAL POLITY

Students of administrative behaviour have critized Weber for failing to take account of the more informal and personal structures and motives of bureaucracies. But Weber was right to insist on the importance of the fact that bureaucracies profess to be formalistic and impersonal, and that the 'creativity' of bureaucratic administration is therefore in theory and at least sometimes in practice subordinate to this formal, impersonal 'rationalism'.[15] Where Weber, Hegel and the bureaucratic mind go wrong is in their radical contrast between private, personal motives (Hegel's particularistic subjectivity) and public, rational motives (Hegel's universalistic objectivity). Why can particular, personal and even passionate motives not be objective and rational? Liberal politics is based less on the stark opposition of passion and reason, than on the identification and cultivation of rational passions. This recognition of rational passions amounts to a recognition that the public can never be totally divorced from the private. As James Madison said in that classic commentary on the American constitution, *The Federalist*, the 'spirit of party' must be permitted to be involved 'in the necessary and ordinary operations of government'.[16] The separation of state and society, and especially of state and economy, cannot be absolute. Liberal government is neither libertarian government, leaving the private alone, nor communistic government, trying to abolish the private. The Hegelian and Weberian identification of the modern state with unspirited bureaucracy tends to assume, in Hegelian language, that history is over, and that the liberal interplay of private and public can be and is being superseded by a public life that is purely formal and dispassionate. Hegel sees wisdom in accepting the bureaucratic state. Weber rebels (albeit somewhat pessimistically) against its lack of vitality, and rather favours the more charismatic possibilities of democratic parties. (In this vein, he comments: 'Those American workers who were against the "Civil Service Reform" knew what they were about. They wished to be governed by parvenus of doubtful morals rather than by a certified caste of mandarins.')[17] But Hegel and Weber agree that the 'precision', 'discipline', and 'reliability' which Weber says constitute the technical superiority of bureaucratic administration are naturally hostile to the uncalculating, loosely-disciplined and unreliable passions and private interests that play a necessary part in liberal politics.

The spirit of bureaucracy, for all its animus against the passionate and the political, is thus itself a species of that frequently passionately pursued political purism which, since Plato's *Republic*, has been diagnosed as a tempting but utopian desire to do away with the mixture of the needs of the body and the needs of the soul. In American politics, the bureaucratic spirit has been upheld and advanced by those theoreticians of public administration associated with the civil service reform movement – and, more recently, by judges who have decided that the spoils system of political parties unjustifiably violates the freedom of speech guaranteed by the First Amendment. In a classic mid-twentieth-century study of *The Administrative State*, Dwight Waldo described the cold, dispassionate, utilitarian 'Heavenly City of the Twentieth-Century Public Administrators' and its appeal to civil service reformers: 'the practices of realistic democracy offended their nostrils and assailed their consciences'.[18] Waldo punctured many of the dogmas of the reform movement, at the same time that he admitted the reasonableness and patriotism of their revolt against official corruption and incompetence and public ignorance and indifference. However, he did not notice the illiberal leap taken by these 'men of finer sensibilities' from righteous indignation at 'the governmental facts' to the desire to cleanse politics of every taint of selfishness. This desire was evident, for example, in Elihu Root's attack on the 'invisible government' of machines and bosses, in a speech at the New York Constitutional Convention in 1915. His polemics reveal the deep revulsion at the mire of party politics felt by many reform politicians in the progressive era, and by many Americans with a progressive cast of mind ever since. Root asserted 'the fundamental principle of good government, which is that men should be selected to perform the duties of the office', and which 'looks upon appointment to office with a view to the service that can be given to the public'. He contrasts this idea with 'the false one', 'which looks upon appointment to office with a view to what can be gotten out of it'.[19]

The sharpness of this contrast is too great. As we shall see in the next chapter, this contrast resembles the mistaken dichotomy of the leading contemporary liberal theorist John Rawls' distinctions between 'egoism' and the 'moral point of view'; and between pursuers of excellence, who try to win more goods for themselves alone, and 'moral persons', who treat all goods as if they were already common. Better models for understanding the psychological and moral relationship between the pursuit of self-interest and the pursuit of the public good are available. Winston Churchill's biography of John Churchill, the first Duke of Marlborough, provides one such model. Churchill explains why what has been made to appear to be the Duke's greed and self-aggrandizement, in the face of Parliament's initial refusal to reward him properly for his military victories, was actually more harmonious with the common good than a more self-effacing attitude would have been:

> It would have been more agreeable to the Muse of History if Marlborough had refused all honours and rewards, and had met the addresses of the Commons by saying that owing to the heavy charges upon the public he had resolved to fight the next campaign on half-pay. But then he would not have been the Marlborough who gained the victories. For certain it is that this same matter-of-fact care for his own interests and desire to found a powerful family in an enduring State was an inherent part of his great deeds. He was a builder for England, for posterity, and for himself. No one of these purposes could be removed without impairing the others, and part of his genius lay in their almost constant harmony.[20]

The more truly liberal principle lies between the opposite extremes of public service *versus* private gain. But it is to these extremes that the perennial American battle between grafters and reformers has driven the American polity. At one extreme is capitulation to selfishness and the private, reducing liberal politics to the new feudalism of mere pluralism (what Theodore Lowi named 'interest group liberalism'), which goes as far as denying that the public interest exists. At the other is neglect of the private and an attempt (which, of course, must fail, except in abstract theories such as Rawls') to subordinate the particular, private and passionate, to the universal, public and 'rational'.

James Madison, in *The Federalist*, describes a polity that transcends this opposition between pure privacy and pure publicity. Madison speaks of methods of obtaining representatives 'who possess most wisdom to discern, and most virtue to pursue, the common good of society', but he is not above including in the motives of such representatives not only their senses of duty and gratitude to their constituents, and interest in re-election, but also 'motives of a more selfish nature': ambition, pride and vanity.[21] A 'realistic' politics need not be untouched by views of the common good.

As it was originally designed, the American constitution's separation of powers reflects a realistic assessment of politicians' motivations, at the same time that it creates places worthy of the ambitions of those whose ambition it is (or, having been elected, it becomes) to gain credit for having steered the country on a wise course. That is why American political reformers in the pro- gressive tradition, including many promoters of the administrative state, have often wished to do away with the separation of powers, which is based on recognition of the necessity of allowing – and therefore of controlling – the lower motives of politicians, and which also creates space in which the higher motives of these same politicians can grow. The separation of powers is today almost universally misunderstood, by its supporters as well as by its critics, as a purely negative device, based on a cynical assessment of political motives. As it was originally designed, the American constitution's separation of powers was also, and primarily, a positive device, to attract into public service those who, while not devoid of selfish ambitions, were capable and inclined to pursue public projects, and constructively to criticize the public projects of others.[22] A constitutionalist separation of powers tries to prevent the exercise of arbitrary will by governing officials, and to check unjust and unwise policies, but it also tries to provide scope for reason to enter – from one branch of government or another – and for just and wise policies to be developed.

BUREAUCRACY AND DEMOCRACY

In the modern world, for a variety of reasons (starting with the greater publicity that liberal constitutionalism gives to the natural fact of human equality), liberal constitutionalism tends to be democratic constitutionalism. So even if we accept the argument of this chapter up to this point, that *liberal* constitutionalism and bureaucracy are, in spite of certain superficial affinities, radically antithetical, we are still confronted with the possibility that bureaucracy is a disease endemic to *democratic* politics. Perhaps bureaucracy is a prominent and threatening feature of modern liberal governments less because of its affinities with liberalism than because of its appeal to democrats. Alexis de Tocqueville argued this case more thoroughly than did Hegel, Mill or Weber, and de Tocqueville's argument is still used by many commentators today who wish to warn us about the dangers of bureaucratization and administrative centralization.

Mill's contrast (quoted in the first section of this chapter) between the characteristics of popular representative assemblies and the needs of administration might suggest, as many critics of bureaucracy have suggested, that bureaucracy, whatever its relationship to liberalism, is at odds with democracy. After all, bureaucracy is by definition rule – or at least government – by the few. Even if it serves liberal ends, it would seem to do so by non-democratic methods. However, some thoughtful observers of democracy and bureaucracy have found affinities here too. Hegel's civil servants are middle class, and every citizen is eligible to become a civil servant.[23] Weber also noted that one typical precondition of bureaucratization was at least a relative 'leveling of economic and social differences', by the removal of 'a closed status group of officials'.[24] But Hegel and Weber saw in democracy a great ambivalence in the face of bureaucracy. Democracy's apolitical, 'rational', liberal side, generally favouring equality before the law and the state's universal interest, is, according to them, favourable to bureaucracy, but democracy's more traditionally political, 'emotional' side, where public opinion favours a particular interest in a particular case, and insists on exceptions to the formal rules, creates what Hegel called 'obvious ruptures and blockages to bureaucratic organization'.[25] Hegel's and Weber's indications of the affinity of modern democracy with bureaucracy would seem, then, to amount to a restatement of the affinity of liberal universalism and formalism with bureaucracy. Democracy for them remains basically opposed to bureaucracy, and they are forced to choose between them. (Hegel chooses bureaucracy; Weber plumps for the greater charisma of democracy – for reasons we have already glanced at.)

A much stronger statement of the connection between democracy and bureaucracy is made by de Tocqueville. De Tocqueville's 'one general idea' controlling most of his observations on *Democracy in America* was the contrast between the 'ages of aristocracy' in which

centripetal and individualistic forces were natural (and it was proper
to combat them with the central state), and modern democratic times
in which 'unity and uniformity' are the natural threat.[26] The battle of
the modern state against feudalism having been won, de Tocqueville
declared war on statism. Close attention to administrative
arrangements dominates the beginning and the end of *Democracy in
America*.[27] De Tocqueville observed that both intellectually and
sentimentally democracy naturally promotes the centralization,
hierarchy and scope of administration. 'Democratic man' welcomes
simple ideas; does not claim any privileges or right to rule by virtue
of birth, education or wealth; and 'sees himself little different from
his neighbors'. Therefore he tends to think it natural for government
to take the form of a single central power, imposing uniform rules on
all citizens. Centralization may begin in aristocratic times, but
democracy finds it tempting to retain and to magnify this particular
element of the old regimes.[28] Moreover, as every citizen becomes
'lost in the crowd', democratic society dwarfs individuals, so the
central and uniform power becomes comprehensive; everyone agrees
'that it is its duty, as well as its right, to take each citizen by the hand
and guide him'. Democratic Americans 'can hardly conceive any
limits' to a state's power. Democracy thus suggests the idea of a
central power 'which can and should administer directly according to
a uniform plan all affairs and all men'.[29] Democratic sentiments and
passions tend to favour this logic. By nature democrats lack the taste
and the time for public business, and are inclined to leave it to the
state. Individuals are proud of their independence but also aware that
they and their fellows are individually weak; therefore their pride is
accompanied by a lack of confidence in themselves and in other mere
individuals, and so can easily reconcile itself to servility to the state.[30]
These natural inclinations can be retarded by certain 'accidental'
circumstances. If people become accustomed to liberty before they
reach equality, if they can reach a state of equality without class
warfare and revolution, if their degree of education helps them retain
their independence from the state, if geopolitics shields them from
the necessity of large and frequent wars, if social stability reduces
their natural love of order and well being, and (most importantly) if
the central power is not itself of democratic origins and inclinations,
then the centralization and expansion of political power will at least
advance more slowly.[31] But 'in the dawning centuries of democracy
individual independence and local liberties will always be the
products of art. Centralized government will be the natural thing',[32]

as will centralized administration, for the sake of the uniformity and comprehensiveness of that government.

In contrast to Hegel and Weber, de Tocqueville thus suggests that democratic humans will be all too ready to subordinate their particular interests to the state and its apparatus. They will do so because they trust themselves only as a mass, and therefore allow public opinion to rule.[33] Hegel argues that public opinion is necessarily insufficiently organized and universal to rule the state. Likewise, Weber insists that democratization does not mean rule by the *demos*; public opinion only serves as a context for the conflicts of party leaders.[34] Because de Tocqueville takes more seriously the possibility of real rule by the mass, he can see the compatibility or even the identity of democracy and a highly organized state. The loss of individualism rightly understood – in other words, the mistaken impression that everyone is not only politically equal but also humanly identical – leaves humans with no reason and no means to organize themselves in any other than the one, central, mild but all-embracing state. (And, as Weber points out, who says centralization says bureaucracy.)[35] In the United States, de Tocqueville saw bureaucrats who 'dare to do things which astonish a European, accustomed though he be to the spectacle of arbitrary power'. He sees this bureaucratic power as a product of the omnipotence of the majority – that is, as a democratic phenomenon, subject to the power of mass opinion. However, he also sees that these discretionary habits 'may one day become fatal to that freedom' in which they were formed. De Tocqueville argues, then, that democracies naturally create bureaucracies, and that their bureaucratic creatures may become their gentle but enervating masters if citizens lapse into that '*general apathy*' which is the fruit of individualism wrongly understood.[36]

De Tocqueville's grim picture of the paternalistic 'soft despotism' to which modern democracies are prone is powerful stuff, and it is often deployed by current proponents of the decentralization of American public administration. De Tocqueville praised the USA's decentralized administration as one of the main advantages of American over European government in the modern world, that is, in the age of equality. Aristocracies that have no provincial institutions still have aristocratic families and privileges as barriers to central despotism; but democracies without such institutions have no such barriers. De Tocqueville's argument is compelling; his authority is legitimate. However, as a current tract for the decentralized

American state, de Tocqueville's analysis is inappropriate and somewhat misleading.

In the first place, it must be remembered that de Tocqueville was
aware that decentralization could go too far, and was in some senses
already going too far in the United States in the 1830s.[37] In the
second place, it is not clear that de Tocqueville believed that
decentralization could be a successful policy in a centralized state, or
that decentralization once lost could be retrieved. In de Tocqueville's analysis, the township is the basis of American decentralization. 'The township is the only association so well rooted in
nature that wherever men assemble it forms itself'. Not only its
existence but also its local freedom (where this exists) seems to owe
more to nature and history than to 'human efforts': 'It is seldom
created, but rather springs up of its own accord'.[38] So although de
Tocqueville's 'new science of politics' is designed to counteract the
natural centralizing tendencies of democracy, and in spite of what he
says about 'individual independence and local liberties' always being
'the products of art' in democratic ages,[39] 'the art of association' –
that is, the art of encouraging voluntary associations of 'private
citizens'[40] – appears to be more universally useful and more fundamental than the decentralization of public administration. In the
United States, local political institutions help stop social atomization
by providing 'continual reminders to every citizen that he lives in
society', but it is the voluntary 'civil associations' that 'must take the
place of the powerful private persons whom equality of conditions
has eliminated'. Therefore 'in democratic countries knowledge of
how to combine is the mother of all other forms of knowledge'.[41] It
is these associations, rather than political or administrative decentralization on its own, that can maintain the habit of thinking socially
that de Tocqueville seeks to cultivate as an antidote to the democratic poison of individualism. Administrative decentralization cannot function properly unless local citizens are 'enlightened, awake to
their own interests, and accustomed to take thought for them'.[42] In
de Tocqueville's analysis, administrative decentralization also
requires a substantial degree of civil homogeneity, making it easy for
different localities to agree ('the difference in civilization between
Maine and Georgia is less than that between Normandy and
Brittany'[43]). If decentralization is conceived as a merely formal,
institutional contrivance, ignoring the necessary substantial elements
of uniformity and common outlook, and abstracting from the quality

of citizens, it is in a sense a too bureaucratic solution to the problem of bureaucracy, overlooking substance for form.

It is worth adding that de Tocqueville's whole account of decentralization, for all its valuable insight, is somewhat defective as a liberal democratic theory. For de Tocqueville, the important thing is not diversity within unity, but self-determination. He thinks that uniformity and agreement are necessary to political life, but that efforts to enforce these from the top are deadening and ultimately self-defeating. (De Tocqueville even tries to follow this principle with his readers, when he encourages them to 'reach, unguided and by other roads, the conclusion to which I have pointed'.[44]) De Tocqueville's difficult message is that spontaneous sociality must somehow be encouraged. Far from being too enamoured of diversity, he is a little too ready to see it dissolved, as long as this is done without direction from the top. A stronger yet balanced case for a degree of decentralization can be built on an appreciation not (as de Tocqueville has it) of the human need both to determine oneself and simultaneously to mold oneself into a social being but of the need to preserve and to cultivate both one's naturally-given, unique, non-uniform qualities, and one's naturally-given, shared, human qualities. De Tocqueville seems too ready to admit the impotence of individuals and their natural differences in the face of modern mass society. He attributes the 'intractability' of individuals not to human nature but to the democratic state of society, which also gives rise to conformist tendencies, which he thinks are unfortunately more powerful.[45] De Tocqueville clearly overstates the novelty of the modern world. He denies that even the most profound thinkers in the classical world ever 'managed to grasp the . . . conception of the likeness of all men'.[46] But, as we have already seen (and will see again in Chapter 6), some of them did manage to do that, and to draw out the constitutionalist implications of this conception. In western political philosophy, the age of political equality began in pagan Athens, not in Christian Europe. The idea of human equality (as will become more apparent in the arguments in Chapters 5 and 6) need not be understood as excluding natural differences among humans, however much more these differences were celebrated in pre-modern times than in the modern age. Therefore it need not give rise as inevitably as de Tocqueville thought to mass society and its 'soft despotism'. Decentralization – deference to local differences and, ultimately, to different individuals

– can survive in modern democratic times. Democracy's instinct for bureaucracy need not be as inevitable or as fatal as de Tocqueville feared.

PUTTING BUREAUCRACY IN ITS PLACE

There are three basic ways one can look at the role of bureaucracy in liberal governments. Hegel and Weber see it as the inevitably central and dominant part of all modern states. Like Hegel (but unlike Weber), American proponents of the administrative state also look favourably upon such a development. But they have had reason to despair. The halting progress of centralizing administrative reform in the United States in the nineteenth and twentieth centuries shows how the separation of powers (among other things) has been an effective obstacle to the rationalization and centralization of American bureaucracy,[47] helping to keep the de Tocquevilleian nightmare of 'soft despotism' at bay. This suggests the second view: instead of replacing other kinds of government administration, bureaucracy can be an adjunct to them, appearing not as a single corps but as a collection of shadows of legislatures, executives, courts, parties and pressure groups. This second view has greater empirical plausibility; even the most alarming portraits of the growth of American bureaucracy acknowledge the fragmented condition of American public administration, and nowadays every political organization – every fragment of American politics – has its professional staff to help or to hinder it. Finally, rather than being seen as a replacement of or a fragmented adjunct to the other parts of the political system, bureaucracy can be seen as a branch of government in its own right, not dominating the political system (as the first view has it) but simply adding a useful step and therefore certain characteristically bureaucratic influences to government actions. Such a scheme is visible in Mill's thinking, and it has long been described – as an ideal if not as a reality – by commentators on the British constitution. It assumes, in Graham Wallas' early twentieth-century formulation, that 'electoral opinion' and the political branches of government immediately responsive to it need to be moderated by a prudent body of civil servants; it depends on civil servants having 'the right and duty of making their voice heard, without the necessity of making their will, by fair means or foul, prevail'.[48] Following this line of thought, commentators on the American political system such as Herbert Storing have suggested that

American bureaucracy, too – if 'properly schooled' – could serve as an antithesis to the party system, and be 'a solidly-based source of the intelligence, stability, equity, and public-spiritedness that a democracy needs'.[49] Hugh Heclo's recent analysis of the dispositions of Washington's higher bureaucrats, revealing their gradualism, indirection, political caution and desire to maintain long-term working relations, shows that at least some of the desired schooling already takes place on the job[50] – as any student of Hegel or Weber would have predicted. But perhaps formal education could also be directed more towards producing politically moderate and moderating bureaucrats. One of Storing's students has recently published a book that outlines what such education might look like, and that tries to find a legitimate constitutional role for career civil servants as a modern (though more subordinate) replacement for the original Senate, which has now become too democratized to serve its original function as a 'balance wheel' in the governmental mechanism.[51]

These three views of how to accommodate bureaucracy in liberal constitutions correspond to our two extremes, public administration purity and private interest pluralism, and our liberal constitutionalist middle way.

If politics is to be purified, and if there is (at least for the moment) no natural harmony that makes government unnecessary, then pure bureaucracy, as little hampered by external control as possible, is desirable. But how can such a bureaucracy arise? Twentieth-century communist regimes characteristically developed a 'privilegentsia' based on the party. But liberal reformers dislike political parties, which often smack of private interests and always act as carriers of them. (Thus, the reformers who espouse a theory of allowing the party system to cure the mischiefs of separated powers do not usually follow this theory in practice.) If a pure bureaucracy is to take over American government, it would seem that it must do so by default, that is, by the abdication of political responsibility by the political branches of government and by citizens. (In the concluding section of this chapter, some of the current implications of just such an abdication will be brought out.)

Bureaucracy – more accurately, bureaucracies – as shadows of other political institutions can be a description and prescription for mere pluralism, in which various private interests contend in the public arena with nothing but a poorly-grounded set of 'rules of the game', no vision of the common good, to guide them. Such a purely pluralistic arrangement may be more attractive than pure bureaucracy, since its unambitiousness and inefficiencies allow a measure of freedom. Its drawbacks are indicated by this negative attractiveness and reactionary character. If it is sufficient for the United States to be on automatic pilot, a fragmented political system and bureaucracy may be adequate, but what if positive domestic and foreign policies are needed? Fragmentation of government and the multiplication of public bureaucracies may protect private interests, but it makes no positive contribution to the identification and pursuit of public interests. Just as the public cannot be totally divorced from the private, neither should the private be totally divorced from the public: in Madison's phrase, 'the regulation of . . . interests forms the principal task of modern legislation'.[52] Mere pluralism elevates the private at the expense of the public. Let us give the early public administration reformers their due. No doubt they were too extreme, but they were reacting against an extremely unscrupulous party machinery. As Leon Epstein has remarked, 'Nowhere else in the western democratic world did parties look so evil'.[53] Similarly, because government regulation is necessary, both to correct the inefficiencies and inequities of a superficially freer political system[54] and to pursue the common good, current arguments for complete deregulation in American politics are not so much serious political schemes as they are expressions of desperation. Deregulators conclude that regulation must be abolished, because they conclude (one must hope too readily) that nothing can be done to control regulation to ensure that it is in the public interest. The case for deregulation and decentralization can be built on a stronger psychological grounding than de Tocqueville gave it, but even so it is politically too negative.

The third view, bureaucracy as moderator, seems more suitable to liberal democratic constitutionalism. In this scheme, spirited politicians can be allowed to be attuned to both private and public interests, and bureaucrats can place their perhaps less high-spirited but more sage advice into public deliberations without claiming to be representatives of pure rationality or disinterested agents of historical progress. The hope is that coupling the spirited with the anti-spirited in this way can satisfy the paradoxical but vital requirement that liberals remain political, and that liberal governments, while limited to the end of securing liberal rights, be energetic, capable of interfering with society and economy whenever necessary for that end. Elements of fragmentation and decentralization could coexist with this arrangement, but the liberal democratic ideal looks also towards a unified corps of public administrators, although they would be unified primarily by their determination to be *éminences grises* who are politically more grey than eminent.

THE NEW ANTIPOLITICAL SYSTEM

As Wallas' formulation made clear, this ideal view of the possibility of accommodating, perhaps even welcoming, bureaucracy in liberal politics makes certain crucial assumptions about the character of bureaucrats and the qualities of other elements of the political system, and if these assumptions are wrong, then the political negativity of the second view can infect this more suitable third view as well. On its own each view is insufficient. Like the prudent fragmentation proposed in the second view, the braking effect of a somewhat unified but cautious bureaucracy in this third view assumes that the politicial machine also possesses a means of acceleration and steering. It presupposes healthy and active citizens, legislatures and executives; it presupposes, in other words, education of citizens and of politicians. However, precisely because of this presupposition, the third view rather than the second corresponds to the middle way; in ideal circumstances, bureaucracy is not expected to do everything, but it is expected that there will be things for governments to do, and that bureaucracy can make its contribution.

The circumstances required for this middle way are not currently prominent in the USA. In the last twenty years, a much more cynical portrait of American government and citizens has become established. Today even those few political scientists who paint *A Hopeful View of American Government* (the subtitle of a recent book by Steven Kelman[55]) do so at least partly simply to try to reduce the downward spiral caused by a cynical political science interacting with an admittedly pretty cynical political reality. In this more cynical climate, it is difficult to see American bureaucracy as a moderating element in a liberal system of government. This vision seems somewhat archaic in the face of the 'new American political system' that emerged in the 1960s and 1970s, a system that is characterized by the opposites of the presuppositions of our ideal middle way.[56] This new American political system is complex and if anything even more chaotic than the old one, but it is not misleading to summarize much of its novelty simply as a decline in politics. The new American political system is an antipolitical system, a product of a flight from politics by American politicians and people, which has brought closer to realization the conditions that would be necessary for purely bureaucratic government and soft despotism to prevail. Thus, American government currently has less need of moderation from its bureaucracy than of energizing from its representative system.

In the new American political system, as the political branches of government have declined, the non-political branches of government have risen in political importance. As legislators and executives have become less effectively active, certain unelected officials and judges have become hyperactive. Neither the judicial courts nor the public bureaucracies have been particularly well equipped to take on their greater policy-making role, and public disenchantment with their actions and inactions is high. The problem is not simply with the policy-making 'iron triangles', those survivors of the old American political system in which fragments of the economy and fragments of the public bureaucracy collude with each other, out of view of the public: not even the new economy-wide bureaucracies created in the 1970s, addressing widely publicized problems of environmental and safety standards, are credible pursuers of the public interest, because they are detached from political responsibility, but of course not detached from particular human interests (theirs and their clients').

These developments have been overseen by the legislative branch of American government (at the state level as well as at the federal level) with some hand-wringing, but also with no little cause for complacency by legislators. The more active bureaucracy and jurocracy enable federal and state legislators to avoid political responsibility and still to claim political credit, if only for making exceptions to bureaucratic policies being applied to their constituents. So legislators have little incentive to change these arrangements – little incentive, that is, to consider the public interest, on top of their attentive consideration of private interests. Incumbent legislators do very nicely out of what amounts to their political demotion, from legislators to constituent servicers. Beginning in the late 1980s there have been signs of great public dissatisfaction with incumbent legislators. A few states have even decided to limit the number of terms that legislators can serve, and there are moves to amend the federal constitution to apply such a limitation to members of congress as well. However, Americans' public outrage at legislative incumbents in general is often accompanied by satisfaction with their particular incumbent, so it is not yet clear to what extent the American people have been weaned away from their dependency on this new political system.

Behind the institutional shifts away from political towards non-political branches of government is another, more fundamental move away from politics: the decline of political parties, and the rise of candidate-centred electoral politics and minorities-centred policy making. The 'new politics' liberalism of the 1960s was less party-oriented partly because it was much less majoritarian than the New Deal liberalism of the 1930s, and much more inclined to emphasize the necessity of institutionalizing protection of minorities from the hopelessly backward 'silent majority'. Robert Eden has pointed out that New Deal liberalism, in contrast to more recent liberal projects, clearly set out to establish a ruling ethos, a democratic notion of virtue and honour, self-consciously opposed to the minority ethos of the industrial entrepreneur. This majoritarian ethos cut across the divisions between the public and the private, the governmental and the social.[57] More recent liberalism has been much less confident and successful in carrying out this necessary feat of engineering in liberal politics, the intricate task of bridging the gap between public and private, in order to keep these spheres separate but connected.

Behind the decline of party politics, then, lies a defective philosophy of liberal politics. In public attitudes towards government and morality, there has been a flight from politics, and this flight is – as we shall see in the next chapter – encouraged by the extreme tendencies of liberalism in the academy. At one extreme, pluralism and privatism encourage a narcissistic withdrawal from politics. Communalistic thinking, the opposite extreme, requires citizens to be public-spirited, but does not allow them to taint this public persona with any private-spiritedness. When private interests are made to seem irrelevant to 'the moral point of view', political partisanship – loyalty to a party not only because of its ideals but also because of its protection of one's interests – also seems immoral. If one votes at all, one must vote 'independently'. This political escapism has resulted in a decline both in political controversy (many moral purists do not like arguing) and in political compromise (most moral purists do not like bargaining). It has also resulted in a stalemated political system, in which established institutions and legislative incumbents have become much more immune to pressure from the partisanship that has not yet been removed from the American electorate. The electorate and public opinion have developed a bad case of schizophrenia: conservatism – the new right reaction against the new left – finds favour in general terms, but on specific policy questions the new apolitical liberalism – the protection of 'discrete and insular' minorities, with no majoritarian cement – still appeals. The consequence is the election of conservative (usually Republican) Presidents and liberal (usually Democratic) Congresses. Split minds split tickets. This tears the separated powers of the Presidency and Congress into isolated bodies – the superego and the id, as it were, of the American government psyche – pulling in opposite directions, rather than cooperating (as they were designed to cooperate) to articulate a national and public interest that is acceptable to local and private interests. The result is too purely pluralistic and exclusively private-spirited in practice, even or especially when it is too communalistic and exclusively public-spirited in theory.

Thus, behind the current diseases of American political practice, which make the accommodation of bureaucracy in American government more difficult than it might be, lies the disease of contemporary liberal theory, on which we focus our attention in the following chapters.

Chapter 5

Unnatural liberalism

Our brief survey of liberal political practice has shown how crucial for sound practice is a certain amount of sound theory. In ethnic policy, in sexual politics and in arranging and running the institutions of government, liberals need a clear insight into human political equality, and a firm theoretical grasp of some associated facts of human nature: the formal unity of the human species, alongside its ethnic and sexual diversity and the uniqueness of its individual members; the interpenetration of human biology and culture; the sometimes conflicting but ever undeniable claims of body, rationality and spiritedness. Not everyone in liberal polities needs to be an advanced student of political theory, biology and psychology, but there are times when liberal lawmakers and policymakers need to be informed by sound theory if laws and policies are to be well made; and at all times liberal civic education needs to aim at maintaining a liberal political creed that can touch citizens' lives and act as the sheet anchor of public opinion.

The currently most fashionable liberal theories offer little if any of this support to liberal political practice. During the last quarter of the twentieth century there has been a resurgence of liberal political theory, but this theorizing, for the most part, has deliberately and systematically avoided the question of natural standards for political life. In this chapter I explain how and why this avoidance of nature has appeared so attractive to liberal political theorists, and explore the disastrous effects of that avoidance. I argue that this avoidance appeared reasonable, but was not; and that it accounts for the major shortcomings of current liberal theory, namely the failure to provide support for liberal middle ways in political practice, and the tendency to veer off, in spite of its moderate intentions, towards the extremes of excessive political unity or excessive individualism and plurality.

Of course, one can always find extreme positions expressed in political theory; that is in the nature of theoretical activities. The point I am making is the difficulty of finding anything *but* extremes, even in the thinking of those theorists who try hard to articulate golden means. So there is a change of procedure (though not of strategy) in this chapter: instead of looking directly at the extremes and teasing out a middle way, we look mainly at mainstream liberal theory (especially as represented by John Rawls and his allies and critics), in order to see how quickly the apparent moderation of this theory dissolves before our eyes. We shall see that the main reason for the ephemeral moderation of this theory is its attempt to substitute the standard of moral personality for that of natural humanity: fictitious 'moral persons', not real human animals, are its subject matter.

The argument of this chapter is not that current liberal theory is the main cause of the practical troubles traced in the preceding chapters (although it may well be one of the causes of some of these troubles), but that it doesn't help the situation, and moreover that it could help if it took off the blindfold that it has insisted on wearing, and allowed itself to contemplate some of the admittedly mysterious but undeniably relevant natural facts. This chapter is therefore pathological and rather destructive. The next chapter will be less so; it will sketch the possibility and desirability of reconstructing a more natural liberalism.

THE UTILITARIAN CRITIQUE OF CLASSICAL LIBERALISM

The classical liberalism of the seventeenth and eighteenth centuries was based on a confident view of the natural equality of human beings. The self-evident truth of this natural fact of human equality most famously affirmed in the American Declaration of Independence in 1776 agreed with the position that had been stated by John Locke in his *Second Treatise of Government*, published in 1689: humans are naturally in a state of freedom and equality, 'there being nothing more evident, than that Creatures of the same species', with 'the use of the same faculties, should also be equal one amongst another without Subordination or Subjection'.[1] Seventeenth- and eighteenth-century liberals often spoke of a 'state of nature', in contrast to the state of civil society, and (as we have already had occasion to notice, when reflecting on Locke's views on sexual equality) they understood human civilization to be in many ways an improvement on this primitive state of nature, with civil society based on some sort of original contract that moves humans out of the state of nature. However, unlike the nineteenth- and twentieth-century historicism that proclaims a much more absolute distinction between human moral and political life on the one hand and the natural world on the other, classical liberalism held up the state of nature not only as a primitive condition that humans need to transcend, but also as a state of affairs that could recur within civil society (for example, in cases of justified forceful self-defence). The state of nature was also seen as a continuing source of standards of justice for civil society: the natural equality of human beings – most visible in the state of nature, outside of the deferential hierarchies set up by human conventions – demands two (often conflicting) things: that civilized government must operate by consent of the governed, and that it must act to secure equal natural human rights to 'life, liberty and the pursuit of happiness'. Because of its natural basis, classical liberalism was at the same time a philosophy of rights, a philosophy of consent and a philosophy of utility. Its natural basis prevented the split that is characteristic of later political philosophy into the contending camps of rights-based theorists ('deontologists'), contractarians (basing all on consent) and utilitarians.

The story of the liberal abandonment of natural standards – the history of unnatural liberalism – begins not with John Rawls in the late twentieth century but over two hundred years before. By the middle of the eighteenth century, some of the natural bases of liberal political philosophy were already being criticized and rejected by philosophers like David Hume. The first steps of the abandonment of the natural basis of liberalism seemed to be sensible, down-to-earth corrections of early liberalism, by utilitarian critics such as Hume and (a little later) Jeremy Bentham. Twentieth-century utilitarianism pursues the lines of attack laid out by these thinkers. To appreciate the reasonableness and the unreasonableness of the first, utilitarian departure from nature-based liberalism, we must pay attention to the arguments of these earlier utilitarians.

Hume's investigation of human nature led him to regard social and political life as a great departure from mere nature. In his *Treatise of Human Nature* (1739–40), he does not hesitate to speak of a state of nature, but he insists that this is 'a mere philosophical fiction'.[2] This imagined 'wretched and savage condition'[3] serves to demonstrate the usefulness of society and justice, but it is merely an analytical construction, not a reality, for it abstracts from human 'understanding', in order to show how the 'blind motions' of human 'affections' on their own would 'incapacitate men for society'.[4] Of course, human understanding is a part of human nature, and political conventions invented by the understanding are in one sense natural: 'nature provides a remedy in the judgement and understanding, for what is irregular and incommodious in the affections'.[5] But even though political conventions are not arbitrary, and have such a predictable logic that they could even be called 'Laws of Nature, . . . inseparable from the species',[6] Hume emphasizes their dependence on human artifice. For one thing, they take the form of 'universal and perfectly inflexible' laws, which are unnatural restraints on human conduct. By nature 'the mind restrains not itself by any general and universal rules; but acts on most occasions as it is determin'd by its present motives and inclination'.[7] The device of inflexible rules is a remedy for the natural human predicament, and it relies more on the inventiveness of the human species than on natural providence. Moreover, Hume observes that the original motive for the invention and acceptance of these conventional rules – 'a general sense of common interest' – would be insufficient in a 'numerous' society, where the temptation to ride free would be too strong.[8] Happily, the original motive is soon overlaid by a common 'moral sense',[9] a relatively unreflective but strong social pressure. Hume says this second motive is more natural than the first, but only because it requires little (albeit some) artificial augmentation by political and private education.[10] Humans in society naturally develop social definitions of virtue and vice, and it is these social artifices rather than calculations of interest or even natural sentiments and sympathy (which exist, but are too limited in extent) that maintain society and political conventions.

In both his *Treatise* and in his *Essays: Moral, Political and Literary* (1742)[11], Hume applies this general view of the distance between nature and politics in a famous critique of the classical liberal explanation of the authority of government on the basis of consent. He points out the implausibility of that explanation: neither magistrates nor subjects act as if the obligation to obey political authorities depends on consent (whether express or tacit). Such a dependence would imply that there was an obligation to perform the promise of obedience made in a contractual agreement between governors and governed. But even where such an agreement may exist, why, asked Hume, is there an obligation to abide by it? The obligation to obey government is found to be 'requisite to preserve order and concord in society'; the duty to perform promises is equally an artificial convention, 'to beget mutual trust and confidence in the common offices of life'.[12] Political obligation begins and ends with the common interest in 'security and protection'; it needs and can tolerate no additional motive in the duty of promise-keeping.[13] The virtue of political obligation may initially be supported by 'the obligation of promises', 'yet it quickly takes root of itself'.[14] Hume's critique of the liberal 'creed'[15] of natural rights and the social contract is based on this deflation of the claims of political voluntarism. He admits that 'the voluntary convention and artifice of men'[16] are the original source of political conventions, including the establishment of legitimate government, but he allows none of the force of this genesis of government to carry forward into established political society, which is maintained not by consciousness of the way government and other political conventions are invented but by the power of social opinion, which 'takes root of itself'. He grants that 'the people still retain the right of resistance; since 'tis impossible, even in the most despotic governments, to deprive them of it'.[17] But he denies the possibility of philosophy's establishing any particular rules 'by which we may know when resistance is lawful',[18] and admits that 'an absolute government'[19] can have as much claim to allegiance as a free one, since not the formality of consent but the end of 'security and protection' is the general criterion for allegiance or resistance.

Hume's critique of classical liberal consent thinking overlooks the extent to which that thinking actually concurs with his own concern for the end of security. As John Rawls has remarked, Hume's critique of Locke's contract doctrine 'never denies, or even seems to recognize, its fundamental contention'.[20] John Locke, the leader of the 'party' of philosophers that Hume criticized, successfully combined voluntarism and utilitarianism; Locke's doctrine of consent was not (as Hume believed it was) purely a doctrine of actual (as opposed to hypothetical) consent.[21] A recent study of liberalism has pointed out that the 'sharp distinction between the deontic considerations specified by claims of right and the aggregative or teleological considerations specified by arguments from welfare . . . was alien to the liberal tradition'.[22] The question for Hume and later utilitarians who follow in his footsteps is this: is it not necessary for utilitarianism itself to favour the establishment of a liberal 'creed' in order to ensure that political societies, with their independent roots,

do not grow in illiberal directions? 'Time and custom', Hume
remarks, 'give authority to all forms of government'.[23] What but a
liberal creed can ensure that 'time and custom' favour free government? Like Edmund Burke, Hume wanted to accept the benefits of
the Revolution of 1688 (which 'had such a happy influence on our
constitution')[24] without accepting its liberal justification and
constitutional democratic implications.

In comparison to Hume, Jeremy Bentham was a more sweeping –
not to say a deeper – critic of classical liberalism. He denounces the
natural rights doctrines of the American Declaration of Independence and the French Revolutionary Declarations of Rights as
'anarchical fallacies'. Against their 'terrorist language', he opposes
'the language of reason and plain sense', which says that only
consideration of the advantage of any given society – with due
attention to time and circumstances – can determine which rights
should be established, maintained or abolished.[25] 'Natural rights',
wrote Bentham, 'is simple nonsense: natural and imprescriptible
rights, rhetorical nonsense, nonsense upon stilts'.[26] Bentham agreed
with Hume's critique of the social contract doctrines of earlier
liberals; after reading it, he 'felt as if scales had fallen from [his]
eyes'.[27] The 'season of fiction' is now over, because 'the universal
spread of learning' has made such fictions unnecessary and impossible
to propagate.[28] Appeals to justice, right reason, or the law of nature,
can now be seen as admissions that one simply cannot explain the
true reason for one's opinions. 'The recognition of the nothingness
of the laws of nature and the rights of man' is an essential part of
modern education, needed to counteract the tragic, anarchical
theory and practice of the French Revolution.[29] Bentham hopes that
the misusage of the word 'right' as a noun rather than an adjective
eventually will be removed from the English language.[30]

Bentham grants that the doctrine of the original contract had been
a useful and admirably successful *ad hominem* argument when it was
first deployed.[31] He does not make such a concession in the case of
natural rights doctrines, which he pronounces to be 'a moral crime'
in his day, and 'in the times of Grotius and Pufendorf', 'little more
than improprieties in language, prejudicial to the growth of
knowledge'.[32] In neither case does he appreciate that the rhetoric of
natural rights might have any present or future use. He does not
recall that Grotius and Pufendorf had developed the modern concept
of universal individual 'rights' (in the sense of just claims that one
possesses) in order to defend the sanity of politics in a world where

that sanity was threatened by universal religious claims. Natural rights were essential in order to moderate politics under pressure from such claims. Even in Bentham's day, natural rights doctrines could have served to defend politics from the anarchical and tyrannical perversions of such doctrines. Bentham's retreat to social judgement of the balance of utility shares with Hume the difficulty of not being able to defend the liberal ground inherited from earlier liberals, should social judgement drift away from that ground. For all his rationalism, Bentham's distrust of natural rights reasoning borders on a distrust of reason altogether. Holding up as a model of political language the practical-minded proceedings in the House of Commons – in contrast to the theoretical style of French politicians – Bentham asserts: 'A jealousy of abstract propositions is an aversion to whatever is beside the purpose – an aversion to impertinence'.[33] Aversion to 'natural and imprescriptible rights' can easily become an exaggerated deference to 'prescription', transforming utilitarian liberalism into Burkean conservatism. Bentham's rational retreat from nature prepared the way for the critique of rationalism and the embrace of historicism that are evident in twentieth-century conservative thinking such as that of Michael Oakeshott and Friedrich Hayek.[34]

The same kinds of objections confronting early utilitarianism apply to twentieth-century utilitarianism. The liberal credentials of utilitarianism are now frequently questioned, partly because utilitarianism has retreated even further from the natural foundations of liberalism. Post-Benthamite utilitarianism tries to dispense with the controversial or difficult-to-measure psychological criteria of classical utilitarianism, by substituting preference satisfaction for happiness or some more substantive notion of utility. This has revealed and deepened the radically individualistic and antinaturalistic outlook of utilitarianism. Utilitarianism is often criticized for not taking seriously enough the distinction between persons: it too readily justifies a social (perhaps majoritarian) tyranny. But the reason it does this is its radical moral individualism. In utilitarianism, especially in its twentieth-century form of welfare economics, human beings with common natural species characteristics are replaced by preferring individuals, each *sui generis* and each the sole judge of his or her own welfare. At the same time, the various human goods that these individuals prefer are replaced by the less restricted but somehow more homogeneous (and therefore more mathematically expressible) category, sources of utility.

Welfare is all in the mind. On this basis, it is not surprising to see how easily utilitarian arguments can justify disregard not only for human rights, whether of majorities or of minorities (what is this human species that has rights?), but also for the significance of differences of political regime (what is the difference, as long as utility is maximized?).[35]

BEYOND UTILITARIANISM

The problems of liberal utilitarianism have encouraged attempts to go beyond it. In their return to questions of value during the last twenty years, professional philosophers in the English-speaking world have frequently gone beyond utilitarianism in order to defend human rights, but they have seldom gone so far as to question the utilitarian rejection of nature and natural rights. Therefore the revival of rights talk or 'deontology' (by Rawls and Rawlsians), which has found its roots in Kantian philosophy, has in turn been challenged by a more or less conscious revival of Burkean and Hegelian philosophy (by 'communitarian' writers such as Michael Walzer, Michael Sandel and Charles Taylor), which has emphasized the historical and cultural rootedness of human selves, not the trans-historical nature of human beings. Current challenges to the deontological challenge to utilitarianism reject not its Kantian contrast between human morality and nature, but its Kantian universality. When (as in Kantian deontology) reason rather than nature is the source of principles, principles begin to be too formal, and (as in Hegelian philosophy) history comes to be looked upon as a supplier of more substantive principles. The Continental movement in the nineteenth century away from utilitarianism through Kantian deontology to Hegelian historicism seems to be repeating itself in the English-speaking world of the twentieth century. To break out of this cycle, we need to return to a pre-Kantian and pre-utilitarian view of human rights as natural rights, but neither the deontologists nor their critics want to bear the burden of maintaining that human rights are natural. It seems doubtful that liberalism can relieve itself of that burden – or, rather, dispense with that support – without collapsing into a conservative or radical historicism.

Most of the rest of this chapter is devoted to understanding and criticizing the political philosophy of John Rawls. With the publication of *A Theory of Justice* in 1971 (based on work he had been doing since the 1950s), Rawls more than anyone is responsible for setting in motion the current cycle of normative political theory. His timing was good: the troubles of 'the sixties', along with sound philosophical critiques of positivism, had broken the spell of the positivistic idea that values, as opposed to facts, could not be discussed rationally. At the same time, there was a felt need for a moderate liberal response to radical critiques of liberalism. Rawls' work responded to that need. The conclusions of his theory appealed to a broad slice of academic opinion, and they were in demand in the political marketplace. (Ronald Dworkin has spoken of the 'intuitive appeal of his [Rawls'] conclusions to people of good will'.)[36] Rawls' theory supported welfare state liberalism, by supporting two 'principles of justice': the provision of equal basic liberties for each person, and the arrangement that all social and economic inequalities work for the greatest benefit of the least advantaged. Apart from the fact of the wide influence or appeal of Rawls' thinking, what makes it interesting for our purposes is its determined attempt to provide a moderate way of responding to the question of what needs to be unified and in common, and what needs to be diverse and private in liberal polities; and the failure of that attempt, because of Rawls' unswerving opposition to natural political standards.

Before examining Rawls' theory, it may be helpful to place it into its current academic context, and to consider in particular the view of that theory from the vantage point of its communitarian critics. The terrain of academic liberal political theory is now occupied by four armies: the two main forces, Rawlsians and communitarians, and two lesser ones, utilitarians and libertarians. The utilitarians (including legions of economists) are massed in the dry but fertile plains, while Rawlsians hold the commanding if somewhat airless heights. Communitarians camp in the villages and the countryside, and a motley assembly of libertarians (along with a few anarchists) hang around the frontiers. None of these armies would feel at home in the natural ground, the cities, although that is where liberal theory used to thrive, and although it is where most civilians still live (the theorists and the people therefore have trouble communicating with each other). Even the libertarians (as will become clear when we look at Robert Nozick's critique of Rawls) have abandoned the strong views about human nature and natural rights that used to define their cause.

There have been skirmishes but no large battles between the two main forces, the Rawlsians and the communitarians. This may be because they are engaged in negotiations of their differences, and are beginning to realize that their differences are not all that great. In particular, the Rawlsians – including Rawls himself – are beginning to emphasize how much of the substance of communitarianism they actually agree with. Rawlsianism is capable of conceding much to communitarianism, because from the beginning it has actually shared much with that doctrine. The communitarians are not very aggressive, but they may win by default, by the inner collapse of the enemy. Rawlsians are looking more and more like communitarians these days, and they are more and more open about the historicist ground that they share with communitarianism.

The tendency of unnatural liberalism towards historicism – a doctrine that one might have thought more appropriate for Marxists and conservatives than for liberals – is currently perhaps most visible in what the editors of a recent collection of essays on contemporary liberalism call the search for 'a mature liberal theory' that will incorporate 'public and social elements' as well as private and individual ones.[37] This search is presented as a concession to the criticism that has been levelled at what are regarded as the hyper-individualistic assumptions of contemporary deontological thinkers, led by Rawls. The liberals who make this concession and join this search reject the 'thin self' of Rawls' 'ultra-liberalism', and replace it with the 'thickly constituted' selves of a 'civic republic'. These 'thick selves' are encumbered with 'loyalties and obligations'[38] – but not to humanity or nature, only to particular human histories, for these somewhat dubiously liberal liberals accept the historicist idea that without social (and therefore – at present – unequal) definition, human selves are nothing: 'isolated, vulnerable, insupportable'.[39] In their battle against Rawls' Kantianism, they turn for support not to any philosophy of nature but to writers such as T. H. Green and John Dewey, progressivist philosophers of growth as mere change, unconstrained by nature.[40] Like Kant and Hegel, Rawlsians and post-Rawlsians inhabit the same unnatural world. The post-Rawlsians (in Walzer's self-description) simply replace the Rawlsian notion of persons as 'moral and psychological blanks, neutral bearers of accidental qualities', with 'persons-in-the-social-world', 'in [their] communit[ies]'.[41] They call themselves and are called 'communitarians' rather than 'liberals', because they think that individuals can derive worthy identities only from communities – (in Sandel's generous but still parochial formulation) 'whether family or city, tribe or nation, party or cause'.[42]

Michael Sandel has published the most elaborate critique of Rawls from the communitarian position. Sandel is aware of some of the differences between Rawls and Kant, but his critique of Rawls nevertheless focuses (misleadingly, as we shall see) on Rawls' rather Kantian notion of the autonomous subject. He questions the plausibility of this agent who acts – or at least thinks – 'in an ideal, unconditioned realm wholly independent of our social and psychological inclinations'.[43] However, he makes it clear that he is concerned to reinject into political philosophy the 'social' or communal, not the 'psychological' or natural. He argues that Rawlsian liberalism 'goes wrong' because 'it tries to do without . . . a theory of community'.[44] The virtue of Sandel's critique is not its complex contrast between Rawlsian individualism and an allegedly superior communitarianism, but its uncovering of some of the ground that Rawls actually shares with his communitarian critics, in spite of his 'official' individualism. By thinking through Rawls' work, Sandel lets us see that Rawls himself is at least unconsciously communitarian. Sandel argues that Rawls is unaware that his own 'theory of justice requires for its coherence a conception of community in the constitutive sense',[45] a conception that defines selves rather than merely facilitating their plans. Sandel is (unreasonably) happy with this conclusion, because he is happy with a radically communitarian, merely intersubjective understanding of political life. He agrees with the Kantian (and Rawlsian) attempt to liberate humanity from a 'disenchanted', ateleological nature;[46] he disagrees – or is more precise and forthcoming – on what is necessary to achieve this liberation: namely, the bonds of community, which are needed 'to prevent the lapse into arbitrariness which the deontological self is unable to avoid'.[47] Thus the avoidance of nature, which (as we shall see when we glance at Robert Nozick's work) can lead modern liberals towards an extreme, atomistic individualism reminiscent of Hobbes, more often drags them towards the communitarian extreme. Sandel goes the communitarian route, and he plausibly claims that Rawls is ripe for recruitment into the ranks of communitarian republicans.

RAWLSIAN COMMUNITARIANISM

Sandel is right about Rawls, but for the wrong reasons. Rawls and his defenders have been able to respond to Sandel's and other communitarians' criticism by pointing out that Rawls' *Theory of Justice* is not as metaphysical or as Kantian as these critics have assumed. In the words of the title of a recent article by Rawls, 'justice as fairness' is 'political, not metaphysical': it 'has no metaphysical implications concerning the nature of the self'.[48] For all its Kantian and deontological trappings, for all its assertion that the just is prior to the good, Rawls' theory of justice is actually based on his theory of 'primary goods'. One of his most recent statements about 'The priority of right and ideas of the good' emphasizes that 'a political conception of justice . . . *must* draw upon ideas of the good'.[49] Moreover, Rawls is not as individualistic as the communitarians claim. The ease with which Sandel transforms Rawls' logic into communitarian logic is due to the fact that Rawls is rather communitarian without undergoing extensive transformation by Sandel. As we shall see, the priority of justice in Rawls' theory presupposes the priority of society over individuals, and the most primary of the 'primary goods' – self-respect – reinforces that priority. Rawls is not ripe for recruitment by Sandel, because he himself is a chief recruitment officer, although he would deny that he is.

Rawls' political theory represents another step in the modern retreat from nature, and it is this step – shared by the post-Rawlsians – that undermines his liberalism and encourages the post-Rawlsian collapse into communitarianism. Rawls' theory is criticized from left and right for its universalistic, 'pancultural aspirations'[50], but his continuation of the retreat from nature actually makes his theory too weakly universal. He urges us not to try 'to find a conception of justice suitable for all societies regardless of their particular social or historical circumstances', but 'to find a conception of justice for a democratic society under modern conditions'.[51] We are to 'look to ourselves and to our future, and reflect upon our disputes since, let's say, the Declaration of Independence'.[52] But while this Rawlsian reflection leads to the assumption that 'the methods and conclusions of science play an important role' in the 'public culture',[53] it does not allow any role for the Declaration's self-evident truths about humanity and nature. It does not 'search for moral truth interpreted as fixed by a prior and independent order of objects and relations, whether natural or divine'.[54] Political philosophy simply 'hopes to uncover, and to help to articulate, a shared basis of consensus on a political conception of justice drawing upon citizens' fundamental intuitive ideas about their society and their place in it'.[55]

At times Rawls' reflection leads him into positions that resemble the atomistic individualism that communitarians find so offputting, but generally and decisively he places himself within the communitarian tendency of contemporary liberalism, because his overriding concern is with social unity. He does not aim for a society of 'saints agreeing on a common ideal',[56] a society 'beyond justice', 'however desirable it may be'.[57] But he does seek to make fraternity a more operative ideal in liberal democracy, pushing the ties of the political community closer to those of the family.[58] His 'well-ordered society' is so united that penal sanctions might never need to be applied within it.[59] Throughout his book, as well as in his recent reflections on his intentions in the book, he emphasizes his 'avoidance' strategy: he tries 'to avoid disputed philosophical, as well as disputed moral and religious, questions', because of the difficulty or impossibility of resolving them politically.[60] In other words, he tries to apply the liberal principle of toleration not only to religious beliefs but also to moral and philosophical opinions. 'Philosophy as the search for truth about an independent metaphysical and moral order cannot', he believes, 'provide a workable and shared basis for a political conception of justice in a democratic society'.[61] He fears that if politics concerns itself with overly 'comprehensive . . . conceptions of the good', the results will be as disastrous today as they were when wars between Catholics and Protestants devastated Europe.[62] The state would be given 'a sectarian character'. Even if a 'comprehensive doctrine' were 'widely . . . shared' in a society, it would tend 'to become oppressive and stifling'.[63] Given 'the fact of pluralism' in the modern world, the need for political consensus 'forces political philosophy to be, so far as possible, independent of and autonomous from other parts of philosophy, especially from philosophy's long-standing problems and controversies'.[64] The blind men must somehow be forced to agree on the shape of the elephant, or at least they must stop arguing about it in public. Rawls has no time for a liberal politics in which philosophical questions are present without being resolved. Such controversial matters must be kept 'off the political agenda'. When confronted by contending claims – for example, those of individualism and communitarianism – the Rawlsian strategy is not to try to combine them, recognizing the elements of truth in each, but to try to avoid them, to relegate the questions that they raise to the private sphere, and to base politics on neutral ground.[65]

All this may sound like a preface to an individualistic case for extending and protecting private freedom, but in fact it is simply the minor premise of Rawls' argument in favour of greater socialization.

He speaks of the separation of morality and citizenship, but proposes what amounts to a radical merger of these concepts, because he doubts the possibility of combining selfishness and citizenship. He sees only a stark alternative between the anarchy of 'general egoism' and acceptance of his version of social justice. Although he admits that he has no way of persuading the rational egoist to adopt a 'sense of justice', he insists that a strong 'sense of justice' must rule (like Hobbes' sovereign) if society is to work, so there will be sufficient social 'stability' – that is, so the temptation of egoistic non-cooperation is removed, or at least overpowered by social guilt in the few instances that it erupts. He distinguishes his theory of justice from the kind of 'social theory' that favours any stability whatever, but he has little toleration for ambiguity in relations between individuals and communities, and no sense of the vitality that can result from such tension. Society is the fundamental good, determining the 'primary goods' and the principles of justice.[66] Rawls' concern for social equilibrium and stability is connected with his elevation of society over the individual, convention over nature, and the democratic 'self' over the human soul.

The avoidance strategy appears attractive to Rawls less because of his acceptance of moral diversity in modern societies than because he insists on attaining a very high degree of social unity and public agreement on principles of justice. Moral diversity simply makes the political philosopher's search for a basis for social unity much more urgent and difficult. For all its tolerant postures, Rawls' work aims above all at intensifying individuals' 'sense of justice' so that they will cooperate willingly within a 'social union'.[67] This aim is the end of his work, and its major premise. Combined with the minor (that philosophy as the search for truth cannot provide the basis of social unity), it yields the conclusion that we need a theory of 'justice as fairness' that is built not on trans-cultural and trans-historical philosophical appreciation of human nature, or even on Kantian claims about the nature of 'persons' or 'selves', but on 'ideals' that are already 'implicit or latent in the public culture of a democratic society'.[68]

Both of Rawls' premises are doubtful. Such a degree of social unity as he seeks seems unavailable, even if it were desirable (and it is not clear why social unity based on Rawlsian justice would be less 'stifling' than 'comprehensive' doctrines of the human good); and the 'creed' of natural rights liberalism, while it is safe to guess that it will never be as universally accepted as Rawls thinks a 'political conception of justice' ought to be, does offer a philosophical basis for liberal democracy, a basis from which liberals can judge various contending 'comprehensive' moral doctrines, instead of just hoping they will go away (even while recapitulating them, as a Rawlsian pursuit of a culture's intimations may threaten to do[69]). Like his utilitarian precursors in the history of unnatural liberalism, Rawls wants the benefits of liberal democracy without the trouble of establishing the truth of its principles. Thus, Rawls resists Ronald Dworkin's suggestion that his (Rawls') theory is 'right-based'. Rawls himself had toyed with that suggestion in his book.[70] But now, on reflection, he sees that justice as fairness is not a 'right-based' view but a 'conception-based' view.[71] Rawls explores existing, socially accepted conceptions, trying to find within them – or rather, in their common ground – a basis for greater agreement and cooperation,[72] and therefore cannot take natural rights too seriously. Methodologically, at least, Rawls is not so much a deontologist as a liberal democratic sociologist. He modestly writes *A* (not *The*) *Theory of Justice*. He strives for a 'strictly deductive . . . moral geometry', but achieves only a 'highly intuitive' and highly culture-bound account of justice.[73]

This is not to say that Rawls is a political quietist, meekly accepting and analysing given ideas and trends. He greatly favours some of these (however 'latent') at the expense of others, for his methodological modesty is not matched by moderation in his ambitions for political society. If the effort to construct a workable conception of justice from the available materials turns out to be hopeless, then 'the practical task of political philosophy is doomed to failure'.[74] Nothing short of justice will do. Rawls does not build on popular notions of justice that oppose his own principles, particularly his 'difference principle' (that all inequalities must serve to benefit the less advantaged). He does not share de Tocqueville's admiration for the individual 'intractability' and 'love of independence' inspired by modern egalitarianism, which de Tocqueville depended upon to counterbalance the more powerful egalitarian tendency towards soft social despotism, a tendency that Rawls promotes.[75] While in his *Theory of Justice* he 'leaves aside' the controversy between proponents of negative and positive liberty, and leaves the initial impression that he is interested in establishing the justice of negative liberty,[76] that impression is removed once we see the extent of his hunger for social unity. He has more recently stated that he sees himself as one who is trying 'to adjudicate between these contending traditions', the traditions (briefly) of Locke – 'freedom of thought and conscience, certain basic rights of the person and of property, and the rule of law' – on the one hand, and of Rousseau on the other – 'equal political liberties and the values of public life'.[77] But in fact, he quickly finds himself drawn into the Rousseauian camp (although – like many admirers of Rousseau – he sometimes tries to avoid some of the harsher disciplines of that camp):

> Justice as fairness starts from the idea that society is to be conceived as a fair system of social cooperation and so it adopts a conception of the person to go with this idea. . . . a person is someone who can be a citizen, that is, a fully cooperating member of society over a complete life. We add the phrase 'over a complete life' because a society is viewed as a more or less complete and self-sufficient scheme of cooperation, making room within itself for all the necessities and activities of life, from birth until death. A society is not an association for more limited purposes; citizens do not join society voluntarily but are born into it.[78]

Rawls even goes beyond Rousseau, by removing completely the voluntary quality of citizenship. Society cannot 'be a scheme of cooperation which men enter voluntarily in a literal sense'.[79] Only hypothetical consent, not actual consent, can legitimize political society. A just society simply 'comes as close as a society can to being a voluntary scheme, for it meets the principles which free and equal persons would assent to under circumstances that are fair . . . . The theory of justice is a part . . . of the theory of rational choice';[80] it elaborates 'principles that would be chosen by rational persons'.[81] Rawls (committing an error opposite to the one that he spotted in Hume, noticed in the first section of this chapter) would interpret even Locke's doctrine of consent as a doctrine of merely hypothetical consent.[82]

INDIVIDUALITY, EQUALITY AND MORAL PERSONALITY

The most important device used by Rawls to select and to refine just principles from the stock of available ideas is the 'original position', an imagined situation in which all are deprived of knowledge of their natural and social assets and liabilities. Reflection on the original position is supposed to provide 'an Archimedean point for assessing the social system', so that we are 'not at the mercy, so to speak, of existing wants and interests'.[83] However, we remain at the mercy of culturally available ideas. The original position, in contrast to the state of nature, is not a condition in which nature is revealed, and in which culturally available ideas are subjected to critiques from the natural point of view. (As John Dunn has noticed, Rawls' contractarianism, in contrast to classical contract theories, thus 'offers an abstract and philosophically debilitated reverie on how ethical and political value should be conceived – not a relatively powerful account of how human beings have good reason to act in the political settings in which they find themselves'.[84]) Rawls would exclude from the original position 'the knowledge of those contingencies which sets men at odds'.[85] In order to reach a sufficiently unified and 'homogeneous' society with a 'moral consensus', Rawls has to begin by hypothetically eliminating natural human heterogeneity, so that the divisive effect of awareness of this heterogeneity can be eliminated in actual societies. He 'nullifies the accidents of natural endowment and the contingencies of social circumstance', factors which he claims are 'arbitrary from a moral point of view'.[86] The basic structure of society must not incorporate 'the arbitrariness found in nature': 'In justice as fairness men agree to share one another's fate'.[87] 'The arbitrariness of the world must be corrected for'.[88] The principles of justice 'are equivalent to an undertaking to regard the distribution of natural abilities as a collective asset so that the more fortunate are to benefit only in ways that help those who have lost out'.[89] Although persons must accept responsibility for any 'expensive tastes',[90] they can claim no credit for any natural talents. Needs, not desires or deserts, 'define appropriate claims in questions of justice'.[91] What about the traditional notion of claims based on contributions to the common good? As we have noticed in Chapter 4, such claims could include the claims of human excellence (like those of a Marlborough), if these were understood in a less exclusively selfish way than in the 'perfectionism' that Rawls sets up and rejects. Citizenship could be combined with selfishness in theory – as it almost always is in practice. But in Rawls' theory, as in the bureaucratic mentality examined in Chapter 4, there is no such combination; and in Rawls' theory, by means of the original position, claims to honour based on public-serving but private, individual human excellence are ruled out by treating everything good as if it were already part of the commonwealth. Greater natural (or social) assets of an individual must be regarded as 'a social asset to be used for the common advantage', eventually perhaps even as a product of the well-ordered society's 'eugenic policies'.[92] It is not clear how some qualities can be recognized as natural 'assets' if nature is arbitrary. Presumably society will judge.

This cavalier attitude to natural human differences and natural human individuality (at least as glaring as utilitarianism's disregard of the distinction between persons) follows from Rawls' purely conventional notion of human − or rather, personal − equality. The priority of society over the individual, and of homogeneity over heterogeneity, follows from Rawls' account of the priority of convention over nature. Rawls tries − but fails − to give an account of 'the natural basis of equality'.[93] He rightly senses that liberal politics must recognize 'that men have equal dignity', but he means by this only that 'the parties [in the original position] are equally moral persons'.[94] Not actual, natural human beings but hypothetical, abstract, artificial 'moral persons' are equal, and 'entitled to equal justice'.[95] Moral persons are 'rational beings with their own ends and capable . . . of a sense of justice'[96] − that is, they are beings who are capable of using reason in a way that Rawls says they should, so that they can agree on the principles of justice and 'desire to act in accordance with' these 'principles that would be chosen in the original position'.[97] A moral person who actualized their capacity for a sense of justice would be 'a morally good person'. This 'good person, . . . or a person of moral worth', is someone with a highly developed social conscience: the complete good colleague, deeply convinced of the necessity and the desirability of 'engaging in many forms of cooperation'.[98] The imperative of social unity − a greater problem in liberal, pluralistic societies than in those in which the good is more authoritatively defined − dictates this kind of moral personality and the kinds of 'primary goods' (liberty, wealth and self-respect) that such persons would require.[99] Never mind that the 'psychological premises' of these primary goods 'may prove incorrect'[100]; they are required for social cooperation. The 'veil of ignorance' that descends upon parties in the original position is necessary in order to ensure that moral persons (potentially good persons) actually choose to be good persons. Rawls does not ask us to believe that parties in the original position are mutually benevolent, for that would be too 'strong a condition'; but the veil of ignorance (which is so 'thick' that no particular information is available except that which is 'necessary for a rational agreement to be reached'[101]), combined with the stipulation that no party act on motives of envy, 'achieves the same purpose as benevolence'.[102]

Neither the ignorance nor the lack of envy that Rawls forces upon moral persons in the original position is a natural characteristic of human beings. It is misleading for Rawls to call these properties of his imaginary original parties 'natural capacities' or 'natural attributes'. They must be artificially simulated and encouraged, so that they become characteristics of abstract moral persons and actual good persons. This simulation may solve (or dissolve) the classic problem of non-cooperation in rational choice theory, but it hardly suffices to establish 'the natural basis' of human equality and dignity. Moral personality is both too strong and too weak to do that. Too strong, because it disallows individuals' claims to dignity that are based on their natural differences and uniqueness, which they lose sight of as moral persons. Too weak, because it does not tell us why and how human beings, in spite of their natural differences, are naturally equal, with a shared species dignity; the relations of moral persons 'to animals and to nature' are 'outside the scope of the theory of justice': 'moral persons' as such are not part of animate nature.[103] No wonder there are such disparities between them and us human animals.

On the shortcomings and overreachings of moral personality, Robert Nozick's radically individualistic critique of Rawls is very revealing. Rawls does not see individual dignity; Nozick does not see common human dignity. Nozick pours cold water on the idea (an idea that Rawls, unlike Nozick, needs but, like Nozick, fails to appreciate) that humans can obtain dignity 'from their common human capacities by comparing themselves to animals who lack them. ("I'm pretty good; I have an opposable thumb and can speak some language.")'.[104] This is amusing. Yet Nozick's cogent argument against Rawls' view that natural individual endowments are morally arbitrary depends on his demonstration that such natural facts are no less morally arbitrary than the natural human species characteristics that are necessary for moral personality itself: after all, he points out, it is an accidental 'physical fact that those particular gametes [that produced 'persons in the original position'] contained particular organized chemicals (the genes for people rather than for muskrats or trees)' that produced such features as 'rationality, the ability to make choices, having a life span of more than three days, having a memory, [and] being able to communicate with other organisms like themselves'.[105] If nature is regarded simply as an arbitrary 'lottery', human equality and dignity have as little natural support as human inequality and debasement. Rawls needs a stronger argument for human equality to support his condemnations of unjust, oppressive human desires and plans. He also needs a principle of equality that is not merely conventional, so that it can less easily become a tyrannical demand, unlimited by nature. Nozick, on the other hand, needs to see that appeals to rights are not necessarily atomistic: as one commentator has maintained, they need not be 'demands only for more shares of whatever pie [is] available, nor are they inherently hostile to social conscience'.[106] Natural rights are appeals to a common human nature; if that nature has no inherent dignity, why should such rights be respected, why should such appeals be listened to? It is not enough to refer as Nozick does to 'the fact of our separate existences',[107] unless we want to extend human rights to other animals. And why stop there? What about the rights of separate trees and rocks?

Rawls anticipates his Hegelian, communitarian critics by interpreting 'justice as fairness' as a Kantian doctrine that is less transcendental and less dualistic than Kant's own doctrine. By lowering Kant, Rawls risks losing the main advantage that Kant's doctrine enjoys over utilitarianism, namely, the ability to avoid judging actions or rules merely by their consequences.[108] Rawls seeks to relate 'justice as fairness to the high point of the contractarian tradition in Kant and Rousseau',[109] but goes much further than Kant or Rousseau in advocating the claims of society. He makes a greater departure from nature and privacy, in order to make morality and publicity seem less problematic. Although persons in the original position are assumed to be averse to taking unnecessary risks (that is why it is rational for them to play it safe and to opt for Rawls' principles), they cannot avoid the big risk of the social project itself: like lovers, fellow citizens ('simply a special case' of lovers) become so dependent on each other that they must thereby incur great 'dangers of injury and loss'.[110] In Rawls' highly socialized world, a 'good person . . . is someone who has to a higher degree than the average person the broadly based features of moral character that it is rational for persons in the original position to want *in one another*' (my emphasis).[111] Moral virtue is socially defined. There are no human excellences that are not 'goods from everyone's point of view'.[112] The 'full theory of the good' is subordinate to society's theory of justice.[113] The higher is constrained by the lower. We have only Rawls' bland assurance that 'a sufficiently wide range of ends can be accommodated'[114] in this scheme, and no assurance at all that a moral version of Gresham's Law might not drive out good characteristics to accommodate baser ones.[115] (In fact, Rawls has recently conceded that 'there is no social world without loss – that is, no social world that does not exclude some ways of life that realize in special ways certain fundamental values'.[116]) As Rawls acknowledged a few years after his *Theory of Justice* was published, 'justice as fairness', in contrast to Kant's philosophy, 'assigns a certain primacy to the social'; rather than starting with the conscientious individual, it starts with the 'unanimous collective agreement regulating the basic structure of society within which all personal and associational decisions are to be made in conformity with this prior undertaking'.[117] 'Justice as fairness' also requires greater 'publicity' than Kant's doctrine: it must assume 'a wide role as part of public culture', so 'citizens are made aware of and educated to this conception', and are 'presented with a way of regarding themselves that otherwise they would most likely never have been able to entertain'.[118]

To establish this ambitious, deeply social concept of political justice, Rawls relies on a psychology that overlooks some highly relevant facts of human nature. In *A Theory of Justice*, he describes moral development as a sequence of stages, from 'the morality of authority' (accepting precepts) through 'the morality of association' (accepting roles), to 'the morality of principles' (understanding morality).[119] Even in the first stage, Rawls sees remarkably little difficulty in the process of socialization. After all, he argues (in an excessively rationalistic way), 'a child does not have his own standards of criticism, since he is not in a position to reject precepts on rational grounds', so if a child loves its parents, 'he will tend to accept their injunctions', or at least to feel guilty if it does not.[120] Rawls has little appreciation of *thymos* (spiritedness), which as we saw in Chapter 4 is politically crucial. *Thymos* in the form of self-righteous resistance to domination leads humans (even young ones) both to insist on their own equality and freedom and to try to domineer over others. This natural political spiritedness of human beings is at the heart of the classical liberal recognition of natural human equality and liberty. Overlooking it, Rawls massively understates the perennially problematic status of civil society and its claims on individuals.

RAWLSIAN POLITICS

As John Locke noticed, the most interesting and politically problematic feature of the human insistence on equal liberty is that it inspires the love of both freedom and despotism.[121] Humans are naturally tempted to lord it over others even while claiming the right to their independence from others. The natural love of liberty is one of those human characteristics that can produce great harm as well as great good. Abraham Lincoln reflected on this troubling psychologico-political fact: 'With some the word liberty may mean for each man to do as he pleases with himself, and the product of his labor; while with others the same word may mean for some men to do as they please with other men, and the product of other men's labor'.[122] There is a certain logic in this confusion, because while neither the absolute liberty of total individual independence nor the total dependence sought by the tyrannical impulse is politically liberal, neither tendency can be totally avoided without changing human nature (unless Rousseau was right to deny that humans are by nature wilful, and to assert that their *amour propre* is a completely social rather than a natural characteristic[123]). The total independence of libertarianism is as utopian as the total dependence of communitarianism. Rawls never finds the liberal middle way between independence and dependence – between negative and positive liberty (or between de Tocqueville's anarchical individual intractability and egalitarian social despotism) – because he insists on a humbling social dependence, based on something like the Hobbesian rationale that 'because men that think themselves equall, will not enter into conditions of Peace, but upon Equall termes, such equalitie must be admitted'.[124] Like Hobbes, Rawls fails to see that the mixture of independence and dependence can also be a politically fruitful combination: stubbornness well understood can be the basis of political unity and reform, when humans' stubborn, spirited defence of their immediate interests goes so far that it detaches them from those interests sufficiently to combine with others,[125] or even to sacrifice their lives. Righteous indignation loves company.

The failure of Rawls to incorporate natural human spiritedness in his doctrine, and the bent towards social tyranny in that doctrine are slightly disguised by his strong support for judicial toleration of civil disobedience. However, he views civil disobedience only as 'a way of setting up, within the limits of fidelity to law, a final device to maintain the stability of a just constitution'.[126] He does not think of it as a means of dealing with deep injustice. Perhaps this is reasonable; civil disobedience is at the mercy of the majority's sense of justice. More worryingly, Rawls also explicitly excludes consideration of more collective forms of resistance, for his assumption throughout is that the ideal of an almost perfectly just society is the place to look to discover the principles of justice. Like Socrates in the *Republic*, he pushes into the background the tension between what is good for individuals or groups and what is good for political communities, by concentrating on the construction of a perfect community. Rawlsian civil disobedience is merely the action of individuals calmly pointing out departures from the communal sense of justice; it is not the action of angry political groups.[127]

Alongside the Rawlsian tendency towards social tyranny lurks a tendency towards governmental or judicial–bureaucratic tyranny. Rawls does not have a well-developed sense of the ways in which individuals and groups can and should continually consent to liberal government. Voluntarism is important only in the original position. Once the hypothetical consent of parties in the original position is secured − that is, made to seem reasonable − consent takes a very subordinate place in the political process. Rather than admitting the continuing problem of gaining consent to just policies, Rawls comes down firmly on the side of justice, to the neglect of consent. The group compromising and bargaining of pluralistic politics is to give way to judgements about justice by 'rational legislators', or to judges dealing with conscientiously disobedient individuals and to bureaucrats devising and administering just policies. There is some sense in Rawls' criticism of pluralistic proceduralism; procedures alone cannot transform group selfishness into public-spirited policies. However, the value of a well-considered respect for formalities as a barrier between the strong and the weak in democratic societies should not be overlooked.[128] And Rawls clearly goes too far the other way. He has no appreciation of the usefulness of groups as intermediaries, imparting public spirit to private individuals and making public policy secure the rights of individuals. Especially in reflecting on American politics, with its long tradition of decentralization and powerful 'mediating structures', one might expect Rawls to show some awareness of the quasi-public role of groups. However, the second stage in Rawlsian moral development − 'the morality of association' − produces a merely private morality. In Rawls' well-ordered society, associations are private; they do not contribute to the public good, they merely provide 'a secure basis for the sense of worth of their members'.[129] Although 'the morality of association quite naturally leads up to a knowledge of the standards of justice' by requiring individuals 'to take up the point of view of others',[130] the standards of justice themselves are viable only when individuals and groups lose their individuality and 'points of view' by being stripped down to 'parties in the original position', bereft of knowledge of anything that distinguishes them from any other 'party'.[131] Unless this leap from wholly private to wholly public can be accomplished, 'a greater reliance on the coercive powers of the sovereign might be necessary to achieve stability'.[132] The absolute separation of private and public (or of 'egoism' from 'the moral point of view')[133] may lead pluralistic proceduralists (the 'interest group liberals' of Chapter 4) to support a tyranny of private groups; it clearly leads Rawls to prepare a tyranny of public officials ('the sovereign'!), against which a bloodless, atomized civil disobedience would be no match. It is not, as Rawls asserts, when 'the basic law is thought to reflect the order of nature' that citizens become 'subjects' who 'have only the right of suppliants',[134] but precisely when the law tries to ignore the necessarily somewhat private nature of human beings.

Of course, Rawls is not proposing to set up a society of disembodied philosophers. As several commentators have observed,[135] Rawls' 'Kantianism' is not even as true to Kant as he thinks it is. It is too earthy. His parties in the original position are not autonomous, but heteronomous, in Kant's way of thinking, because reason is purely instrumental for them, and they act on motives of desire and self-interest. Although they do not know their own social position, they do know that they have interests in the 'primary goods', and that they have a certain life plan they want to pursue: moral persons, in addition to their capacity for a 'sense of justice', are defined by their capacity of having 'a conception of their good (as expressed by a rational plan of life)'.[136] However, Rawls' original parties do share the Kantian predicament of not being able to get beyond a formal description of the acceptable content of a life plan. Rawls tries but fails to avoid 'a reductionism which regards religion and morality as mere preferences'.[137] So while Rawls' 'moral persons' turn out to be people like the rest of us with quite ordinary, bourgeois desires, they do not have any particular goals beyond these primary desires such as might be thought necessary to justify their elevation as ideal types or even as a 'sovereign' over those of us who have not managed to think ourselves into the original position. The same abstraction from nature that leads Rawls to neglect human individuality leads him to embrace a radical moral individualism in which 'selves' unprompted and unlimited by nature rather than souls with natural ends are the moral agents. Without natural standards, not only are the human good and 'the aims of the self . . . heterogeneous',[138] they are unlimited, as long as they conform to certain empty, formal criteria of rationality. The pursuit of a *summum bonum* strikes Rawls 'as irrational, or more likely as mad'.[139] Lifelong dedication is irrational; the pursuit of happiness is madness. Rawls demands that 'persons . . . have at any given time a particular conception of the good that they try to achieve'.[140] Otherwise, 'social cooperation' would not be useful; ditherers and layabouts should not expect to find a place in the well-ordered society. But while insisting that everyone have a plan, Rawls can offer little guidance as to what the plan should contain. He preaches the necessity of 'taking thought and seeing ourselves as one person with a life over time', but he thinks that 'very little can be said about the content of a rational plan, or the particular activities that comprise it'.[141] He briefly notes the existence of 'broad features of human desires and needs' and 'the requirements of human capacities and abilities',[142] but he sees these not as sources of moral values but merely as sources of the (to him) unquestionably rational preferences for the 'primary goods', and of 'such non-moral values as friendship and affection, the pursuit of knowledge and the enjoyment of beauty, and the like'.[143] Rawls' pseudo-'Aristotelian principle' simply adds to this 'thin theory of the good' the curious twist that the more complex realizations of human capacities are to be preferred to the less complex; it does not add any substance to the notion of 'human capacities', which remain anything that selves 'rationally' discover.[144] Even the 'full theory of the good' will 'leave a person unsettled as to what to do':[145] 'We eventually reach a point . . . where we just have to decide'.[146]

SELF-RESPECT, COMMUNITY AND HUMANITY

Rawls' morality is thus rather empty, but it is not as relaxed as such emptiness might imply. Rawls has had no trouble in defending his liberalism against the charge that it is a doctrine 'purely instrumental to individual or associational ends'; recently – attempting to split the communitarian opposition – he has even compared his liberalism with 'classical republicanism', the view that 'widespread participation in democratic politics by a vigorous and informed citizen body' is necessary for the preservation of liberty.[147] Rawls' well-ordered society, a 'social union of social unions',[148] is not a Nozickian, libertarian utopia of utopias, an 'environment in which people are free to do their own thing'.[149] However, the moral seriousness and social strictness in Rawls' project come not from the intrinsic gravity of moral choices,[150] but from the subordination of individual plans to the dictates of society. Rawls realizes that if 'we feel that our plans are of little value, we cannot pursue them with pleasure or take delight in their execution. All desire and activity becomes empty and vain, and we sink into apathy and cynicism'.[151] But his solution to this difficulty is not to try to sort out natural hierarchies of plans, but to make 'self-respect' (that is, social esteem) a – indeed, *the* – 'primary good': not nature but social convention is to save us from apathy and despair. In spite of the indeterminacy of morality, there is no place in 'justice as fairness' for the 'notion of radical choice, commonly associated with Nietzsche and the existentialists',[152] because individual selves define themselves not out of their inner depths, but only in their relations with others. They are no solitary Zarathustras, they are all 'last men', pursuing their little 'subplans' within the constraints of 'the larger comprehensive plan that regulates the community as a social union of social unions'.[153] In order for the plurality of the good to be corrected by the rather empty but nevertheless binding unity of justice, it is not the drive for self-preservation or the will to power but the drive for 'self-respect' that must be or must become fundamental. 'Self-respect' is 'the most important primary good'.[154] Rawls' two principles of justice – equal basic liberties and the arrangement for any inequalities to advance the greatest good of the less advantaged – are designed primarily to ensure everyone's self-esteem: 'persons express their respect for one another in the very constitution of their society'.[155] This makes material inequalities easy to accept, since the poorer 'have no cause to consider themselves inferior'.[156] To 'affront the self-respect of others' is the most 'evil' desire, worse even than the 'bad' desire for an inordinate amount of esteem and sense of self-mastery, which in turn is worse than the merely 'unjust' desire for too much wealth and security.[157] (As we saw in Chapter 2, this highly subjective moral hierarchy rules in contemporary arguments in favour of reverse discrimination, on the grounds that 'stigma' – which is lacking in such 'benign' discrimination – is worse than the material harm that is present; it also figures in defences of welfare spending that hinge on not asking citizens to accept sacrifices that require them to abandon their 'sense of equal worth'.[158]) 'Self-respect' is dependent upon a person's not being 'found unworthy of his associates'.[159] It must not be allowed to blow itself up into a drive for 'social acclaim', but this vital prop to one's self-esteem is a social product; 'self-respect normally depends upon the respect of others'.[160] The social tyranny of vanity, a watered-down *amour propre*, pervades Rawls' well-ordered society, however much he seeks to dampen envy and the drive for 'social acclaim'. Rawls' thinking shows how this is inevitable when society is elevated and nature is ignored. Here we can see how Rawls' abandonment of nature actually leads him towards both of the extremes that he had hoped to avoid: 'dogmatism and intolerance on the one side, and a reductionism which regards religion and morality as mere preferences on the other'.[161]

Rawls' doctrine of self-respect stands in sharp contrast to the understanding of self-respect in classical liberalism. In this understanding, individual assertions of dignity can appeal to natural human standards, such as the rights to 'life, liberty and the pursuit of happiness', rather than merely to social conventions. This means that assertions of dignity are in principle universally available (as Rawls would require). But it also means that they are not necessarily always appropriate or even good: if one fails to live up to a human standard, that is, if one acts inhumanly, or – more familiarly – if one is not yet perfectly human in some way, then (as William Galston has put it) 'unalloyed self-respect can be an impediment to self-improvement, and the ability to feel and respond to shame must be considered beneficial'.[162] From this point of view, Rawlsian liberalism debases self-respect by assuming that it is always good, by making it a universal, unconditional right, and by thinking of it simply as a product of social recognition, involving no natural, human standards.

The extent to which Rawls prepares the ground for his Hegelian, communitarian critics is particularly evident on this crucial topic of self-respect. This is a topic on which there is substantial agreement between Rawlsian and post-Rawlsian thinking. Consider the apparent contrast between self-esteem and self-respect as defined by one of those communitarian critics, Michael Walzer. Self-esteem, he tells us, is a matter of 'relative standing', resulting from and in a competition in which 'we live in the opinions of others'; but self-respect is less competitive: it 'is a matter of our own qualities:

hence of knowledge, not opinion, and of identity, not relative standing'. There is something here – but not enough. Walzer's certainty about the distinction and the distance between self-respect and self-esteem stems from his certainty about the solidity of the social sources of self-respect. In spite of his allusion to the counter-example of Epictetus, Walzer adopts a Hegelian analysis of recognition, and denies that knowledge of humanity in general can be relevant to self-respect. 'Self-respect requires . . . some substantial connections to the group of members, to the movement that champions the idea of professional honor, class solidarity, or citizen rights, or to the larger community within which these ideas are more or less well established'. The notion 'of what it might mean to be a self-respecting . . . human being . . . lacks concreteness and specificity'. Yet if such sentences as Walzer's 'No self-respecting doctor would treat a patient like that', and 'No self-respecting trade unionist would agree to such a contract' are intelligible signs of professional or other group or community standards somewhat independent from the competitive vanity fair, is it not also intelligible, as evidence of natural, human standards, to say, for example, 'No self-respecting human being would commit rape or murder', or 'No self-respecting human being would destroy their mind'? Why cannot one be 'a particular member' of the human race as well as a doctor, trade unionist, or whatever? 'No substantive account of self-respect will also be a universal account', according to Walzer. If that is so, how can the 'social meaning' of self-respect be immune to the Hobbesian relationality and relativism that Walzer charges only to self-esteem? Walzer's more historically and sociologically sensitive account of human self-respect is still missing the human dimension, and is therefore no different in principle from Rawls' account, which more openly equates self-respect with socially generated self-esteem. Walzer's search for more solid ground on which to base self-respect is reasonable, but doomed to failure because, unlike the authors of the Declaration of Independence, he does not let self-respect base itself on a decent regard for 'the opinions of mankind', aware of 'the laws of nature', but only on 'the freely given recognition and the honest verdict of one's peers'.[163]

CONCLUSION

The difficulties confounding Rawlsian liberal theory arise from the determination of that theory to avoid depending on natural truths.

This leads as surely in our time as in Socrates' to reliance on mere consensus: convention unattentive to nature, politics unmoderated by philosophy. It is clear, even from our brief glance at the communitarian theory that is the major alternative to Rawlsian liberalism in today's battles of the books, that the 'thickening' of the Rawlsian moral 'self' by the communitarians results from their intensification of the very conventionalism that leads Rawls into so many dubiously liberal positions. Therefore Rawls' communitarian critics push liberalism further down the road away from the complex unity of liberal politics. Can liberals resist this push? Only, it would seem, if they can reconsider their abandonment of nature: a prospect that we explore in the next chapter.

If I have exaggerated the illiberal tendencies of contemporary academic liberalism, I have done this in order to show that the extreme tendencies are there, not only more obviously in those libertarian and communitarian theories that suppose humans are or can be either totally autonomous or totally social, but even in the thinking of such an anti-extremist, middle-way seeking theorist as John Rawls. The main point I am making in this chapter is that it is difficult for liberal political philosophers to avoid the extremes of plurality and unity these days, because of their avoidance of political philosophy in the sense of thinking about what is naturally right, as opposed to what is conventional or merely logical. The great resurgence of political philosophy in the last twenty years, for all the renewed relish for talking 'normatively', has not renewed many political philosophers' taste for talking about nature. Yet the ambition to justify liberal democracy without recourse to natural standards remains unfulfilled. Without a natural basis, liberalism persists at best as a weak residue, a kind of conservatism that just happens to conserve liberal traditions, without fully understanding them and without being able fully to defend them. Precise knowledge of natural right may never be commonplace, even in modern liberal democracies; but can these regimes survive if that knowledge is cultivated nowhere within them?

Chapter 6

Liberty and nature

There is no obvious reason why political thinking should conform to the elegant economics of a free market, but an economic metaphor can summarize our findings up to this point. The market research presented in Chapters 2 to 4 has shown that the demand for natural standards for liberal policies and institutions is potentially quite buoyant, but in Chapter 5 we have seen that even if demand is insistent, the shops have few supplies on their shelves. Perhaps part of this supply-side problem can be ascribed to the rarity of the commodity. But I suggest that the supply can be increased, and the price brought down, if some of the artificial barriers to trade can be removed. Many of those barriers have been erected unnecessarily, and can be removed safely. What are often perceived as grave dangers of naturalistic political thinking turn out to be less great than imagined, and we have seen throughout this book how dangerous it can be to try to avoid such thinking.

The argument of the previous chapter was that the most serious weaknesses of liberal thinking in the nineteenth and twentieth centuries have stemmed from the dismissal of the classic natural rights doctrines of the seventeenth and eighteenth centuries. But – as the wisest members of that classic natural rights school were aware – recourse to appeals to natural rights is not opposed to, but is dependent on the idea of natural right, and in this final chapter I argue more fully that the natural standards needed for liberal politics go beyond the natural rights traditionally proposed by liberals (before utilitarians and historicists tried to banish such rights). Liberals need not only natural rights, but also natural right, a regard for the proper cultivation of human nature. They need this both for a fuller self-understanding of liberalism itself, and for self-defence of liberalism against the conventionalism of utilitarian and post-utilitarian attacks.

Modern *physiphobia* is a fear less of natural rights than of a more substantive natural right. A return to nature, it is feared, will mean a return to a demanding, illiberal, teleological understanding of humanity. Let us assume the worst, then, and see just how terrible such a return would be.

This fuller theoretical thesis was implicit in the survey of practical and institutional problems in Chapters 2 to 4, where it became clear, for example, that liberal citizenship has to be a sufficiently deep development of human character to justify the priority of its claims over those of ethnicity, and (for another example) that the rights and wrongs connected with human sexual differences depend on decisions about the aspects of human sexuality that are more or less desirable and more or less human. In Chapter 5, it also became clear that many of the most interesting arguments of contemporary liberal theorists concern – in spite of themselves – arguments about what type of human character it is best to cultivate. This concluding chapter does not begin to provide a full account of natural right (were such a thing possible), to make good the shortages that have been accumulating for some time in the political thought market. It merely offers a more complete sketch of the outlines of the kind of thinking that can bring nature back into the picture and help to harmonize the claims of individuality and communality, of political plurality and unity, claims that recent liberal thinking has failed to accommodate because of its opposition to thinking about nature. What might a more natural liberal theory look like and do? In particular, what would it require or permit in the way of views about the natural ends of human life, and how could such views of human flourishing be compatible with a liberal political regime? My argument here will be that concern for natural human flourishing, far from being opposed to liberal politics, is actually the best reason for maintaining the complex political unity of liberal constitutions and policies. In the circumstances of the modern world, natural right is still morally and politically relevant, but it demands liberal politics.

THE MODERATION OF NATURE

Thinking about nature as a possible source of standards for human life makes us uneasy. So it should. Natural standards can be counted upon to challenge conventional ones (some more than others). But one great cause of anxiety – one great barrier to the supply of natural considerations – can and should be removed. Appeals to nature are commonly assumed to be dangerous not because of their inevitable challenges to convention, but because of their alleged association with dogmatism, fanaticism, and tyranny. 'We now realize', one scholar has recently observed, that appeals to nature are a kind of 'theocratic' device, 'sufficiently un-neutral as to be illiberal', and, if we are as consistent as that scholar, we therefore place 'the American founding fathers' and their 'beliefs about . . . the purpose of human creation' on a level with tyrants such as 'the Ayatollah Khomeini' and their 'beliefs about God . . . [or] the goal of history'.[1] However, in fact, this association of twentieth-century tyranny with natural standards is not only mistaken, it is the very opposite of the truth. For it is the emphatic denial of natural standards by historicist theories that has supported these tyrannies. As Alexander Solzhenitsyn has pointed out, the unprecedented political cruelties of the twentieth century have indeed been based on theoretical orthodoxies, but these have been precisely those nationalistic and internationalistic orthodoxies that have been nurtured by 'the notion that there are no fixed universal human concepts called good and justice, that they are fluid, changing, and that therefore one must always do what will benefit one's party'.[2] Political partisanship is in principle more moderate when it looks to a natural standard, external to social convention, than when its standards are thought to be generated solely by human convention, based on reason or will autonomous from nature. In particular, the moderating force of the idea of human equality is clear; one can more easily push one's partisanship to an extreme if one denies that one's opponents are human.

Of course, naturalistic dogmatism is possible; but while a sensible naturalist can be aware of the limits of reason, a thoroughly sceptical denial of the possibility of any correspondence between the subjective human mind and the objective natural world is less immune to dogmatism. For if human reason has no capacity at all to regard the natural world, it can only occupy itself with logical or merely wilful projects that do not even claim to have any natural basis or limits. A good model of a sensible naturalistic approach to political life is James Madison's case for political moderation in *The Federalist*; Madison bases his case for political moderation on epistemological moderation, not on epistemological scepticism: what should 'moderate . . . our expectations and hopes from the efforts of human sagacity' is the observation that nature is impossible to know perfectly with our imperfect minds, not that it is impossible to know at all.[3] The more radical scepticism of the latter position can easily transform itself into a fanatical insistence that human conventions can and should be made perfect, precisely because they are subject only to internal, purely conventional standards. When human standards are considered to be merely human constructions, it is more reasonable to insist that perfect knowledge of them is available to humans, at least to those who have constructed them.

One meaning of the classical observation that humans are the most political animal is that they are the most mutually destructive of the social animals; that is why they naturally need to extend their logical capacities (which often encourage their tyrannical destructiveness) to philosophical awareness of the natural right (and natural rights) that human nature implies. Humans are naturally political, but politics is not naturally human; human effort is needed to humanize political life. Ever since Socrates took on Thrasymachus and Callicles in Plato's dialogues, the political philosopher's appeal to natural right has been an appeal for political moderation – specifically, for moderation of the self-destructive, tyrannical tendencies of political conventions left to themselves, unaffected by philosophical examination. Thrasymachus (in Plato's *Republic*) and Callicles (in the dialogue *Gorgias*) both present themselves as radical sceptics of conventional standards, but Socrates shows that in fact their admiration of tyrants' freedom from conventional restraints accurately represents the underside of the respectable conventions themselves. Moral and political life has a sneaking admiration for the tyrannical freedom that it also condemns. The same phenomenon is illustrated on a more common, sub-tyrannical level, when those who flout conventional standards and wind up rich and famous as a result are envied as well as criticized. This corrosive, potentially destructive self-contradiction seems intrinsic to moral and political life, and its destructive force is greater where that life is untouched by the philosophic appeal to nature.[4] The conventional restraints need reinforcement by natural restraints if they are to survive the challenge of the widespread conventional temptation to tyranny. Political life needs the natural guidance discerned by the philosophical life. Because of the strong appeal of the *appearance* of happiness, not everyone can be brought to see the folly of the ways of tyrants (and jetsetters), but some can, and everyone can benefit from this moderate success of philosophical moderation. It is not the conflict between philosophy and politics, but the attempt to live political life without philosophy, that is essentially tragic.

RADICAL AND MODERATE MODERNITY

Radical modern political thought has moved in the opposite direction to the sobering Socratic movement from potentially self-destructive convention to convention informed and moderated by nature. The outlines of the story of the development of this radical modernity can be told very briefly. At the cutting edge of radical modernity were the philosophies of Thomas Hobbes in the seventeenth century, Jean-Jacques Rousseau in the eighteenth, and G. W. F. Hegel in the nineteenth. The story begins most clearly with Hobbes' attempt to understand nature as a source of merely negative ends for human beings. 'For there is no . . . *Summum Bonum*, (greatest Good,) as is spoken of in the Books of the old Morall Philosophers', Hobbes found, so the guidance that nature furnishes to human life is therefore not positive but merely negative: there is no greatest good, only a greatest evil, death. What is naturally right is simply the intelligent but endless pursuit of bodily self-preservation.[5] Rousseau protested against this pedestrian Hobbesian view, claiming that it had abandoned nature as the source of every good thing, but he then proceeded to show how nature must be abandoned even more completely. According to Rousseau, the culture or 'general will' of a legitimate civil society can have little basis in human nature, even in the negative sense accepted by Hobbes, because the natural integrity of the human psyche is unavoidably destroyed by the historical passage from a primitive state of nature into civilized life. Nature provides not even negative ends for humans living in society. Human nature changes as humans 'perfect' themselves through time – in other words, as they create their own nature by means of their social interactions and artifices. Rousseau's insight was pursued by the Kantian attempt to replace nature with autonomous reason as the source of human ends (an attempt still pursued by many moral philosophers today), and subsequently by the Hegelian and Marxian substitutions of history – that is, conventions – as that source.

Although the rationality and providence of history have become less credible in the twentieth century than they appeared to Hegelian philosophers, any appeals against the authority of the conventions developed and established by history have tended to accept the lack of natural political standards, and to fall back upon individual searches for authenticity, often through psychoanalysis or creative art. Occasionally efforts have been made to combine the questioning of convention by Freudian psychology or Nietzschean creativity with a revolutionary Marxian politics. The failure of these efforts is eloquent testimony to the modern divergence of the natural and the political. It is much more difficult to maintain a healthy tension between convention and nature in politics and the possibility of individuals' critical distance from their own and their communities' projects, when nature is understood, as much of modern science understands it, as an arbitrary chaos devoid of order and purpose. Within this radically modern perspective, it seems that individual choices of ways of life, even if based on profound analyses of the human 'self', must appear as merely idiosyncratic, not as attempts to exemplify humanity. Any reintegration of nature and humanity – any relation of human conventions to nature – would seem to require the refutation of modern natural science.

However, there have been moderate as well as radical moderns. (One might cite such political thinkers as Locke, Montesquieu, Madison and J. S. Mill.) It is these moderate moderns who provided – and can still help provide – the basis for a moderate liberal politics. While radical moderns have largely discarded the natural as well as the political thought of antiquity, moderate moderns have been less dogmatic about making such a clean break with the past. The radical moderns have a reputation for philosophical ruthlessness and profundity; they, like Rousseau and Nietzsche, accept that true natural science is amoral and even nihilistic, but then try to construct a poetic vision that can conserve or create a space in which humans can live. Nietzsche remarked in one of his early essays that the morally relativistic historical sense produced by modern science and philosophy is 'true but fatal'. The modern scientific knowledge of the meaninglessness of life makes living impossible, except in the worthless fashion of those that Nietzsche's Zarathustra calls 'last men', who exist but do not truly live, for they experience no longing, and therefore neither failure nor fulfillment.[6] The conclusion is that in order to live, one must create one's own 'values' (Nietzsche's word, now on everyone's lips), in the full knowledge that human values have no natural support. Moderate moderns see less radical opposition between nature and truly human lives. They sense the support for human life and happiness that the natural world provides, even in some cases the natural world as depicted by modern natural science. This moderate position does not deny that the natural world cries out for industrious human improvement; for example, there is little complacency in John Locke's description of the necessity of hard human labour in order to make up for the fact that 'Nature and the Earth furnished only the almost worthless Materials, as in themselves';[7] and J. S. Mill, although clearly relying on natural standards in his political writings, also published a very sceptical essay on 'Nature' (still cited today in many epistemological sceptics' dismissals of natural standards), in which he made much of the fact that nature's 'powers are often towards man in the position of enemies, from whom he must wrest, by force and ingenuity, what little he can for his own use'.[8] (After all, even Aristotelian thinking emphasizes the need for human art and education to compensate for nature's failings.)[9] What the moderate modern position does deny is the radical modern contention that the very form and functions of the human species are human creations, artificial constructions with no foundation in nature. To take the example of Locke again, whatever might be the more sceptical conclusions of his epistemological writings, his political writings depend quite clearly on such propositions as the naturalness of the human species, which is the basis for the political equality and the natural rights of individual members of that species.

The hardest question confronting liberals, then, is how well they can defend this moderate position from the radical critique. In the remainder of this chapter I contend that liberals can find it easier to defend their position if they arm themselves not only, and not primarily, with a doctrine of natural rights, but also with an account of natural right: not so much a dogmatic doctrine as a powerful awareness of the reality and the political relevance of natural human teleology. I do not claim to establish the truth of that contention in this brief space, only to show that it is a more plausible and coherent view than is the opposite and currently more fashionable liberal avoidance of natural rights and right.

NATURAL TELEOLOGY AND HUMANITY

C. S. Lewis' philosophical etymology, *Studies in Words*, begins with a long and revealing chapter on 'nature', wherein he shows the connection between the Latin word 'natura' and the Anglo-Saxon word 'kind', both the noun and the adjective.[10] He shows that there *is clear etymological support for understanding 'nature' as something* that is politically and epistemologically 'kind' to human beings. That understanding can moderate the human desire (the *thymos* that we have run across in Chapters 4 and 5) to domineer, to punish and to hate, that despotic underside of the love of freedom: if humans can see that nature is kind, that human life is good, perhaps even that the world is a fairly hospitable place, they can more easily avoid an angry rebellion against the human condition, a rebellion that can destroy individual happiness and brutalize political life.[11] But is such a vision of the place of humans in the natural world accurate? Have modern philosophy and science not made such naïvety untenable? Even natural *human* teleology, apart from anything more cosmic, now seems incredible.

Etymologically, the word nature refers to growth, but it is also linked to the goals or ends of growth: nature signifies being as well as becoming.[12] Are human beings natural beings? Do they have natural ends? Asking ourselves the question 'What are people for?' is still natural enough in one sense. That is the form that the question was once put to me by one of my sons. But that was when he was only three years old, and when we are older we are generally taught to accept that such a question is unintelligible. But this acceptance is a bit hasty. The estrangement of moral humanity from the natural world studied by modern science often appears more massive than it actually is. Many studies by modern biologists, anthropologists, neurologists and psychologists assume and enhance our awareness of the natural teleological character of human life. Modern science is by no means unanimous in rejecting the relevance of natural teleological considerations when thinking about humanity. This is one reason why it is becoming less common for natural scientists to concur with Hobbes' confident rejection of ancient natural philosophy as 'rather a Dream than Science, and set forth in senselesse and insignificant Language'.[13]

Natural teleology – the recognition of natural ends – is logically connected with the recognition of natural forms, or species. This recognition of natural species, at least, seems to be still possible, in spite of the challenge of evolutionary biology. Living nature is not totally chaotic. Even if we accept that natural biological species evolve, and do not exist eternally, they are no less real during their very long lives. There may be fuzziness at the origins of species, and (as Aristotle already noticed) many species are very similar to each other, but species have great stability, and there is cross-cultural recognition of that stability, as well as great cross-cultural agreement on the classification of species.[14]

Whether species must be understood teleologically is a more controversial question. However, it seems clear that teleological interpretation of the natural human species could easily be more coherent than the modern approach that would have us postulate a moral world unrelated to (although somehow occupying the same universe as) the natural world. This modern dualism is much more demanding than classical teleology on our powers of doubting our senses: whereas Aristotle only suggests (and this only in his more theoretical writings) that a mysterious, divine 'agent intellect' might be somehow beyond nature, modern moral philosophy, by denying that nature provides any basis for morality, asks us to treat the whole moral life of humans as something beyond nature. The incoherence of modern ateleological natural science and modern moral philosophy is a serious problem, involving modern thinkers in a self-contradictory enterprise, which treats humans either purely mechanistically or purely morally but never both together. As de Tocqueville remarked, modern thinkers, having reduced humans to the subhuman, then 'seem as proud as if they had proved that they were gods'.[15]

But is a more coherent view available? In fact, it is less remote than is usually assumed. Many perceptive modern scientists recognize that biology must be teleological in order to be complete. For example, embryologists and molecular biologists find that they need to use teleological explanations in conjunction with mechanical ones, in order to explain the way that matter is organized into forms that are shaped with a view to certain activities of living beings. Biologists – in contrast to organic chemists dealing with the same material – properly ask 'why?' as well as 'how?'.[16] Teleological enquiries are necessary even to expand non-teleological biological knowledge. Ernst Mayr remarks that Aristotle's consideration of 'the study of ends as an essential component of the study of nature' makes him 'amazingly modern' from the perspective of biologists.[17]

Non-reductionist, teleological interpretations of human life and health are also essential to some of the most interesting work of psychologists, psychiatrists and neurologists, who find human standards in such natural facts as the upright posture and the mental balance between levity and gravity. One of the most profound reflections on the relationship between the natural human form and ends is Erwin Straus' essay on 'The upright posture'. The upright posture – a uniquely human phenomenon (other primates merely ape it) – is based on a host of physical facts; Straus maintains that:

the shape and formation of the human body are determined in

almost every detail by, and for, the upright posture. The skeleton
of the foot, the structure of the ankle, knee and hip; the curvature
of the vertebral column; the proportions of the limbs – all serve
the same purpose. The purpose could not be accomplished if the
muscles and the nervous system were not built accordingly. While
all parts contribute to upright posture, upright posture in turn
permits the development of the forelimbs into the human
shoulders, arms and hands and of the skull into the human skull
and face.[18]

Upright posture is a species characteristic, but it requires individuals'
efforts and awareness to achieve and to maintain it. It can exact a
painful toll: flat feet, hernias, varicose veins, backaches. However, its
benefits are also evident.[19] It is 'a specific mode of being-in-
the-world'.[20] Among other things, it 'has lifted the eye and ear from
the ground', and made seeing and hearing dominant over smelling,
thereby augmenting the natural human capacity for distancing.[21]
Modern philosophical anthropology – reflective inspection of the
human physique – confirms classical views of the nobility of sight
among the human senses, and of the centrality of language, speech
and reason in being human. In contrast to other animals, 'Man in
upright posture, his feet on the ground and his head uplifted, does
not move in the line of his digestive axis; he moves in the direction
of his vision'.[22] The form of the human mouth and ear makes
possible the separation of acoustical form from matter and the
intentional reproduction of sounds for speaking communicatively.
'Upright posture . . . lifts us from the ground, puts us opposite to
things, and confronts us with one another'.[23] Straus' observations
confirm the Aristotelian argument that human flourishing in moral
and political communities involves the perfection of the nature of
human beings as the rational animals. (Robert Ornstein's and David
Sobel's intriguing account of the close relationship between human
health and social connectedness is also based largely on the evidence
of the human form.[24]) At the same time, they suggest ways in which
the human form maintains the dual nature of humans, who (like
some other animals)[25] are both social and solitary beings, communicating and interdependent but also distancing and independent.
    The political scientist Larry Arnhart has recently been
encouraging his colleagues to consider the teleological assumptions
made in the work and popular writings of the neurologist Oliver
Sacks. Sacks' work, like Straus', highlights the function of natural,

physiological facts in determining and in maintaining the natural states – the natural human ends – of psychological health and happiness. Reflecting on the causes of disease can uncover the causes of health. Modern medical practice, with its impressively precise knowledge of the chemistry of health, still illustrates this truth. Sacks tells us an illuminating story about Ray, a man with Tourette's syndrome, a disease that 'is characterised by an excess of nervous energy, and a great production and extravagance of strange motions and notions: tics, jerks, mannerisms, grimaces, noises, curses, involuntary imitations and compulsions of all sorts, with an odd elfin humour and a tendency to antic and outlandish kinds of play'. The 'organic base' of this disease is 'an excess of excitor transmitters in the brain, especially the transmitter dopamine' and the frenetic symptoms can be controlled by the administration of a counteracting drug, such as haldol. Sacks treated Ray with haldol, and – in conjunction with three months of analysis – it worked. But while Ray became a happier human being, he also missed the bubbling freedom of his Touretter self; in particular, he became musically dull, unable to play his drums in such an extravagantly accomplished fashion. The treatment of his Tourette's syndrome had transformed his personality too much in the opposite direction: his 'haldol self' was, in his own judgement, too 'sober, solid, square'. In the end, Doctor Sacks and his patient agreed to a compromise: Ray would confine himself to a haldol existence during the working week, but would enjoy haldol-free weekends. The resulting 'artificial balance' between levity and gravity was, for Ray, the best approximation to the 'natural balance' produced by the 'natural, animal physiological health' that his disease had denied to him.[26] Without such a disease, the natural psychological balance is maintained, on the basis of a natural chemical balance. Body and mind thus serve each other, when health is naturally secured; when they do not, they can in some cases be encouraged to do so by human agency, but the end remains the one given to humans by nature.

Such teleological interpretations of life as these do not demand acceptance of a cosmic teleology, in which non-living things are also understood teleologically (nor did Aristotle's).[27] In other words, these interpretations still distinguish life from non-life. But they avoid the radical break between human and non-human life. Therefore they have little difficulty in combining the insights of mechanical physics with the recognition of natural norms for human psychic health. They avoid what Sacks has referred to as that split between 'a soulless neurology and a bodiless psychology' that makes the bare recognition of diseases such as Tourette's syndrome difficult. (Sacks notes that Tourette's syndrome was widely mis-understood and in fact rarely recognized after this split occurred in psychology, some time after Gilles de la Tourette first described the syndrome in 1885.)[28] They account for the fact that humans are not only rational and moral 'persons', but also rational and moral animals, whose various cultures have a common physical basis: various languages, various economies, etc., are based on identical physical capacities and needs. They also account for the fact that some ways in which the human body and mind function are diseases or disturbances of their natural functioning. When we recognize ways in which the human mind sometimes goes badly wrong, we can better appreciate the marvellous way in which it generally goes right. We are surrounded by – and take too much for granted – such minor miracles of human nature as the mysterious way in which the common noun captures meaning and makes possible the passage of that meaning from one human mind to another.

Natural human teleology should not and need not reduce humans to the level of other animals or to transparently intelligible machinery, nor raise them to gods. Humans can be understood teleologically not only by noticing the naturally-given ends that they share with other animals (such as preservation and reproduction) but also by noticing their ability to be detached and deliberately to choose their ends. These uniquely human abilities are what make them the uniquely moral animal, uniquely capable of pursuing happiness. They also make humans somewhat mysterious animals. Natural teleology informs human choices without dictating them. (That is one reason why liberal politics can be seen as the most appropriate kind of politics for human beings.) If all the mystery of human nature were removed, humans would no longer be free. A modern science of natural teleology is likely to portray a world that is friendlier to human life than the chaotic world depicted by radical modernity, but – in contrast to the poetic constructions of some radical moderns (e.g. Rousseau's Emilian education, or Marx's communistic future) – it is not likely to present to us a vision of a resolution of the contradictions of the human condition. A truly scientific account of the human condition would not be so nihilistic, so deadeningly prosaic. It would not relieve us of our vital tensions – nor of our need for a poetry that acknowledges these tensions and perhaps relieves them in our imaginations.

Human freedom itself prevents human nature from being understood in a wholly determinate way. This indeterminacy helps to prolong human levity and playfulness. The playfulness that humans develop during their unusually long infancies (which are physiologically related to their upright posture[29]) naturally extends into their later lives, which can be dreadful when they jettison playfulness to follow determinedly a 'career path'. It is not in an Aristotelian teleology but in the ateleological doctrines of a radical modern such as Hobbes (echoed in this respect, as we have seen, by John Rawls) that the attempt is made to remove all the mystery of human life, and to settle political controversy once and for all. The virtues recognized and recommended by Hobbes are simply rational deductions from the fundamental right of self-preservation, and this right is founded by Hobbes on a principle of motion in humans that admits of no exceptions: a human being shuns death, Hobbes claims, 'by a certain impulsion of nature, no less than that whereby a stone moves downward'.[30] Hobbes' example silently comes from Aristotle's *Ethics*: 'it is the nature of a stone to move downwards, and it cannot be habituated to move upwards'. But Aristotle had used this example not in comparison with but in contrast to the moral virtues, which do not arise in humans by nature, but have to be acquired through choice and habituation (like skills that can be learned only on the job), 'neither by nature nor contrary to nature'.[31] Humans are by nature capable of becoming virtuous or vicious, but they acquire their moral characters through habits of choosing, not by natural necessity.[32] After all, not even human bodily health (which is not, of course, entirely separable from psychic health) can be easily defined – although it can be recognized – and it too must be an object of choice; for, as Leon Kass observes, habits that damage bodily health appear more easily among humans: '[t]he inherent tendencies toward wholeness are much more precarious in human beings than in our animal friends and relations'.[33] The moral freedom of humans means that they can be the worst and most savage of the animals as well as the best.[34] This 'moral ambiguity of many distinctive human characteristics' is often cited as evidence of the 'formidable' or 'insuperable' difficulty of 'grounding . . . morality . . . on . . . human nature',[35] but this ambiguity is an inevitable result of human freedom, which freedom is itself a part of human nature. Morality requires freedom, but freedom can be understood as a natural phenomenon. C.S. Lewis points out that when a human excuses an act by saying 'it was only natural', this is not to say 'I had no choice', but rather: 'I have been foolish or faulty at least in human, not in bestial or diabolical, fashion. What I did was *natural*, spontaneous, I have not gone out of my way to invent new vices'.[36]

If human action were wholly naturally determined, the human mind itself would be determined, and therefore not free to choose among courses of action. There would be no way and no reason to establish and to maintain one's individual identity, one's responsibility for one's choices. Utilitarian and Rawlsian diminutions of human responsibility and individual desert in the distribution of honour are implausible mainly because (in Michael Walzer's words) they ask us to 'view . . . capacities and achievements as accidental accessories, like hats and coats' that people 'just happen to be wearing'.[37] Human beings naturally insist on their individual identities and responsibility. When they are deprived of these by psychological disease, their lives are reduced to (in Oliver Sacks' description) 'phantasmagoric fluttering with no centre or sense', which they are often driven to replace with 'pseudo-narratives, in a pseudo-continuity, a pseudo-world, peopled by pseudo-people'.[38] They are repelled by the prospect of living their lives plugged into an 'experience machine' (Robert Nozick's thought experiment)[39] that would give them the illusion of having any desired set of experiences, while they were actually floating unawares in a tank of sustaining chemicals, their brains attached to stimulating electrodes. As Aristotle notes, no one would even choose *really* to have every good thing in the world, if the precondition were loss of identity, becoming someone else.[40] Why is this so? Is this a point, as one contemporary natural right thinker has suggested, 'at which the metaphysical category of "nature" is inadequate to the reality which is grasped by ethics'?[41] That suggestion seems to be an unnecessary concession to the Kantian notion that our consciousness of our freedom cuts us off from nature. Is it not better simply to say that humans are one part of nature that is to an extent free? It does seem to be part of the nature of humans that they resist tampering with their freedom, even if such tampering were truly in their best interests. If the human mind were determined, it would not even have the mental freedom and detachment needed to know anything. For a human mind to claim that the human mind is determined is self-contradictory. If human teleology were wholly transparent, there would be no good questions, no moral problems, no moral arguments, and in any case no one capable of asking the questions, understanding the problems, or making the arguments.

On the other hand, if human teleology were totally opaque, there would be no good answers, and humans would be cut off from nature in the implausible manner posited by modern dualism. They would be not free but merely adrift – and politically organized by some convention originating merely in autonomous reason or will, not subject to the moderating influence of an imperfect but powerful awareness of natural standards. That is neither an attractive nor a sensible view of the human condition. Human freedom is freedom to live well or badly. This does not mean that there is only one way to live well. In fact, bad lives seem to display less genuine diversity than good ones. We do not command perfect knowledge of our condition and of our choices. But our lack of ability to demonstrate that this or that choiceworthy way of life is the most choiceworthy does not mean that we can have no knowledge relevant to moral choices at all, apart from purely instrumental 'rational choice' considerations. Conflict among 'the various components of human flourishing' does not seem to be as 'decisive against . . . a natural law ethics' as it is often taken to be.[42] Aristotle's suspicion about a total moral relativism still seems warranted: no one, he says, could admire someone with

> no particle of courage, moderation, justice, or wisdom, who is afraid of the flies buzzing around him, cannot refrain from any extreme when he desires to eat or to drink, destroys his dearest friend for a trifle, and similarly in matters of mind, is as senseless and as thoroughly deceived as a child or a madman.[43]

We do not – and, unless we were gods rather than humans, could not – know everything about humanity, but we do know some things. One thing that we know is that we are questioning beings. Questioning implies that one is not completely bewildered; it implies knowledge of ignorance, and assumes the possibility of answers that correspond to an intelligible and not wholly arbitrary, merely humanly-constructed order. To question that assumption itself would be self-contradictory. As Erwin Straus observed, a logical nominalism 'would not stop with the individual thing; rather, it would have to demand that names be applied as designations only to each of the individual perspectives, to the unendingly changing aspects of the individual things – if one could even speak of individual things any longer'.[44] If the universe were so unintelligible, if nature could not be apprehended at all by the human mind, then questioning, thinking and speaking would be pointless. However much such absurdity may appeal to Nietzscheian 'free spirits', it is difficult and unnecessary to build political thought on such an abyss.[45]

LIBERTY AND NATURE

At this point, even a sympathetic reader might well object: do not such arguments about the existence of natural ends of human life, if they are right, prove too much? Perhaps it is true, such a reader might concede, that the abandonment of nature by modern liberalism leads liberals into great difficulties, but do not even greater difficulties threaten to flow from a return to nature? Especially if it is to be a return to nature not only in the minimal sense, asserting natural human rights, but in a more demanding, teleological sense, asserting the reality and the moral and political relevance of natural human right. Is the teleological view of humanity, even if it is more coherent than non-teleological views, not uncongenial to liberals and liberal politics? If human nature is understood teleologically, even if moral freedom can be maintained within such an understanding, is political liberty not undermined? Is the right not an enemy of rights? Is Aristotle not an unlikely ally for liberals?

It is true, of course, that rights have become much more central in modern than they were in ancient political thinking. In a moment we shall see some of the reasons why that has been so, and why it is right that rights should now be more widely understood and more emphatically stated. But first it is important to see the essential connection between natural rights and natural right. A political claim on the ground of a natural human right carries with it a claim that it is right to respect the claim, that respecting the claim would lead to a rightful state of affairs, and that denying it would be wrong – that is, ultimately, that it would lead to a state of affairs in which the proper flourishing of human nature is not encouraged. If nothing were naturally right, then no one could claim a natural right. The idea of natural rights thus depends on the idea of natural right. Perhaps we can see this most easily if we consider the right of children to self-development: obviously, a right that makes little sense unless we are thinking of some substantive ends, or human conditions. But we can also see it if we reflect on the most fundamental natural right, the right to life itself. Why is it right to respect human life? (Why is murder wrong? Why is there such a moral and legal controversy surrounding the questions of capital

punishment and euthanasia?) We have noticed above the
defectiveness of the Hobbesian attempt to base this valuing of life on
the fact of the universal striving for self-preservation, an 'impulsion
of nature' that cannot be denied (as if self-sacrifice were always a sign
of madness). Nor do arguments about social utility or voluntary
consent really justify it: society serves life, not the other way around;
and if the rights based on the respect of human life depended on
voluntary agreements then they would be merely conventional, not
natural rights, and could be violated at will – but why should human
will be respected if human life is not respected first? As Leon Kass has
argued, it is only the potential for moral and intellectual flourishing
that makes all human life as such intrinsically respectable. Among the
animals, 'man has special standing because he shares in reason,
freedom, judgment, and moral concern, and, as a result, lives a life
freighted with moral self-consciousness'.[46] The dignity of the natural
human right to life depends on the rightness of human lives; only the
admirable human possibilities justify the respect rightly accorded to
all human life. The value that we place on human life is based on the
fact of the possibility of good human lives.

The presumption in favour of a radical division between ancient
natural right thinking and modern natural rights thinking is very
powerful among scholars today. But it is not unquestioned, and on
the historical evidence as well as on logical grounds it is clearly
questionable. One need only recall how Thomas Jefferson described
the authority of the liberal principles of the American Declaration of
Independence. 'All its authority', wrote Jefferson, 'rests . . . on the
harmonizing sentiments of the day, whether expressed in
conversation, in letters, printed essays, or in the elementary books of
public right, as Aristotle, Cicero, Locke, Sidney, etc'. Jefferson
acknowledged that the 'common sense' of the Declaration's
arguments about natural and political rights flowed from classical as
well as modern sources.[47] Or consider John Adams' description of
the principles of the American revolution, fifty years before
Jefferson's: 'the principles of Aristotle and Plato, of Livy and Cicero,
of Sydney, Harrington and Lock. – The principles of nature and
eternal reason'.[48] The common ground of classical humanism and
constitutionalism and modern humanism and constitutionalism made
it possible, even necessary, to appeal to Aristotelian thought to
support liberal claims.

What is that common ground? We can begin to see it if we take
our bearings from the language of the Declaration of Independence.

It would appear to contain at least three important elements: the assertion of human equality, the recognition of the natural inclination of humans towards 'the pursuit of . . . safety and happiness', and the necessity of 'prudence' in political arrangements designed to secure those natural ends. It is only with regard to the third of these elements that ancient and modern natural right thinkers need to part company, and even there they can share the principles and differ only in their application, because of the different circumstances of the ancient and modern worlds.

Equality and constitutionalism

The idea of human equality is less prominent in classical than in modern political thought, but (as we have noticed above, in Chapter 4) it is equally central. For classical no less than modern political thought depends on the idea of a common human nature. As Aristotle explained, politics is a serious, dignified activity only because it concerns relations among beings who are in an important sense equals, and have the right to be treated as such. Thus, political (constitutional) rule, as opposed to despotism whether private or public, is the government of and by those who are by nature free and equal.[49] The liberal view of the problematic nature of government is not purely modern; it was already present in Aristotle's thought. It was this classical insight into human equality that Algernon Sidney had in mind when he cited Plato and Aristotle as defenders of natural equality and republican government, against 'the impudence and prevarication of those, who gather small scraps of good Books' to justify patriarchy and monarchy.[50] It is this shared classical and modern doctrine that makes sense of Jefferson's and Adams' allusion to Aristotle and Cicero alongside Locke and Sidney. It also makes it less shocking to learn that John Witherspoon (James Madison's teacher at Princeton) 'taught politics straight from Aristotle'.[51] Human equality has essentially the same meaning in Aristotelian politics as it has for these modern liberals. Aristotle's reputation as a defender of human slavery is not justified. He accepted the political necessity of slavery in his world – a world in which civilization was rare and modern technology absent – but he indicates clearly enough his view that this slavery was conventional, not natural, and that it violated that fundamental human equality that is the basis of civilized politics. (Thus he recommended that these slaves should have their freedom set before them as a goal.[52]) Aristotle makes it clear that

despotism (slave management) – however much it must be tolerated
– can be natural and just only in the unconventional sense of cases of
mental incompetence (of the 'slave'). Apart from that exceptional
case, human beings differ from each other much less than all
members of the human species differ from beasts.[53] This equality
makes friendship and justice possible among all human beings as
such, including those unnaturally held as slaves.[54]

Likewise, apart from the theoretically possible but practically
non-existent case of a single human being so much more virtuous
than the rest of the community that this god-like person must be
made an absolute monarch[55], humans do not differ from each other
as widely as gods are believed to differ from humans.[56] Therefore the
intra-specific differences among human beings cannot justify
governing humans as if the governed were beasts, or the governors
gods. As Jefferson put it, 'the mass of mankind has not been born
with saddles on their backs, nor a favored few booted and spurred,
ready to ride them legitimately, by the grace of God'.[57] The shared
nature of the human species means that no humans can rightly claim
god-like pre-eminence, just as none can rightly be treated as
domestic animals. The appropriate tone for politics is that of an
amateurish give and take, not that of a professional dictation or
management. The Hobbesian distrust of political controversy and
rhetoric has its more liberal counterparts, but at their best moments,
liberals encourage civil conversation that avoids captious wrangling
but thrives on enlightening differences of opinion.[58] Even if there
were really a class of god-like, all-knowing humans, the rest of us
would resist domination by them, asserting our freedom and
individual responsibility for our identities. Human resistance to
political despotism is based on this natural human inclination to
assert one's responsibility and dignity. Thus understood, natural
human equality is the basis for individual dignity but also for the
shared specific dignity of humanity, so it supports resistance to
despotism but also precludes an atomistic individualism in which the
uniqueness and separateness of human individuals would completely
overshadow the uniqueness of the human species. The truth of
human equality is self-evident, in the sense that the proposition is
contained in the definition of what it is to be a human being. It is not
a trivial truth (except in the older sense of the word trivial, meaning
that evidence for it is widely available), and unfortunately it does not
go without saying. The twentieth century is full of instances of its
denial not only in practice but also in scientific theories justifying

that practice, raising a class of scientific rulers over the as yet unenlightened masses.

Liberal defenders against such theories need to reassert this natural basis of constitutionalism and the rule of law, in order both to refute the deniers of equality, and to understand their own constitutionalism. Constitutionalism – modern as well as ancient – allows superior talents to be employed in government, but its basic advantage is that it is the only truly political system because it is the only truly human system of government, the only kind of government suitable to beings who are by nature equally free. The equality or homogeneity of humanity makes it natural for humans to take turns in ruling.[59] The rule of law is a kind of this ruling and being ruled, since those who make the rules are also subject to them. Unlike purely rational and impartial gods, humans cannot be trusted always to judge fairly in their own cases. Even when the rule of law is understood as a 'negative value', 'compatible with gross violations of human rights', it is based on the recognition of equal humanity (which, independently, requires that natural rights be respected).[60] Given human moral and intellectual limits, it is prudent to have more than one officer administering the law as well, for judgements of specific cases can then be better informed and more impartial.[61] Modern liberal constitutionalism shares these principles with classical political philosophy, because it shares the underlying principle of natural human equality.

Liberal prudence

The idea of happiness as a natural *summum bonum* for humans, although rejected by the libertarian tendency of contemporary liberal theory and avoided by the communitarian tendency, is not incompatible with liberalism. (Jefferson's phrase 'the pursuit of happiness' has Aristotelian origins.) However, in the modern world, liberal prudence looks for less direct connection between political power and the pursuit of happiness through moral education than classical political thinkers looked for. One of the hallmarks of modern liberalism is its reliance on discussion and persuasion rather than coercion (by state or society) as the more effective means of encouraging the habits that are the conditions of political and individual happiness. Liberals assert that liberty is the only or the most effective way to encourage human development. In its sanest forms, liberalism does not deny the reality of human virtues and happiness; it privatizes them in order to protect them. This privatization is not meant to be total, nor is it meant to marginalize human excellence. (The same strategy is applied to morality as is applied by *laissez-faire* liberals to the economy; but who thinks these latter deny either the reality or the centrality of the economy and economic goods?) Classical political thinkers – and some radical modern ones such as Rousseau – admired the illiberal ideal of the Spartan system of public definition and coordination of moral education. However, Aristotle noticed that this way of nurturing humans was very imperfectly established in Sparta (where education concentrated too exclusively on cultivating the military virtues), and he also admitted that such a strategy was entirely neglected in all or almost all other regimes; therefore, being practical, he did not overlook the strengths of private educational strategies.[62] Even Plato drew attention to the advantage of a liberal democratic regime, in which a variety of ways of life – including the best – are tolerated. Modern liberalism, at its best, expands upon these suggestions, without losing sight of the reasoning behind them.

The primary motives for this expansion were not differences of principle, but different circumstances of political life in a world of Christian nations, rather than pagan cities. The classical (and Rousseauian) admiration of a Spartan integration of politics and ethics was geared to a political world of small cities. Even there it was acknowledged to be an ideal that in practice was rarely pursued and never perfectly achieved. In a political world of large nations and multinational countries, such integration is much less practicable. It is therefore less prudent to accept Aristotle's quick dismissal of the idea of the political community as a mere compact guaranteeing safety and justice rather than a common pursuit of the good life,[63] for that less aspiring definition of political life is sometimes the only feasible one for the large nation (or multinational) state itself, as opposed to the smaller communities within it. The separation of moral education from politics is more prudent in these circumstances. The narrowing of political life at the level of the sovereign state, and its separation (not isolation) from ethical life seem necessary so that both politics and ethics can prosper, not because either is unreal. This liberal strategy for encouraging the separate (but connected) health of politics and morality in the modern world – a strategy that leaves room for many tactical interminglings of the two – has often been mistaken for a principle of public moral indifference or neutrality. But liberal politics need not strive to be as uncontroversial and morality-free as such a principle would imply. Arguments about what is right and wrong are bound to be part of liberal politics; even arguments about rights can be expected to recur. As Stephen Macedo has pointed out in criticism of John Rawls' suggestion that a liberal constitution should fix 'once and for all, the content of our basic rights and liberties', taking them 'off the political agenda', American constitutional liberties, for example, have been and remain 'a matter of lively disagreement' within the political life of the country.[64]

The second and greater change in circumstances in the modern world was that the power of Christianity created problems unknown to classical natural right. The political problems associated with universal revealed religions and their internal and external conflicts are not as simply analagous to the political problems associated with moral conflicts as modern theorists such as Rawls have assumed.[65] The fundamental modern political circumstance is not moral pluralism but transpolitical religions. Christianity's transpolitical, universal claims threatened political authority much more than the more politically adaptable Aristotelian natural right moral doctrines could. These latter specified universal natural ends but not means, which might vary greatly and could be determined only by prudent judgement. The more determinate and more general modern liberal natural right principles – equal rights, government by consent, religious freedom – furnish secular politicians with their own universal principles, to counter those of Christian politicians. Liberal political principles (especially the doctrine of the social contract) provided the grounds for large but still separate, particular, political societies in a world dominated by supra-political religion. Instead of alleviating the problem of religious conflict by the formula 'one country, one religion', liberals constructed the twin principles of religious toleration and limited government, not only to ensure that 'one country, many religions' would no longer be a recipe for civil war and to remove religion as a cause of war between nations – in other words, not only to prevent the corruption of politics by religion – but also to prevent the corruption of religion by politics. The liberal separation of church and state goes beyond a Machiavellian subordination of church to state. There *is* an analogy between the liberal attitudes towards religion on the one hand and morality on the other, but it is an analogy that focuses not only on the unhappy controversies but also on the intrinsic advantages attached to these human activities. The separations of church and state, and of ethics and politics, recognize religion and moral virtues not only as politically necessary even for the liberal state (and therefore never entirely separable from politics), but also as valuable human possibilities, which can be spoiled *either* by being too politicized *or* by being too privatized. Liberals can and must be concerned with 'human flourishing', and this concern does not need to diminish their appreciation for 'the splendours of human liberty and autonomy'; they do not need to become 'defensive and nervous' liberals rather than 'confident and crusading' ones (as recently suggested by John Dunn[66]). Liberals do not have to choose between liberty and morality.

Subscribing to the notion that there can and should be a sharp and easily defined distinction between the state and society, between politics and morality, has been one of modern liberalism's great temptations, ever since John Locke argued in *A Letter Concerning Toleration* that a proper understanding of the relationship between political and religious matters would make it 'easy to understand to what end the legislative power ought to be directed'. It would be nice if things were that simple. But the logic of this particular piece of liberal optimism has always been shaky. It generally depends (as in that particular instance of Locke's thinking – though not often elsewhere in Locke's work) on the idea that the separation of religion and politics requires or implies the restriction of politics to concern with material matters – 'the temporal good and outward prosperity of society' – so that the state should be as neutral on moral questions as on questions of religious belief. But even if religion is ruled out of bounds for politics, why should non-material moral issues be ruled out of bounds at the same time? Morality need not depend on religion. Besides, Locke's argument in his *Letter*, immediately after his optimistic claim, went on to demonstrate that maintaining the proper liberal policy even on religion was bound to be tricky and controversial.[67]

In Chapters 2 and 3 it became clear that the precise relationship between a liberal polity and moral education is neither simple to prescribe nor easy to predict. A liberal state and society, like non-liberal regimes, obviously must be able to claim some authority over the education of citizens, to encourage a degree of law-abidingness and loyalty to the regime, as well as to cultivate citizens' inclination and ability to participate in public deliberations (if only by informed voting). On the other hand, unlike its non-liberal counterparts, liberal education, public or private, must also cultivate the more purely liberal virtues, especially the habit of respect for different interests and ways of life within the regime; this involves controlling the spirited desire to insist on one's own ways being preferred, and tolerating moral diversity, following the liberal preference for example and persuasion to coercion. William Galston's incisive comments on the liberal virtues have pointed out that these virtues are not merely instrumental to the operation of a liberal polity, but are also intrinsic virtues, looking (from various viewpoints) towards the perfection of humans as 'individuals who in some manner take responsibility for their own lives'.[68] While liberal politics must seek to avoid the totalitarian quality of communitarianism or civic republicanism, it must do this not because it doubts the reality or relevance of considerations of the perfection of human nature, but precisely because it has strong notions about that perfection.

In the relationship between liberal politics and human (including liberal) virtues, just as in the policy and institutional areas explored in Chapters 2 to 4, we have an instance – the most classic instance – where liberals need to balance carefully the rights of individuals and of communities. Or, to look at it less as a problem and more as an opportunity, we can here discern a way in which the modern liberal polity is better equipped than any other kind of regime – ancient or modern – to serve the conflicting demands of the dual nature of human beings, to cater to their needs as both individual and social beings. Whether it is considered as a problem or as an opportunity, maintaining this balance is surely a large and characteristic part of liberal politics, and not something that should be expected to disappear from the political agenda in a healthy liberal polity. As long as it does not, considerations of human nature and its perfections will remain on that agenda too, and liberals would do well to recognize them as such.

Of course, it would be foolish to deny that there are deep differences between modern liberal principles and classical natural right doctrines. These differences largely revolve around the distinction between aristocratic and constitutional democratic ethics and politics. The modern liberal principles, because of their universality, allow and demand less prudence in their application to any given modern circumstances. They are more specific on the means, and they rule out in advance the super-Spartan option of aiming at moral perfection directly through comprehensive and intolerant legislation. Constitutionalism becomes more detailed, and the rule of law more firmly established, with less easy recourse to exceptional statecraft. Being universal, the modern principles also demand more popular enlightenment, more public recognition and acknowledgment of the self-evident truths about human beings. Modern technology can serve this demand (well or badly). (As Locke remarks, in more advanced societies the examination of the origins and rights of government is done 'more carefully';[69] as Ken Masugi has added, in large modern states the friendship that perfects politics can no longer be based [as in the classical *polis*] on citizens' mutual recognition from sight, but can be based on mutual knowledge of a common nature – a liberal 'ideology'.[70]) Eventually, the public enlightenment itself, along with the economic democratization that accompanies it, become circumstances that make the way that classical writers applied natural right principles even more inappropriate to the modern world. They make active consent less optional, and reduce the aristocratic presumption[71] against mass educability. They bring out more clearly the affinity of middle-class virtues with the virtues required for political life (that is, for the ability to be ruled and to rule) – an affinity noticed by Aristotle in his discussion of the most universally practicable regimes.[72] My point is not that all these differences between antiquity and modernity are insignificant, but that they neither flow from nor require an abandonment of natural right by us moderns. Even if one concludes that modern constitutional democracy demands less perfection of human nature than classical aristocracy, there is no reason to conclude that this is because constitutional democracy makes no such demands at all. Modern democratic dignity is more universally available than traditional aristocratic dignity, but (except in conventionalist theories such as Rawls') it still has to be earned.

CONCLUSION

In the modern world, natural right generally favours the natural rights of liberal democratic regimes. From the classical point of view, liberal principles, even liberal democratic principles, can be regarded as prudential adaptations of natural right to the circumstances of the modern world. But they can be so regarded only as long as they are not reduced to libertarian moral indifference or advanced to radical moral emptiness, by denying that nature is a source of the human form and ends. In reflecting on several perennial political problems in Chapters 2 to 4, we saw that avoiding that denial is necessary for the kind of liberalism that is characteristic of much of what is best in

American law and politics, not only in the founding generation, but also in our time. In Chapter 5 we saw that avoiding that denial is necessary to avoid the liberal slide into a conservative or a radical conventionalism, which promotes either extreme individualism or extreme communitarianism. We can now conclude that avoiding that denial is possible, because the arguments in favour of the natural basis of liberal politics are more convincing than the arguments against it; and that it is not the recognition of that somewhat mysterious basis but the attempt to dispense with it that threatens to lead us towards quiet despotism and away from liberty and political dialogue.

Notes

1 Introduction

1 Francis Fukuyama, *The End of History and the Last Man*, London, Hamish Hamilton, 1992, p. 63.
2 Francis Fukuyama, *The End of History and the Last Man*, p. 138.
3 Francis Fukuyama, *The End of History and the Last Man*, p. 201.
4 Francis Fukuyama, *The End of History and the Last Man*, p. 202.
5 Francis Fukuyama, *The End of History and the Last Man*, p. 337.

2 Unity and plurality in ethnic politics

1 Aristotle, *Politics*, tr. Carnes Lord, Chicago, University of Chicago Press, 1984, 1325b 33–1326a 9; 1332a 28–33.
2 Abigail M. Thernstrom, 'Language: issues and legislation', in Stephan Thernstrom (ed.) *Harvard Encyclopedia of American Ethnic Groups*, Cambridge, Massachusetts, Harvard University Press, 1980, pp. 619–29; 'E pluribus plura – Congress and bilingual education', *Public Interest*, Summer 1980, No. 60, pp. 3–22; and 'Bilingual miseducation', *Commentary*, February 1990, pp. 44–8; Rosalie Pedalino Porter, *Forked Tongue: The Politics of Bilingual Education*, New York, Basic Books, 1990.
3 414 US 563, 1974.
4 Rosalie Pedalino Porter, *Forked Tongue*, pp. 227f.
5 Richard Rodriguez, *Hunger of Memory*, Boston, David R. Godine, 1981, pp. 26, 35. The poignancy of the division within the souls of those torn between immigrant family cultures and American culture is powerfully portrayed in John Okada's story about Japanese Americans and the Second World War: *No-No Boy*, Seattle and London, University of Washington Press, 1979 [1957], pp. 15f., 33f.
6 'In US, a debate on language', *International Herald Tribune*, 22 July 1986, pp. 1f.
7 Sherry Buchanan, 'Weighing the pros and cons of bilingual education', *International Herald Tribune*, 10 November 1987, p. 5; Rosalie Pedalino Porter, *Forked Tongue*, p. 35.
8 Thorough accounts of the origins of affirmative action and affirmative

discrimination can now be found in Hugh Davis Graham, *The Civil Rights Era – Origins and Development of National Policy, 1960–72*, New York and Oxford, Oxford University Press, 1990; and Herman Belz, *Equality Transformed: A Quarter Century of Affirmative Action*, New Brunswick and London, Transaction Publishers, 1991.

9 *Regents of the University of California v. Allan Bakke*, 438 US 265, 1978.

10 488 US 469, 1989.

11 110 S Ct. 2997, 1990.

12 Local 28 of Sheet Metal Workers' International Association v. Equal Employment Opportunity Commission, 478 US 421, 1986.

13 Michael Walzer, 'Pluralism: a political perspective', in *Harvard Encyclopedia of American Ethnic Groups*, pp. 781–7.

14 "60's civil rights activist calls integration a "sham, con job"', *International Herald Tribune*, 22 February 1985, pp. 1f.

15 Richard Rodriguez, *Hunger of Memory*, p. 152. This point was fleetingly recognized in the *Bakke* case, in note 47 of Justice Powell's opinion.

16 Frank Del Olmo, 'This English-only rumpus is a bad joke', *International Herald Tribune*, 1 September 1986, p. 5.

17 443 US 211, 1979. The logical weakness of this position is demonstrated by its use *against* the 'liberals' on the Court in Justice O'Connor's concurring opinion in *Firefighters v. Stotts* (467 US 561, 1984).

18 E.g. Ronald Dworkin, 'Let's give blacks a head start', *The Times*, 12 December 1981, p. 6.

19 *Plessy v. Ferguson*, 163 US 551, 1896.

20 *Wygant v. Jackson Board of Education*, 476 US 267, 1986, Justice O'Connor's partly concurring opinion.

21 Ronald Dworkin, *A Matter of Principle*, Cambridge, Massachusetts, Harvard University Press, 1985, p. 295.

22 *United Steelworkers of America, AFL-CIO-CLC v. Brian F. Weber et. al.*, 443 US 193, 1979.

23 Hugh Heclo, 'Issue networks and the executive establishment', in Anthony King (ed.) *The New American Political System*, Washington, DC, American Enterprise Institute, 1978, pp. 119f.

24 Mike Royko, *Boss: Richard J. Daley of Chicago*, New York, New American Library, 1971, p. 42.

25 Edward J. Erler, 'Equal protection and personal rights: the regime of the "discrete and insular minority"', *Georgia Law Review*, 1982, vol. 16, pp. 407–44.

26 Justice Stevens' opinion, note 19. But Justice Stevens seems to have abandoned this point, if he ever actually took it on board; see his dissenting opinion in *Wygant v. Jackson Board of Education*, note 10, which accepts the Burger Court's version of the 'discrete and insular minority' doctrine (which originated in Justice Stone's famous note 4 in the *Carolene Products* case, 304 US 144, 1938), and requires strict judicial scrutiny of racial classifications not because of the *principle* of individual equality, but merely to correct a defect in democratic *procedures*: the 'prejudice against discrete and insular minorities . . . tends seriously to curtail the operation of those political processes ordinarily to be relied upon to protect minorities'. On the Burger Court's excessive reliance on

and misconstruction of this doctrine, see Edward J. Erler, 'Equal protection and personal rights'.

27 Edward J. Erler, 'Sowing the wind: judicial oligarchy and the legacy of *Brown v. Board of Education*', *Harvard Journal of Law and Public Policy*, 1985, vol. 8, p. 415.

28 'Are quotas unfair to whites?', *Washington Post National Weekly Edition*, 17 March 1986, pp. 31f.

29 *Wygant v. Jackson Board of Education*, Justice Stevens' dissenting opinion.

30 *Wygant v. Jackson Board of Education*, Justice Stevens' dissenting opinion, note 14.

31 *Regents of the University of California v. Allan Bakke*, 438 US 265, 1978.

32 163 US 551, 1896.

33 *Brown v. Board of Education*, 347 US 494, 1954.

34 Edward J. Erler, 'Sowing the wind', pp. 412f.

35 *Regents of the University of California v. Allan Bakke*, 438 US 265, 1978.

36 Derek Bok, 'Goals aren't quotas', *Washington Post National Weekly Edition*, 10 March 1986, p. 29.

37 Glenn C. Loury, 'Goals are quotas', *Washington Post National Weekly Edition*, 24 March 1986, p. 28.

38 Richard Rodriguez, *Hunger of Memory*, p. 153.

39 Howard Brotz, *The Black Jews of Harlem: Negro Nationalism and the Dilemmas of Negro Leadership*, Glencoe, Free Press, 1963, pp. 131ff. More recently, Shelby Steele has emphasized the same theme: professions of guilt by whites (as the civil rights establishment and its doctrine of affirmative discrimination require) may be preferable to professions of innocence (like Ronald Reagan's), but neither attitude particularly encourages blacks 'to find their true mettle or develop a faith in their own capacity to run as fast as others . . . . Selfish white guilt is really self-importance . . . . The selfishly guilty white is drawn to what blacks least like in themselves – their suffering, victimization, and dependency. This is no good for anyone'. (*The Content of Our Character: A New Vision of Race in America*, New York, St. Martin's Press, 1990, pp. 9f., 89–92.)

40 Michael Walzer, 'Pluralism: a political perspective'. Walzer's opposition to affirmative discrimination is based not on its violation of *natural* rights, but only on its violation of the United States' individualistic traditions and conventions. See his *Spheres of Justice: A Defence of Pluralism and Equality*, Oxford, Martin Robertson, 1983, pp. 148, 153; on the shortcomings of his argument, see Chapter 5 below.

41 Anthony D. Smith, *The Ethnic Revival*, Cambridge, Cambridge University Press, 1981, p. 54.

42 Michael Novak, *The Rise of the Unmeltable Ethnics*, New York, Macmillan, 1971.

43 Friedrich Nietzsche, *Thus Spoke Zarathustra*, tr. W. Kaufman, in *The Portable Nietzsche*, New York, Viking, 1954, book I, 'On the new idol', pp. 160–3.

44 Harold Isaacs, *Idols of the Tribe: Group Identity and Political Change*, New York, Harper & Row, 1975, ch. 1.

45 William Petersen, 'Concepts of ethnicity', in *Harvard Encyclopedia of American Ethnic Groups*, pp. 234–42.

46 Arthur Mann, *The One and the Many: Reflections on American Identity*, Chicago, University of Chicago Press, 1979, ch. 4. Recent changes in immigration statutes, and legal decisions as old as *Schneiderman v. United States* (320 US 118, 1942), show how loosely the ideological criteria are enforced.

47 Thomas Jefferson, *Notes on the State of Virginia*, in Merrill D. Peterson (ed.) *The Portable Thomas Jefferson*, New York, Viking Press, 1975, pp. 124f.

48 Arthur Mann, *The One and the Many*, pp. 86f.

49 Thomas Paine, *Common Sense*, in Michael Foot and Isaac Kramnick (eds) *The Thomas Paine Reader*, Harmondsworth, Penguin, 1987 [1776], p. 81.

50 See Edward George Hartmann, *The Movement to Americanize the Immigrant*, New York, Columbia University Press, 1948, ch. 10.

51 Horace Kallen, *Culture and Democracy in the United States: Studies in the Group Psychology of the American Peoples*, New York, Arno, 1970, p. 43.

52 Horace Kallen, *Culture and Democracy in the United States*, p. 124.

53 Horace Kallen, *Culture and Democracy in the United States*, p. 116.

54 Horace Kallen, *Culture and Democracy in the United States*, p. 199.

55 Horace Kallen, *Culture and Democracy in the United States*, p. 229.

56 Randolph Bourne, 'Trans-national America', in *The Radical Will: Selected Writings 1911–1918*, New York, Pluto Press, 1977, pp. 248–64.

57 Michael Novak, 'Pluralism: a humanistic perspective', in *Harvard Encyclopedia of American Ethnic Groups*, pp. 772–81.

58 Randolph Bourne, 'Trans-national America', p. 259.

59 Arend Lijphart, *Democracy in Plural Societies*, New Haven, Yale University Press, 1977, pp. 1f., 228.

60 Pierre L. van den Berghe, *The Ethnic Phenomenon*, New York, Elsevier, 1981, ch. 9.

61 Horace Kallen, *Culture and Democracy in the United States*, p. 120.

62 Arthur Mann, *The One and the Many*, p. 169.

63 Howard Brotz, *The Black Jews of Harlem*, pp. 91–4, 125f., 129–31.

64 Horace Kallen, *Culture and Democracy in the United States*, p. 327.

65 Horace Kallen, *Culture and Democracy in the United States*, p. 322.

66 Horace Kallen, *Culture and Democracy in the United States*, p. 332.

67 Thomas Hobbes, *De Cive*, New York, Appleton-Century-Crofts, 1949, ch. 1, section 2; for a current version of Hobbes' view, see Pierre L. van den Berghe, *The Ethnic Phenomenon*, pp. 6f., 251.

68 Alexander Rosenberg, *The Structure of Biological Science*, Cambridge, Cambridge University Press, 1985, ch. 7. Hans Jonas points out that even with DNA, it is the form rather than the matter that counts in determining the identity of a living organism: 'it is still the functional aspect and not that of mere material persistence that matters in organic identity. Furthermore, it is the replicable pattern and not the individuality of its building blocks that matters: each of these *could* be replaced by a like atom or molecule without consequence to the function and thus to the total identity. Here, too, the principle is continuity of form and not of matter, even where material continuity happens to obtain.' (*The Phenomenon of Life: Toward a Philosophical Biology*, New York, Dell, 1966, p. 98).

69 Nathan Glazer, 'The structure of ethnicity', *Public Opinion*, 1984, October/November, pp. 3f.

70 Alexis de Tocqueville, *Democracy in America*, tr. G. Lawrence, Garden City, New York, Doubleday, 1969, vol. I, part II, ch. 10, p. 316.

71 John Jay, *The Federalist*, Number 2, in Alexander Hamilton, James Madison and John Jay, *The Federalist Papers*, New York, New American Library, 1961 [1787–8], p. 38.

72 John Stuart Mill, *Considerations on Representative Government*, in *Utilitarianism, Liberty, Representative Government*, London, Dent, 1968, ch. 16, pp. 360f.

73 John Stuart Mill, *Considerations*, p. 361.

74 John Stuart Mill, *Considerations*, p. 362.

75 John Stuart Mill, *Considerations*, p. 364.

76 John Stuart Mill, *Considerations*, p. 363.

77 John Stuart Mill, *Considerations*, p. 364.

78 John Stuart Mill, *Considerations*, p. 361.

79 John Emerich Edward Dalberg-Acton, First Baron Acton, 'Nationality', in John Neville Figgis and Reginald Vere Laurence (eds) *The History of Freedom and Other Essays*, London, Macmillan, 1922, pp. 270–300, reprinted from *Home and Foreign Review*, July 1862.

80 That Mill was also aware of this is indicated by his remarks on puritanism in *On Liberty*, in *Utilitarianism, Liberty, Representative Government*, ch. 4, p. 143; see also his letter to Pasquale Villari, 26 January 1862, in Francis E. Mineka and Dwight N. Lindley (eds) *The Later Letters of John Stuart Mill*, (*Collected Works of John Stuart Mill*), Toronto and Buffalo, University of Toronto Press, 1972, vol. XV, pp. 770-2.

81 John Emerich Edward Dalberg-Acton, 'Nationality', pp. 288f.

82 John Emerich Edward Dalberg-Acton, 'Nationality', pp. 289f.

83 John Emerich Edward Dalberg-Acton, 'Nationality', pp. 300, 299.

84 John Emerich Edward Dalberg-Acton, 'Nationality', pp. 298.

85 W.E.B. DuBois, 'The conservation of the races', in A.G. Paschal (ed.) *A W.E.B. DuBois Reader*, New York, Collier, 1971, pp. 25f.

86 Plato, *Laws*, tr. Thomas L. Pangle, New York, Basic Books, 1980, 707e–708d; cf. Aristotle, *Politics*, 1303a–1303b, where ethnic conflict in settler societies is described as a cause of revolution.

87 163 US 556f., 1896.

88 John Locke, *A Letter Concerning Toleration*, tr. W. Popple, Indianapolis and New York, Bobbs Merrill, 1955 [1689], pp. 50–2.

89 John Locke, *A Letter Concerning Toleration*, p. 48.

90 406 US 205, 1972.

91 John Emerich Edward Dalberg-Acton, 'Nationality', p. 293.

92 John Emerich Edward Dalberg-Acton, 'Nationality', p. 291.

93 Eli Kedourie, *Nationalism*, third edition, London, Hutchinson, 1966, ch. 2.

94 Abraham Lincoln, speech at Chicago, 10 July 1858, in Roy P. Basler (ed.) *The Collected Works of Abraham Lincoln*, 9 vols, New Brunswick, Rutgers University Press, 1953–5, vol. II, pp. 499ff.

95 Frederick Douglass, oration delivered in Corinthian Hall, Rochester, 5 July 1852, in Herbert J. Storing (ed.) *What Country Have I? Political*

Writings by Black Americans, New York, St. Martin's Press, 1970, p. 35.
96 Niccolo Machiavelli, *The Discourses*, tr. L. J. Walker, Harmondsworth, Penguin, 1970, book I, ch. 6 and book II, ch. 3.
97 William A. Schambra, 'Progressive liberalism and American "community"', *Public Interest*, 1985, Summer, no. 80, pp. 31–48.
98 Karl Marx, 'On the Jewish question', in *Early Writings*, tr. R. Livingstone and G. Benton, New York, Vintage Books, 1975, p. 213; V.I. Lenin, *The National Liberation Movement in the East*, Moscow, Progress Publishers, 1976, pp. 81f., 190–200, 240, 249, 323ff. The Soviets were often great conservationists of pre-Communist cultures, opposed to more heavy-handed Communist opponents of those cultures.

3 Sexual difference and human equality

1 Ursula Le Guin, *The Left Hand of Darkness*, London, Macdonald Futura, 1981 [1969], p. 85.
2 Nancy J. Chodorow, *The Reproduction of Mothering: Psychoanalysis and the Sociology of Gender*, Berkeley, University of California Press, 1978, pp. 4, 37.
3 John Stuart Mill, *The Subjection of Women*, in Stefan Collini (ed.) *On Liberty* with *The Subjection of Women* and *Chapters on Socialism*, Cambridge, Cambridge University Press, 1989 [1869], ch. 2, pp. 164f.
4 'Other voices', *Washington Post National Weekly Edition*, 10 March 1986, p. 38.
5 Glenn Collins, 'Americans like being married', *International Herald Tribune*, 16 June 1987.
6 'Opinion roundup', *Public Opinion*, 1984, February/March, p. 40.
7 'Currents: Women and the professions', *Economic Impact*, 1986, no. 55, p. 5.
8 'Why women go to college', *Washington Post National Weekly Edition*, 17 November 1986, p. 38.
9 E. M. Forster, *A Room With A View*, London, Edward Arnold, 1962 [1904], pp. 52f.
10 Daniel Patrick Moynihan, *Family and Nation*, New York, Harcourt Brace Jovanovitch, 1986, pp. 89f.
11 Plato, *Laws*, tr. Thomas L. Pangle, New York, Basic Books, 1980, 805c.
12 John Stuart Mill, *The Subjection of Women*, ch. 4, p. 200.
13 US Department of Labor statistics, reported in *International Herald Tribune*, 2–3 Feb 1985.
14 Judy Mann, 'No more Ms. Nice Guy', *Washington Post National Weekly Edition*, 30 June 1986, p. 20.
15 Child Trends statistics, reported in Spencer Rich, 'Reports of the American family's death are greatly exaggerated', *Washington Post National Weekly Edition*, 7 September 1987, p. 25.
16 Sylvia Ann Hewlett, *A Lesser Life: The Myth of Women's Liberation in America*, New York, William Morrow & Company, 1986, ch. 15.
17 Judy Mann, 'No more Ms. Nice Guy'. Some companies have found that the provision of high-quality day care is a good way to retain good men

and women employees; Glenn Collins, 'Wooing the 1990s workers', *International Herald Tribune*, 22 July 1988; and Claudia H. Deutsch, 'Good company day care is worth caring about', *International Herald Tribune*, 20 June 1991, p. 9.

18 Joseph H. Pleck, *Working Wives/Working Husbands*, Beverly Hills and London, Sage, 1985, pp. 148–51.

19 'Other voices', *Washington Post National Weekly Edition*, 10 March 1986, p. 38.

20 Joseph H. Pleck, *Working Wives/Working Husbands*, ch. 6, p. 135.

21 Betty Friedan, *The Second Stage*, London, Sphere Books, 1983, p. 159.

22 Joyce Appleby, *Capitalism and a New Social Order: The Republican Vision of the 1790s*, New York, New York University Press, 1984, p. 36.

23 Nancy J. Chodorow, *The Reproduction of Mothering*, pp. 20f.

24 Roger D. Masters, 'Explaining "male chauvinism" and "feminism": cultural differences in male and female reproductive strategies', *Women and Politics*, 1983, vol. 3, pp. 198ff.

25 Ken Masugi, 'Another peek at Aristotle and Phyllis: the place of women in Aristotle's argument for human equality', in Thomas B. Silver and Peter W. Schramm (eds) *Natural Right and Political Right*, Durham, Carolina Academic Press, 1984, pp. 280, 283.

26 Susan Moller Okin, *Women in Western Political Thought*, Princeton, Princeton University Press, 1979, p. 303.

27 John Zvesper, 'Hobbes' individualistic analysis of the family', *Politics*, 1985, vol. 5, pp. 28–33.

28 Allan Bloom, 'Rousseau on the equality of the sexes', in Frank S. Lucash (ed.) *Justice and Equality Here and Now*, Ithaca, Cornell University Press, 1985.

29 A little misleadingly called *The Closing of the American Mind*, New York, Simon & Schuster, 1987. The distinction between radical and moderate modernity is crucial; it will be discussed in greater detail below, in Chapter 6.

30 E.g. Susan Moller Okin, *Women in Western Political Thought*, p. 282.

31 John Locke, *Two Treatises of Government*, Peter Laslett (ed.) Cambridge, Cambridge University Press, 1963, II, section 95.

32 Nathan Tarcov, *Locke's Education for Liberty*, Chicago and London, University of Chicago Press, 1984, p. 210.

33 John Locke, *Two Treatises*, II, sections 90–4, 135–8.

34 John Locke, *Two Treatises*, II, ch. 6.

35 John Locke, *Two Treatises*, II, section 73.

36 John Locke, *Two Treatises*, II, sections 74–6, 94, 105–12.

37 John Locke, *Two Treatises*, II, section 78.

38 John Locke, *Two Treatises*, I, section 58.

39 John Locke, *Two Treatises*, II, sections 63, 67, 170.

40 John Locke, *Two Treatises*, I, section 88.

41 Nathan Tarcov, *Locke's Education for Liberty*, p. 231 n. 363.

42 John Locke, *Two Treatises*, II, section 34.

43 Nathan Tarcov, *Locke's Education for Liberty*, p. 210.

44 Nathan Tarcov, *Locke's Education for Liberty*, p. 139 (see also p. 133).

45 Nathan Tarcov, *Locke's Education for Liberty*, p. 163–71.

46 John Locke, *Two Treatises*, II, sections 57, 67, 68.
47 John Locke, *Some Thoughts Concerning Education*, in James L. Axtell (ed.) *The Educational Writings of John Locke*, Cambridge, Cambridge University Press, 1968 [1693], sections 43–62; Nathan Tarcov, *Locke's Education for Liberty*, pp. 86–107.
48 Thomas Hobbes, *De Cive*, New York, Appleton–Century–Crofts, 1949, ch. 1, sections 2, 4; and *Leviathan*, Harmondsworth, Penguin, 1968, chs 11, 13.
49 Rogers M. Smith, *Liberalism and American Constitutional Law*, Cambridge, Massachusetts, Harvard University Press, 1985, pp. 28–30.
50 John Locke, *Two Treatises*, II, section 78.
51 Lorenne M.G. Clark, 'Women and Locke', in Lorenne M.G. Clark and Lynda Lange (eds) *The Sexism of Social and Political Theory: Women and Reproduction from Plato to Nietzsche*, Toronto, Buffalo and London, University of Toronto Press, 1979, p. 21.
52 John Locke, *Two Treatises*, I, section 47.
53 Lorenne M.G. Clark, 'Women and Locke', pp. 19, 21.
54 John Locke, *Two Treatises*, II, section 82.
55 John Locke, *Two Treatises*, II, section 3.
56 John Locke, *Two Treatises*, II, section 77.
57 Teresa Brennan and Carole Pateman, '"Mere auxiliaries to the common-wealth": women and the origins of liberalism', *Political Studies*, 1979, vol. 27, pp. 193–5.
58 John Locke, *Two Treatises*, II, section 83.
59 John Locke, *Two Treatises*, II, section 78.
60 Lorenne M.G. Clark, 'Women and Locke', pp. 31f., 34.
61 John Locke, *Two Treatises*, II, section 83.
62 John Locke, *Two Treatises*, II, section 84.
63 John Locke, *Two Treatises*, II, section 69.
64 John Locke, *Two Treatises*, II, section 81.
65 John Locke, *Two Treatises*, II, section 65.
66 Lorenne M.G. Clark, 'Women and Locke', p. 35.
67 John Locke, *Two Treatises*, I, section 59.
68 Nancy E. Levine, *The Dynamics of Polyandry: Kinship, Domesticity, and Population on the Tibetan Border*, Chicago and London, University of Chicago Press, 1988, p. 168.
69 Lorenne M.G. Clark, 'Women and Locke', p. 25.
70 Lorenne M.G. Clark, 'Women and Locke', p. 33.
71 John Locke, *Two Treatises*, II, section 80.
72 Nancy E. Levine, *The Dynamics of Polyandry*, p. 169.
73 John Locke, *Two Treatises*, II, section 43.
74 Thomas Hobbes, *De Cive*, ch. 1, section 7.
75 Plato, *Symposium*, tr. W.R.M. Lamb, London, William Heinemann, 1925, 207b.
76 John Locke, *Two Treatises*, I, sections 56–8, 88.
77 Leon R. Kass, *Toward A More Natural Science: Biology and Human Affairs*, New York, Free Press, 1985, ch. 11.
78 Leon R. Kass, *Toward A More Natural Science*, pp. 110f., 315.
79 Ursula Le Guin, *The Left Hand of Darkness*, p. 86.

80 Allan Bloom, 'Introduction', in Jean-Jacques Rousseau, *Emile*, tr. Allan Bloom, New York, Basic Books, 1979 [1762], p. 4.

81 Jean-Jacques Rousseau, *On the Social Contract*, tr. Judith R. Masters, New York, St. Martin's Press, 1978 [1762], book I, ch. 6, p. 53.

82 Jean-Jacques Rousseau, *Emile*, book V, p. 415.

83 Jean-Jacques Rousseau, *Emile*, book V, p. 363.

84 John Stuart Mill, *The Subjection of Women*, ch. 2, p. 160.

85 Leon R. Kass, *Toward A More Natural Science*, pp. 72f., 317.

86 Alexis de Tocqueville, *Democracy in America*, tr. G. Lawrence, Garden City, New York, Doubleday, 1969, vol. II, part III, ch. 12, pp. 600–3.

87 'Other voices', *Washington Post National Weekly Edition*, 10 March 1986, p. 38.

88 Gilbert Y. Steiner, *The Futility of Family Policy*, Washington, DC, Brookings, 1981, p. 8.

89 Gilbert Y. Steiner, *The Futility of Family Policy*, pp. 194ff.; Glenn Collins, 'Americans like being married'; Spencer Rich, 'Reports of the American family's death are greatly exaggerated'; and James R. Wetzel, 'American families: 75 years of change', *Monthly Labor Review*, 1990, March, pp. 4–13.

90 Alison M. Jaggar, *Feminist Politics and Human Nature*, Brighton, The Harvester Press, 1983, p. 37; and see her recent reflections on 'Sexual difference and sexual equality', in Deborah L. Rhode (ed.) *Theoretical Perspectives on Sexual Difference*, New Haven and London, Yale University Press, 1990, pp. 246f., where she accepts that 'a dynamic approach to sexual difference' is needed, in which sometimes the equality of women and men is recognized, and sometimes the differences, but without assuming 'that these differences are presocial or biological givens'.

91 Jean-Jacques Rousseau, *Emile*, book V, p. 362.

92 Plato, *Republic*, tr. Allan Bloom, New York, Basic Books, 1968, 455c.

93 Arlene W. Saxonhouse, 'The philosopher and the female in the political thought of Plato', *Political Theory*, 1976, vol. 4, p. 199. Mary Nichols makes a contrasting but complementary point when she suggests that women, who because of their giving birth can be more aware of the particularity of individual human beings, might be less likely to get caught up in the thymotic quest for communal unity on which Socrates leads his male companions in the *Republic*. Mary Nichols, 'Women in western political thought', *Political Science Reviewer*, 1983, vol. 13, pp. 245–8.

94 Plato, *Laws*, 794d–795d, 804d–805d.

95 On this point, see Sylvia Ann Hewlett, *A Lesser Life*, pp. 144–7, 179f., ch. 9; and Jean Bethke Elshtain, 'The liberal captivity of feminism: a critical appraisal of (some) feminist answers', in Philip Abbott and Michael B. Levy (eds) *The Liberal Future in America*, Westport, Connecticut and London, Greenwood Press, 1985.

96 Some radical feminists agree: Alison M. Jaggar, *Feminist Politics and Human Nature*, p. 341.

97 John Stuart Mill, *The Subjection of Women*, ch. 1, p. 144.

98 Sylvia Ann Hewlett, *A Lesser Life*, pp. 393, 401.

99 'Later motherhood could become stable trend in US', *International Herald*

Tribune, 17–18 November 1984; 'Number of Americans living alone, "nonfamily" households rise sharply', *International Herald Tribune*, 21 November 1985.

100 Sylvia Ann Hewlett, *A Lesser Life*, pp. 177, 399f.

101 'Other voices', *Washington Post National Weekly Edition*, 16 June 1986, p. 38.

102 Bureau of the Census, *Social Indicators III*, Washington, DC, Government Printing Office, 1980, pp. 3, 12; 'US population seen falling in 21st century', *International Herald Tribune*, 2 February 1989, p. 3.

103 For a view of the controversy, see Ben J. Wattenberg, *The Birth Dearth*, new edition, New York, Pharos Books, 1989.

104 Anne Fausto-Sterling, *Myths of Gender: Biological Theories About Women and Men*, New York, Basic Books, 1985, p. 270.

105 Alice Rossi, 'Parenthood in transition: from lineage to child to self-orientation', in Jane B. Lancaster, Jeanne Altman, Alice S. Rossi and Lonnie R. Sherrod (eds) *Parenting Across the Life Span*, New York, Aldine de Gruyter, 1987, pp. 68f.

106 Gilbert Y. Steiner, *The Futility of Family Policy*, p. 190.

107 Melford E. Spiro, *Gender and Culture: Kibbutz Women Revisited*, Durham, North Carolina, Duke University Press, 1979.

108 Alice Rossi, 'Parenthood in transition', p. 60.

109 Alice Rossi, 'Parenthood in transition', p. 69.

110 Alice Rossi, 'Parenthood in transition', p. 69.

111 Alice Rossi, 'Parenthood in transition', p. 63.

112 Larry Arnhart, 'A sociobiological defense of Aristotle's sexual politics', paper delivered at the annual meeting of the American Political Science Association, San Francisco, California, 30 August–2 September 1990, pp. 1–4.

113 Frans B.M. de Waal, 'Commitments and grudges', *Politics and the Life Sciences*, 1989, vol. 8, pp. 27–30.

114 Maggie Scarf, *Intimate Relations: Patterns in Love and Marriage*, New York, Random House, 1987, p. 123.

115 *Bradwell v. Illinois*, 16 Wallace 442, 1873.

116 208 US 412, 1908.

117 198 US 45, 1905.

118 In *Frontiero v. Richardson*, 411 US 677, 1973, at 688.

119 *Craig v. Boren*, 429 US 197, 1976.

120 In *Reed v. Reed*, 400 US 71, 1971.

121 *Royster Guano Co. v. Virginia*, 253 US 412, 1920, at 415.

122 *Michael M. v. Sonoma County Superior Court*, 450 US 464, 1981, at 478 – admittedly, only a plurality opinion, and not a wholly persuasive one.

123 Sylvia A. Law, 'Rethinking sex and the constitution', *University of Pennsylvania Law Review*, 1984, vol. 132, pp. 988–96, 1001–2 n. 180; cf. p. 1004.

124 *Frontiero v. Richardson*, at 692; Edward S. Corwin, *The Constitution and What It Means Today*, thirteenth edition, revised by Harold W. Chase and Craig R. Ducat, Princeton, Princeton University Press, 1973, p. 460.

125 Thomas Hobbes, *Leviathan*, ch. 6; John Locke, *Some Thoughts Concerning Education*, section 107.
126 William H. Chafe, *Women and Equality: Changing Patterns in American Culture*, New York, Oxford University Press, 1977, ch. 5.
127 'The Seneca Falls declaration of sentiments and resolutions', in Henry Steele Commager (ed.) *Documents of American History*, 2 vols, Englewood Cliffs, Prentice-Hall, 1973 [19 July 1848], vol. I, pp. 315–17.
128 Janet Radcliffe Richards, *The Sceptical Feminist*, London, Routledge & Kegan Paul, 1980, pp. 5, 20ff., 44–62.
129 John Stuart Mill, *The Subjection of Women*, ch. 4, p. 212.
130 Ruth Bleier, *Science and Gender: A Critique of Biology and Its Theories on Women*, New York, Pergamon, 1984, p. 206; see also her 'Sex differences research', in Ruth Bleier (ed.) *Feminist Approaches to Science*, New York, Pergamon Press, 1986, p. 162.
131 Nancy J.Chodorow, *The Reproduction of Mothering*, chs 1, 2 and 'Afterword'; and *Feminism and Psychoanalytic Theory*, Oxford, Polity Press, 1989, ch. 5; Carol Gilligan, *In a Different Voice*, Cambridge, Massachusetts, Harvard University Press, 1982, ch. 1; Alison M. Jaggar, *Feminist Politics and Human Nature*, chs 3, 7, and 11.
132 E.g. Sylvia A. Law, 'Rethinking sex and the constitution', p. 968.
133 Cited at note 131, above; see also 'Reply by Carol Gilligan', *Signs*, 1986, vol. 12, pp. 324–33.
134 Carol Gilligan, *In a Different Voice*, pp. 20f.
135 Carol Gilligan, *In a Different Voice*, pp. 33, 63, 173.
136 Ruth Bleier, *Science and Gender*, p. 196; and 'Introduction' to *Feminist Approaches to Science*, p. 15.
137 Carol Gilligan, 'Reply by Carol Gilligan'; 'Preface' and 'Prologue' in Carol Gilligan, Janie Victoria Ward and Jill McLean Taylor (eds) *Mapping the Moral Domain: A Contribution of Women's Thinking to Psychological Theory and Education*, Cambridge, Massachusetts, Harvard University Press, 1988, pp. iv–v, xxiv. Consider in this light the critique of Gilligan by Susan Moller Okin, 'Thinking Like A Woman', in Deborah L. Rhode (ed.) *Theoretical Perspectives on Sexual Difference*, pp. 158f. Okin notices the ambiguity of the 'others' who are the objects of Gilligan's care morality: is the object of caring just one's own family and friends, or is it more universal and impartial? In other words (although Okin might object to this elaboration) is it to do with the recognition of a universal human nature? (Cf. below, Chapter 6 at note 54.) Perhaps that implication is what makes for Gilligan's ambiguity. Her developmental psychology is a kind of historicism, which logically must deny a significant transcultural, transhistorical human nature.
138 Alison M. Jaggar, *Feminist Politics and Human Nature*, p. 388.
139 Alison M. Jaggar, *Feminist Politics and Human Nature*, p. 46.
140 Alison M. Jaggar, *Feminist Politics and Human Nature*, pp. 387f.
141 Shere Hite, *Women and Love: A Cultural Revolution in Progress*, London, Penguin, 1987, p. 761.
142 Alison M. Jaggar, *Feminist Politics and Human Nature*, pp. 387f.
143 Sarah Blaffer Hrdy, 'The myth of the coy female', in Ruth Bleier (ed.) *Feminist Approaches to Science*, pp. 119–46.

144 John Stuart Mill, *The Subjection of Women*, ch. 1, p. 121.

145 John Stuart Mill, *The Subjection of Women*, ch. 2, pp. 152f., and ch. 3, p. 192.

4 Bureaucracy and liberal constitutionalism

1 James O. Freedman, *Crisis and Legitimacy: The Administrative Process and American Government*, Cambridge, Cambridge University Press, 1978, p. ix.

2 John Locke, *Two Treatises of Government*, Peter Laslett (ed.) Cambridge, Cambridge University Press, 1963, II, section 87.

3 Aristotle, *Politics*, tr. Carnes Lord, Chicago, University of Chicago Press, 1984, 1255b 16–21.

4 *From Max Weber: Essays in Sociology*, H. H. Gerth and C. Wright Mills (eds) London, Routledge & Kegan Paul, 1948, p. 299.

5 G. W. F. Hegel, *Philosophy of Right*, tr. T. M. Knox, Oxford, Clarendon Press, 1967, section 294; H. H. Gerth and C. Wright Mills (eds) *From Max Weber*, p. 239; Max Weber, *The Theory of Social and Economic Organization*, Talcott Parsons (ed.) New York, Oxford University Press, 1947, p. 333.

6 John Stuart Mill, *Considerations on Representative Government*, in *Utilitarianism, Liberty, Representative Government*, London, Dent, 1968, chs 5–6.

7 There are books of the series: *Yes Minister* and *Yes Prime Minister*, Jonathan Lynn and Anthony Jay (eds), 4 vols, London, BBC, 1981–3, 1986. The 'editors' shrewdly show the Minister (and then Prime Minister) sometimes holding his own against his Permanent Secretary (and then Cabinet Secretary), and show both of them colluding against the public interest, to save each other's skin.

8 G. W. F. Hegel, *Philosophy of Right*, section 297; John Stuart Mill, *Representative Government*, ch. 5; H. H. Gerth and C. Wright Mills (eds) *From Max Weber*, pp. 232–9; Max Weber, *The Theory of Social and Economic Organization*, pp. 392–423.

9 Ramsay Muir, *Peers and Bureaucrats*, London, Constable & Company, 1910, p. 94; for another early warning see Lord Hewart, *The New Despotism*, London, Ernest Benn, 1929, especially pp. 16f.

10 For a recent collection of essays on politics and *thymos*, see Catherine H. Zuckert (ed.) *Understanding the Political Spirit: Philosophical Investigations from Socrates to Nietzsche*, New Haven and London, Yale University Press, 1988.

11 Aristotle, *Politics* 1264b 5–25.

12 G. W. F. Hegel, *Philosophy of Right*, section 296.

13 John Stuart Mill, *Representative Government*, ch. 6. See also Graham Wallas, *Human Nature in Politics*, London, Constable & Company, 1929 [1908], part 2, ch. 3; and Alexis de Tocqueville, 'Of the methods of administration under the old régime', in *The Old Régime and the French Revolution*, tr. Stuart Gilbert, Garden City, New York, Doubleday, 1955, part II, ch. 6, pp. 61–72.

14 Max Rheinstein (ed.) *Max Weber on Law in Economy and Society*, Cambridge, Massachusetts, Harvard University Press, 1954, p. 351.

15 Max Rheinstein (ed.) *Max Weber on Law in Economy and Society*, p. 355.
16 James Madison, *The Federalist*, Number 10, in Alexander Hamilton, James Madison and John Jay, *The Federalist Papers*, New York, New American Library, 1961 [1787–8], p. 79.
17 H. H. Gerth and C. Wright Mills (eds) *From Max Weber*, p. 71; cf. Max Weber, *The Theory of Social and Economic Organization*, pp. 391f.
18 Dwight Waldo, *The Administrative State: A Study of the Political Theory of American Public Administration*, New York, The Ronald Press Company, 1948, pp. 66, 131.
19 'Elihu Root on invisible government', Speech to the New York Constitutional Convention, 30 August 1915, in Henry Steele Commager (ed.) *Documents of American History*, 2 vols, Englewood Cliffs, Prentice-Hall, 1973, vol. II, pp. 105–7.
20 Winston S. Churchill, *Marlborough: His Life and Times*, 2 vols, London, Harrap, 1934, vol. I, p. 620.
21 James Madison, *The Federalist*, Number 57, in *The Federalist Papers*, pp. 350, 352. In fact, Madison as 'Publius'(the author of *The Federalist*) was a little too inclined towards the extreme of purity; just as Hegel depends on the large size of the modern state to detach civil servants from personal interests and passions (*Philosophy of Right*, section 296), so 'Publius' depends on the extensiveness of the American republic to keep selfishness out of public deliberations. But if Madison erred in this way, he corrected himself by his party government views in the 1790s, which relied less on the detachment of national governing from local political conflicts.
22 Charles R. Kesler, 'Separation of powers and the administrative state', in Gordon S. Jones and John A. Marini (eds) *The Imperial Congress*, New York, Pharos Books, 1988, pp. 20–40; Stephen Macedo, *Liberal Virtues: Citizenship, Virtue, and Community in Liberal Constitutionalism*, Oxford, Clarendon, 1990, ch. 4.
23 G. W. F. Hegel, *Philosophy of Right*, sections 291, 297.
24 H. H. Gerth and C. Wright Mills (eds) *From Max Weber*, pp. 224–6.
25 G. W. F. Hegel, *Philosophy of Right*, sections 294, 301; Max Rheinstein (ed.) *Max Weber on Law in Economy and Society*, pp. 352, 355; H. H. Gerth and C. Wright Mills (eds) *From Max Weber*, pp. 224–6, 231.
26 Alexis de Tocqueville, *Democracy in America*, tr. G. Lawrence, Garden City, New York, Doubleday, 1969, vol. II, part IV, ch. 7.
27 Alexis de Toqueville, *Democracy in America*, vol. I, part I, chs 2–5; vol. II, part IV, chs 2–7.
28 Alexis de Tocqueville, *The Old Régime and the French Revolution*, part II, ch. 5.
29 Alexis de Tocqueville, *Democracy in America*, vol. II, part IV, chs 2, 5.
30 Alexis de Tocqueville, *Democracy in America*, vol. II, part IV, ch. 3.
31 Alexis de Tocqueville, *Democracy in America*, vol. II, part IV, ch. 4.
32 Alexis de Tocqueville, *Democracy in America*, vol. II, part IV, ch. 3.
33 Alexis de Tocqueville, *Democracy in America*, vol. II, part I, ch. 2.
34 G. W. F. Hegel, *Philosophy of Right*, sections 316–18; H. H. Gerth and C. Wright Mills (eds) *From Max Weber*, pp. 225f.
35 H. H. Gerth and C. Wright Mills (eds) *From Max Weber*, p. 221.

36 Alexis de Tocqueville, *Democracy in America*, vol. I, part II, chs 5–7; and Appendix BB (original emphasis).
37 Alexis de Tocqueville, *Democracy in America*, vol. I, part I, ch. 10, pp. 386–95.
38 Alexis de Tocqueville, *Democracy in America*, vol. I, part I, ch. 5.
39 Alexis de Tocqueville, *Democracy in America*, vol. II, part IV, ch. 3.
40 Alexis de Tocqueville, *Democracy in America*, vol. II, part I, ch. 5; and part IV, ch. 7.
41 Alexis de Tocqueville, *Democracy in America*, vol. II, part I, chs 4 and 7.
42 Alexis de Tocqueville, *Democracy in America*, vol. I, part I, ch. 5.
43 Alexis de Tocqueville, *Democracy in America*, vol. I, part I, ch. 8.
44 Alexis de Tocqueville, *Democracy in America*, vol. II, part IV, ch. 5.
45 Alexis de Tocqueville, *Democracy in America*, vol. II, part IV, chs 1, 5, 7.
46 Alexis de Tocqueville, *Democracy in America*, vol. II, part I, ch. 3.
47 Stephen Skowronek, *Building a New American State*, Cambridge, Massachusetts, Harvard University Press, 1982, pp. 210ff.
48 Graham Wallas, *Human Nature in Politics*, p. 249.
49 Herbert J. Storing, 'Political parties and the bureaucracy', in Robert A. Goldwin (ed.) *Political Parties, USA*, Chicago, Rand McNally, 1964; and 'American statesmanship, old and new', in Robert A. Goldwin (ed.) *Bureaucrats, Policy Analysts, Statesmen: Who Leads?*, Washington, DC, American Enterprise Institute, 1980.
50 Hugh Heclo, *A Government of Strangers*, Washington, DC, Brookings, 1977, pp. 142–8.
51 John A. Rohr, *To Run A Constitution: The Legitimacy of the Administrative State*, Lawrence, University Press of Kansas, 1986, pp. 39, 182. It has also been suggested that bureaucracies can serve as avenues for citizens' participation in government decision-making. Francis E. Rourke, 'Bureaucracy in the American constitutional order', *Political Science Quarterly*, 1987, vol. 102, pp. 23–32, notes this suggestion, but also questions it by noticing that it goes against the grain of the argument for bureaucrats as policy experts and political moderates.
52 James Madison, *The Federalist*, Number 10, in *The Federalist Papers*, p. 79.
53 Leon D. Epstein, *Political Parties in the American Mold*, Madison, University of Wisconsin Press, 1986, p. 159.
54 Alan Stone, 'Justifying regulation', in Philip Abbott and Michael B. Levy (eds) *The Liberal Future in America: Essays in Retrieval*, Westport, Connecticut, Greenwood Press, 1985.
55 Steven Kelman, *Making Public Policy: A Hopeful View of American Government*, New York, Basic Books, 1987.
56 Anthony King (ed.) *The New American Political System*, Washington, DC, American Enterprise Institute, 1978.
57 Robert Eden, 'Dealing democratic honor out', in Richard A. Harris and Sidney M. Milkis (eds) *Remaking American Politics*, Boulder, San Francisco and London, Westview Press, 1989, p. 61. New Deal liberalism itself had already gone some of the way down the anti-partisan road, by calling for the transcendence of party loyalty in favour of 'independence'; see Sidney M. Milkis, 'Franklin D. Roosevelt and the transcendence of partisan politics', *Political Science Quarterly*, 1985, vol. 100, pp. 479–504.

5 Unnatural liberalism

1 John Locke, *Two Treatises of Government*, Peter Laslett (ed.) Cambridge, Cambridge University Press, 1963, II, section 4.
2 David Hume, *A Treatise of Human Nature*, Ernest C. Mossner (ed.) Harmondsworth, Penguin, 1969, p. 544.
3 David Hume, *Treatise*, p. 586.
4 David Hume, *Treatise*, p. 544.
5 David Hume, *Treatise*, p. 540.
6 David Hume, *Treatise*, p. 536.
7 David Hume, *Treatise*, p. 583.
8 David Hume, *Treatise*, pp. 538, 541, 590, 594.
9 David Hume, *Treatise*, p. 638.
10 David Hume, *Treatise*, pp. 541, 551, 585, 597.
11 David Hume, *Essays: Moral, Political and Literary*, Eugene F. Miller (ed.) Indianapolis, Liberty Classics, 1985.
12 David Hume, *Treatise*, p. 595.
13 David Hume, *Treatise*, p. 602.
14 David Hume, *Treatise*, p. 614.
15 David Hume, *Treatise*, p. 593.
16 David Hume, *Treatise*, p. 585.
17 David Hume, *Treatise*, p. 614.
18 David Hume, *Treatise*, p. 614.
19 David Hume, *Treatise*, p. 600. This reasoning is repeated in one of his *Essays*, 'Of the original contract'.
20 John Rawls, *A Theory of Justice*, London, Oxford and New York, Oxford University Press, 1971, p. 33.
21 John Zvesper, 'The utility of consent in John Locke's political philosophy', *Political Studies*, 1984, vol. 32, pp. 55–67.
22 John Gray, *Liberalism*, Milton Keynes, Open University Press, 1986, p. 51.
23 David Hume, *Treatise*, p. 617.
24 David Hume, *Treatise*, p. 614.
25 Bhikhu Parekh (ed.) *Bentham's Political Thought*, New York, Barnes & Noble, 1973, p. 269.
26 Bhikhu Parekh (ed.) *Bentham's Political Thought*, p. 269.
27 Bhikhu Parekh (ed.) *Bentham's Political Thought*, p. 315.
28 Bhikhu Parekh (ed.) *Bentham's Political Thought*, p. 316.
29 Bhikhu Parekh (ed.) *Bentham's Political Thought*, p. 289.
30 Bhikhu Parekh (ed.) *Bentham's Political Thought*, pp. 287–90.
31 Bhikhu Parekh (ed.) *Bentham's Political Thought*, p. 316.
32 Bhikhu Parekh (ed.) *Bentham's Political Thought*, p. 290.
33 Bhikhu Parekh (ed.) *Bentham's Political Thought*, p. 260.
34 Eugene F. Miller, 'The cognitive basis of Hayek's political thought', in Robert L. Cunningham (ed.) *Liberty and the Rule of Law*, College Station and London, Texas A & M University Press, 1975.
35 Joseph Cropsey, *Political Philosophy and the Issues of Politics*, Chicago, University of Chicago Press, 1977, pp. 19–31; Philip Pettit, *Judging Justice*, London, Boston and Henley, Routledge & Kegan Paul, 1980, chs

11, 13, 14; John Finnis, *Fundamentals of Ethics*, Oxford, Clarendon Press, 1983, pp. 81f.; and John Dunn, *Rethinking Modern Political Theory*, Cambridge, Cambridge University Press, 1985, p. 165.
36 Ronald Dworkin in programme 13 of the BBC television series 'Men of Ideas', broadcast in 1973.
37 Philip Abbott and Michael B. Levy (eds) *The Liberal Future in America*, Westport, Connecticut and London, Greenwood Press, 1985, p. 13.
38 Philip Abbott and Michael B. Levy (eds) *The Liberal Future in America*, p. 82.
39 Philip Abbott and Michael B. Levy (eds) *The Liberal Future in America*, p. 169.
40 Philip Abbott and Michael B. Levy (eds) *The Liberal Future in America*, p. 9.
41 Michael Walzer, *Spheres of Justice: A Defence of Pluralism and Equality*, Oxford, Martin Robertson, 1983, pp. 261, 279.
42 Michael J. Sandel, 'Introduction', in Michael J. Sandel (ed.) *Liberalism and Its Critics*, Oxford, Basil Blackwell, 1984, p. 6.
43 Michael J. Sandel, *Liberalism and the Limits of Justice*, Cambridge, Cambridge University Press, 1982, p. 6.
44 Michael J. Sandel, *Liberalism and the Limits of Justice*, p. 135.
45 Michael J. Sandel, *Liberalism and the Limits of Justice*, p. 164.
46 Michael J. Sandel, *Liberalism and the Limits of Justice*, p. 175.
47 Michael J. Sandel, *Liberalism and the Limits of Justice*, p. 180. For a critique of the insistence on the totally encumbered – or totally unencumbered – self, see Will Kymlicka, *Liberalism, Community and Culture*, Oxford, Clarendon, 1989, pp. 52f.
48 John Rawls, 'Justice as fairness: political not metaphysical', *Philosophy and Public Affairs*, 1985, vol. 14, pp. 238f.; see also Amy Gutmann, 'Communitarian critics of liberalism', *Philosophy and Public Affairs*, 1985, vol. 14, pp. 311–14.
49 John Rawls, 'The priority of right and ideas of the good', *Philosophy and Public Affairs*, 1988, vol. 17, pp. 252f., original emphasis.
50 E.g. John Dunn, *Western Political Theory in the Face of the Future*, Cambridge, Cambridge University Press, 1979, p. 50 n. 50; and *Rethinking Modern Political Theory*, p. 163; John N. Gray, 'Social contract, community and ideology', in Pierre Birnbaum, Jack Lively and Geraint Parry (eds) *Democracy, Consensus and Social Contract*, London and Beverly Hills, Sage, 1978, pp. 232f., 237f.
51 John Rawls, 'Kantian constructivism in moral theory', *Journal of Philosophy*, 1980, vol. 77, p. 518.
52 John Rawls, 'Kantian constructivism in moral theory', p. 518.
53 John Rawls, 'Kantian constructivism in moral theory', p. 537.
54 John Rawls, 'Kantian constructivism in moral theory', p. 519.
55 John Rawls, 'The idea of an overlapping consensus', *Oxford Journal of Legal Studies*, 1987, vol. 7, pp. 24f.
56 John Rawls, *A Theory of Justice*, p. 129.
57 John Rawls, *A Theory of Justice*, p. 281.
58 John Rawls, *A Theory of Justice*, pp.105f.
59 John Rawls, *A Theory of Justice*, pp. 269, 315.

60 John Rawls, 'Justice as fairness', pp. 230f.; see also p. 223; *A Theory of Justice*, pp. 14, 127, 211, 520f.; 'Kantian constructivism in moral theory', pp. 539–42.
61 John Rawls, 'Justice as fairness', p. 230; see also 'Social unity and primary goods', in Amartya Sen and Bernard Williams (eds) *Utilitarianism and Beyond*, Cambridge, Cambridge University Press, 1982, pp. 159, 183.
62 John Rawls, 'The priority of right', p. 256.
63 John Rawls, 'The idea of an overlapping consensus', p. 4 n. 7.
64 John Rawls, 'The idea of an overlapping consensus', pp. 8, 24.
65 Charles Larmore, 'Political liberalism', *Political Theory*, 1990, vol. 18, pp. 337, 346.
66 John Rawls, *A Theory of Justice*, pp. 74f., 119f., 136, 496f., 568.
67 John Rawls, *A Theory of Justice*, chs 8–9; and 'Social unity and primary goods', pp. 164, 184.
68 John Rawls, 'Justice as fairness', p. 231 n.4.
69 William A. Galston, 'Pluralism and social unity', *Ethics*, 1989, vol. 99, p. 724.
70 John Rawls, *A Theory of Justice*, pp. 31f., 505f. n. 30.
71 John Rawls, 'Justice as fairness', pp. 223, 231, 236 n. 19.
72 John Rawls, *A Theory of Justice*, pp. 21, 123, 580f.
73 John Rawls, *A Theory of Justice*, p. 121.
74 John Rawls, 'Kantian constructivism in moral theory', p. 570.
75 Alexis de Tocqueville, *Democracy in America*, tr. G. Lawrence, Garden City, New York, Doubleday, 1969, vol. II, part IV, ch. 1.
76 John Rawls, *A Theory of Justice*, pp. 201f.
77 John Rawls, 'Justice as fairness', p. 227; see also 'Kantian constructivism in moral theory', pp. 519f.
78 John Rawls, 'Justice as fairness', p. 233.
79 John Rawls, *A Theory of Justice*, p. 13
80 John Rawls, *A Theory of Justice*, pp. 13, 16.
81 John Rawls, *A Theory of Justice*, p. 16.
82 John Rawls, *A Theory of Justice*, pp. 112, 112f. n. 28.
83 John Rawls, *A Theory of Justice*, p. 261.
84 John Dunn, *Rethinking Modern Political Theory*, p. 183.
85 John Rawls, *A Theory of Justice*, p. 19.
86 John Rawls, *A Theory of Justice*, p. 15; see also pp. 72, 136.
87 John Rawls, *A Theory of Justice*, p. 102.
88 John Rawls, *A Theory of Justice*, p. 141.
89 John Rawls, *A Theory of Justice*, p. 179.
90 John Rawls, 'Social unity and primary goods', pp. 168f.
91 John Rawls, 'Social unity and primary goods', pp. 172f.
92 John Rawls, *A Theory of Justice*, pp. 107f.; see also p. 137.
93 John Rawls, *A Theory of Justice*, p. 453.
94 John Rawls, *A Theory of Justice*, p. 329.
95 John Rawls, *A Theory of Justice*, p. 505.
96 John Rawls, *A Theory of Justice*, p. 12; see also p. 19.
97 John Rawls, *A Theory of Justice*, p. 312.
98 John Rawls, *A Theory of Justice*, pp. 437ff.
99 John Rawls, 'Social unity and primary goods', pp. 159–67.

100 John Rawls, *A Theory of Justice*, p. 260.
101 John Rawls, 'Kantian constructivism in moral theory', pp. 549f.
102 John Rawls, *A Theory of Justice*, pp. 148f; see also p. 129. For Rawls, envy flows mainly from the absence of self-respect, so his 'well-ordered society', with its pervasive self-respect, can be made to seem impervious to the corrosive effects of envy (*A Theory of Justice*, pp. 530–41).
103 John Rawls, *A Theory of Justice*, p. 512.
104 Robert Nozick, *Anarchy, State, and Utopia*, Oxford, Basil Blackwell, 1974, p. 243.
105 Robert Nozick, *Anarchy, State, and Utopia*, p. 227.
106 Judith N. Shklar, 'Injustice, injury, and inequality', in Frank S. Lucash (ed.) *Justice and Equality Here and Now*, Ithaca, New York, Cornell University Press, 1985, p. 25.
107 Robert Nozick, *Anarchy, State, and Utopia*, p. 33.
108 John Finnis, *Fundamentals of Ethics*, p. 125.
109 John Rawls, *A Theory of Justice*, p. 252.
110 John Rawls, *A Theory of Justice*, p. 573.
111 John Rawls, *A Theory of Justice*, p. 437.
112 John Rawls, *A Theory of Justice*, p. 443.
113 John Rawls, *A Theory of Justice*, pp. 396, 436f.
114 John Rawls, 'Social unity and primary goods', p. 167.
115 William Galston, 'Defending liberalism', *American Political Science Review*, 1982, vol. 76, p. 515.
116 John Rawls, 'The priority of right', p. 265.
117 John Rawls, 'Kantian constructivism in moral theory', pp. 552f.
118 John Rawls, 'Kantian constructivism in moral theory', p. 553.
119 John Rawls, *A Theory of Justice*, pp. 462–79.
120 John Rawls, *A Theory of Justice*, p. 464.
121 John Locke, *Some Thoughts Concerning Education*, in James L. Axtell (ed.) *The Educational Writings of John Locke*, Cambridge, Cambridge University Press, 1968 [1693], sections 41, 73, 103.
122 Abraham Lincoln, Address at Baltimore, 18 April 1864, in Roy P. Basler (ed.) *The Collected Works of Abraham Lincoln*, 9 vols, New Brunswick, Rutgers University Press, 1953–5, vol. VII, p. 301.
123 Jean-Jacques Rousseau, *Emile*, tr. Allan Bloom, New York, Basic Books, 1979 [1762], book I, pp. 67f. Rousseau had made this point in his *Discourse on the Origins of Inequality Among Men* (note o), in *The First and Second Discourses*, tr. Roger D. Masters and Judith R. Masters, New York, St. Martin's Press, 1964, pp. 221f. Rousseau's is perhaps the most radical of all modern critiques of liberalism, because it traces the origins of inequality and unhappiness in liberal regimes not to material injustices but to the social psychology of *amour propre* (another expression for *thymos*) – absent, he claims, in natural man.
124 Thomas Hobbes, *Leviathan*, Harmondsworth, Penguin, 1968, ch. 15, p. 211.
125 Harvey C. Mansfield, Jr., 'The absent executive in Aristotle's *Politics*', in Thomas B. Silver and Peter W. Schramm (eds) *Natural Right and Political Right*, Durham, North Carolina, Carolina Academic Press, 1984, pp. 171–4.

126 John Rawls, *A Theory of Justice*, p. 384.

127 John Rawls, *A Theory of Justice*, pp. 363–91.

128 Alexis de Tocqueville, *Democracy in America*, vol. II, part IV, ch. 7.

129 John Rawls, *A Theory of Justice*, p. 441; and see p. 4 (justice is not subject to 'political bargaining'); p. 22 ('interest groups' – unlike 'political parties' which 'advance some conception of the public good' – are involved merely in 'petitioning the government on their own behalf'); and p. 537 (on the low public 'visibility' of 'noncompromising' groups in a well-ordered society).

130 John Rawls, *A Theory of Justice*, p. 473.

131 John Rawls, *A Theory of Justice*, p. 136; and see p. 360 ('There seems to be no way of allowing ['citizens and legislators'] to take a narrow or group-interested standpoint and then regulating the process so that it leads to a just outcome.')

132 John Rawls, *A Theory of Justice*, p. 337; and see pp. 356f. ('majority rule, however it is defined and circumscribed, has a subordinate place as a procedural device').

133 John Rawls, *A Theory of Justice*, p. 136.

134 John Rawls, *A Theory of Justice*, p. 383.

135 E.g. Oliver A. Johnson, 'The Kantian interpretation', *Ethics*, 1974, vol. 85, pp. 62–6; and Joe H. Hicks, 'Philosophers' contracts and the law', *Ethics*, 1974, vol. 85, p. 21. Rawls' reply, in 'Kantian constructivism in moral theory', p. 531, is unconvincing.

136 John Rawls, *A Theory of Justice*, p. 505; see also p. 19.

137 John Rawls, *A Theory of Justice*, p. 243; see also p. 214.

138 John Rawls, *A Theory of Justice*, p. 554.

139 John Rawls, *A Theory of Justice*, p. 554.

140 John Rawls, 'Justice as fairness', p. 234.

141 John Rawls, *A Theory of Justice*, pp. 423f.

142 John Rawls, *A Theory of Justice*, p. 424.

143 John Rawls, *A Theory of Justice*, p. 434.

144 John Rawls, *A Theory of Justice*, pp. 424–33.

145 John Rawls, *A Theory of Justice*, p. 450.

146 John Rawls, *A Theory of Justice*, p. 551; see also p. 416.

147 John Rawls, 'The priority of right', pp. 269, 272.

148 John Rawls, *A Theory of Justice*, p. 527.

149 Robert Nozick, *Anarchy, State, and Utopia*, p. 312.

150 Is it merely stylistic taste that leads Rawls to discuss conflicting desires in holiday plans to illustrate moral perplexity? (*A Theory of Justice*, pp. 412, 551f.). Contrast the saner approach of Erwin Straus, *Phenomenological Psychology*, London, Sydney and Wellington, Tavistock Publications, 1966, p. 172.

151 John Rawls, *A Theory of Justice*, p. 440; see also pp. 178, 396.

152 John Rawls, 'Kantian constructivism in moral theory', p. 568.

153 John Rawls, *A Theory of Justice*, p. 563; see also pp. 416, 424, 528f. and 565f. ('Plans that happen to be out of line must be revised').

154 John Rawls, *A Theory of Justice*, p. 396; see also pp. 92, 440.

155 John Rawls, *A Theory of Justice*, p. 179; see also p. 442.

156 John Rawls, *A Theory of Justice*, p. 536; see also pp. 543–6.

157 John Rawls, *A Theory of Justice*, p. 439; see also p. 553.
158 Ronald Dworkin, *A Matter of Principle*, Cambridge, Massachusetts, Harvard University Press, 1985, pp. 205, 301f.
159 John Rawls, *A Theory of Justice*, p. 445.
160 John Rawls, *A Theory of Justice*, p. 178.
161 John Rawls, *A Theory of Justice*, p. 243.
162 William A. Galston, *Justice and the Human Good*, Chicago and London, University of Chicago Press, 1980, p. 114.
163 All quotations of Walzer in this paragraph come from Michael Walzer, *Spheres of Justice*, pp. 272–80; see also the reference to Hegel on p. 259, and the quotation of the phrase from the Declaration of Independence, p. 320. William A. Galston, *Liberal Purposes: Goods, Virtues and Diversity in the Liberal State*, Cambridge, Cambridge University Press, 1991, pp. 44–54, has drawn attention to a minimal kind of universalism lurking within Walzer's recent thinking, but Galston also notices that there are severe limits on this universalism, which cause Walzer 'to risk democratic tyranny' rather than to allow the questioning of communally defined values on philosophical grounds.

6 Liberty and nature

1 James S. Fishkin, *Beyond Subjective Morality: Ethical Reasoning and Political Philosophy*, New Haven and London, Yale University Press, 1984, pp. 153–7. In a similar vein, John Rawls classifies what he calls 'moral perfectionism' together with racism: 'The priority of right and ideas of the good', *Philosophy and Public Affairs*, 1988, vol. 17, p. 265.
2 Alexander Solzhenitsyn, *Nobel Lecture*, tr. F. D. Reeve, New York, Farrar, Straus & Giroux, 1972, p. 22.
3 James Madison, *The Federalist*, Number 37, in Alexander Hamilton, James Madison and John Jay, *The Federalist Papers*, New York, New American Library, 1961 [1788–9], p. 228; for this interpretation, see Jeffrey D. Wallin, 'John Locke and the American Founding', in Thomas B. Silver and Peter W. Schramm (eds) *Natural Right and Political Right*, Durham, North Carolina, Carolina Academic Press, 1984, pp. 143–67.
4 Plato, *Republic*, tr. Allan Bloom, New York, Basic Books, 1968, 344a–344c; *Gorgias*, tr. M. C. Hembold, Indianapolis, Bobbs-Merrill, 1952, pp. 482–4, 513.
5 Thomas Hobbes, *Leviathan*, Harmondsworth, Penguin, 1968, chs 11, 14. The quotation is from ch. 11, p. 160.
6 Friedrich Nietzsche, *The Use and Abuse of History*, tr. Adrian Collins, Indianapolis, Bobbs-Merrill, 1957, p. 61; and 'Zarathustra's Prologue' in *Thus Spoke Zarathustra*, tr. W. Kaufman, in *The Portable Nietzsche*, New York, Viking, 1964, pp. 128–31.
7 John Locke, *Two Treatises of Government*, Peter Laslett (ed.) Cambridge, Cambridge University Press, 1963, II, section 43.
8 John Stuart Mill, 'Nature', in *Nature, The Utility of Nature, and Theism*, third edition, London, Longmans, 1885, p. 20.

9 Aristotle, *Politics*, tr. Carnes Lord, Chicago, University of Chicago Press, 1984, 1337a.

10 C. S. Lewis, *Studies in Words*, second edition, Cambridge, Cambridge University Press, 1967, ch. 2.

11 Harvey C. Mansfield, Jr., 'The absent executive in Aristotle's *Politics*', in Thomas B. Silver and Peter W. Schramm (eds) *Natural Right and Political Right*, pp. 193f.

12 Jacob Klein, 'On the nature of nature', *Independent Journal of Philosophy*, 1979, vol. 3, pp. 101–9.

13 Thomas Hobbes, *Leviathan*, ch. 46, p. 685.

14 Larry Arnhart, 'Aristotle's biopolitics: a defense of biological teleology against biological nihilism', *Politics and the Life Sciences*, 1988, vol. 6, pp. 181f.

15 Alexis de Tocqueville, *Democracy in America*, tr. G. Lawrence, Garden City, New York, Doubleday, 1969, vol. II, part II, ch. 15.

16 Alexander Rosenberg, *The Structure of Biological Science*, Cambridge, Cambridge University Press, 1985, ch. 3; Larry Arnhart, 'Aristotle's biopolitics', pp. 183f.

17 Ernst Mayr, *The Growth of Biological Thought: Diversity, Evolution and Inheritance*, Cambridge, Massachusetts, Harvard University Press, 1982, pp. 56, 88f.

18 Erwin W. Straus, *Phenomenological Psychology*, London, Sydney and Wellington, Tavistock Publications, 1966, p. 138.

19 A comparable trade-off occurs in the human larynx: 'The evolution of the larynx has forced awkward trade-offs between three different functions – respiration, phonation and the ingestion of food . . . . Among mammals, animals such as horses have larynges that are maximally efficient for respiration, which allows fast running. But social animals such as dogs and chimpanzees, who need to communicate with one another, sacrifice some respiratory efficiency in having larynges adapted for rudimentary vocal communication. Human beings have a capacity for even more complex vocalization, yet as a result their supralaryngeal tract is less efficient for breathing, chewing and swallowing. One severe consequence of the extreme adaptation of the human vocal apparatus for speech is that human beings are more prone to choking on food or liquid than are other animals. After the third month of life, the larynx of a human infant moves down the vocal tract to create an airway that can produce certain vowels and consonants beyond the range of other animals. But then food must pass over the opening of the larynx, and thus the human infant loses the ability, which it had during the first months of life, to breathe through the nose and swallow food simultaneously. The glorious consequence of all this is that human beings are better after-dinner speakers than chimpanzees. But the chimpanzees are more likely to enjoy the dinner without choking to death'. (Larry Arnhart, 'Aristotle, chimpanzees and other political animals', *Social Science Information*, 1990, vol. 29, pp. 523f., citing P. Lieberman, *The Biology and Evolution of Language*, Cambridge, Massachusetts, Harvard University Press, 1984.)

20 Erwin W. Straus, *Phenomenological Psychology*, p. 139.

21 Erwin W. Straus, *Phenomenological Psychology*, p. 161.

22 Erwin W. Straus, *Phenomenological Psychology*, p. 162.
23 Erwin W. Straus, *Phenomenological Psychology*, pp. 163f.
24 Robert Ornstein and David Sobel, *The Healing Brain*, New York, Simon & Schuster, 1987, chs 8–9.
25 Larry Arnhart, 'Aristotle, chimpanzees and other political animals', p. 548, citing Aristotle, *History of Animals*.
26 Oliver Sacks, *The Man Who Mistook His Wife for a Hat*, New York, Summit Books, 1985, ch. 10.
27 Ernst Mayr, *The Growth of Biological Thought*, pp. 50, 52, 89f.; Larry Arnhart, 'Aristotle's biopolitics', p. 187.
28 Oliver Sacks, *The Man Who Mistook His Wife for a Hat*, pp. 87f.
29 Robert Ornstein and David Sobel, *The Healing Brain*, pp. 132ff.; Joseph Campbell, *The Masks of God: Primitive Mythology*, New York, Penguin, 1969, pp. 39f.
30 Thomas Hobbes, *De Cive*, New York, Appleton-Century-Crofts, 1949, ch. I, section 7, p. 26; the rational deductions are made in *Leviathan*, chs 14–16.
31 Aristotle, *Nicomachean Ethics*, tr. H. Rackham, Cambridge, Massachusetts, Harvard University Press, 1934, 1103a 14–1103b 3.
32 Support for this Aristotelian idea can be derived from modern quantum physics; see Danah Zohar, *The Quantum Self*, London, Bloomsbury Publishing Ltd., 1990, pp. 165–9.
33 Leon R. Kass, *Toward a More Natural Science: Biology and Human Affairs*, New York, Free Press, 1985, p. 233; see also pp. 169, 173f.
34 Aristotle, *Politics* 1253a 31–7.
35 John Gray, *Liberalism*, Milton Keynes, Open University Press, 1986, pp. 46–8, citing Bernard Williams, *Morality: An Introduction to Ethics*, New York, Harper & Row, 1976, pp. 73f.
36 C. S. Lewis, *Studies in Words*, p. 71.
37 Michael Walzer, *Spheres of Justice: A Defence of Pluralism and Equality*, Oxford, Martin Robertson, 1983, p. 261.
38 Oliver Sacks, *The Man Who Mistook His Wife for a Hat*, pp. 105f., 119; see also pp. 28, 34, 37, 112f.
39 Robert Nozick, *Anarchy, State, and Utopia*, Oxford, Basil Blackwell, 1974, pp. 42–5.
40 Aristotle, *Nicomachean Ethics*, 1166a 20–2.
41 John Finnis, *Fundamentals of Ethics*, Oxford, Clarendon Press, 1983, pp. 39f.
42 John Gray, *Liberalism*, pp. 39, 49, citing Stuart Hampshire, *Freedom of Mind*, Princeton, Princeton University Press, 1971, pp. 78f.
43 Aristotle, *Politics*, 1323a 28–34.
44 Erwin W. Straus, *Phenomenological Psychology*, p. 183.
45 The classical account of the clash between the extremes of unreflective piety and complete conventionalism is (the Greek) Herodotus' presentation of (the Persian) Darius' conventionalist contrast between the attitudes of the pious Indians and those of the thoughtful Greeks towards their respective funeral customs. For a thoughtful commentary, see Leon R. Kass, *Toward a More Natural Science*, ch. 11.
46 Leon R. Kass, 'Death with dignity & the sanctity of life', *Commentary*, March 1990, pp. 33–43.

47 Thomas Jefferson, Letter to Henry Lee, 8 May 1825, in Adrienne Koch and William Peden (eds) *The Life and Selected Writings of Thomas Jefferson*, New York, Modern Library, 1944, p. 719.

48 John Adams, 'Letters of "Novanglus"', 23 January 1775, in Robert J. Taylor, Mary-Jo Kline, Gregg L. Lint and Celeste Walker (eds) *Papers of John Adams*, Cambridge, Massachusetts, Harvard University Press, 1977–, vol. II, p. 230.

49 Aristotle, *Politics*, 1255b 16–21; see also 1279a 9–22.

50 Algernon Sidney, *Discourses Concerning Government*, New York, Arno Press, 1979, ch. II, section 1, p. 66; see also ch. III, section 23.

51 Ralph Ketcham, *Presidents Above Party: The First American Presidency, 1789–1829*, Chapel Hill, The University of North Carolina Press, 1984, p. 113.

52 Aristotle, *Politics*, 1330a 31; Harry V. Jaffa, *Crisis of the House Divided*, second edition, Seattle and London, University of Washington Press, pp. 342–6.

53 Aristotle, *Politics*, 1254b 16–26; cf. John Locke, *Two Treatises*, II, section 60.

54 Aristotle, *Politics*, 1328a 7–10; and *Nicomachean Ethics*, 1161b; Ken Masugi, 'Another peek at Aristotle and Phyllis: the place of women in Aristotle's argument for human equality', in Thomas B. Silver and Peter W. Schramm (eds) *Natural Right and Political Right*, p. 287 n. 41. It is often assumed that Cicero's emphasis on the equality of all members of the human species conflicted with Aristotelian thought. But this was not Cicero's assumption. The famous statement of human equality in his *Laws* (in *De Re Publica, De Legibus*, tr. Clinton Walker Keyes, London, William Heinemann Ltd, 1970, I, x, 28 – xii, 34) claims the authority of the political philosophers in general, including Aristotelians. Cicero's statement here also explains the political inadequacy of the anti-Socratic, hedonistic view that would distinguish between true human utility and the justice that is naturally appropriate to and sensed by all humans equally. This anti-Socratic philosophy could attack the institution of human slavery as a merely conventional imposition resting on force, but could not stop itself from going on to attack and to undermine all political institutions on the same grounds. Those who would base modern liberalism on pre-Socratic philosophy overlook the deeply antipolitical character of that philosophy.

55 Aristotle, *Politics*, 1284b 26–34, 1288a 15–29.

56 Aristotle, *Politics*, 1332b 17–27, 1287b 41–1288a 5.

57 Thomas Jefferson, Letter to Roger C. Weightman, 24 June 1826, in *Life and Selected Writings*, pp. 729f.

58 Consider John Locke, *Some Thoughts Concerning Education*, in James L. Axtell (ed.) *The Educational Writings of John Locke*, Cambridge, Cambridge University Press, 1968 [1693], sections 145, 188–9.

59 Aristotle, *Politics*, 1279a 9–13.

60 Joseph Raz, 'The rule of law and its virtue', in Robert L. Cunningham (ed.) *Liberty and the Rule of Law*, College Station and London, Texas A & M University Press, 1975, p. 14.

61 Aristotle, *Politics*, 1287a 16–b 35, 1318b 38–40.

62 Aristotle, *Politics*, 1324b 5–9, 1325a 1–8; and *Nicomachean Ethics*, 1179b 30–1180b 13.
63 Aristotle, *Politics*, 1280a 25–1281a 5.
64 Stephen Macedo, *Liberal Virtues: Citizenship, Virtue, and Community in Liberal Constitutionalism*, Oxford, Clarendon Press, 1990, p. 58.
65 John Rawls, 'The idea of an overlapping consensus', *Oxford Journal of Legal Studies*, 1987, vol. 7, pp. 15, 18; and 'The priority of right', p. 256; see also above, Chapter 5, pp. 127f.
66 John Dunn, *Rethinking Modern Political Theory*, Cambridge, Cambridge University Press, 1985, p. 168.
67 John Locke, *A Letter Concerning Toleration*, tr. W. Popple, Indianapolis and New York, Bobbs-Merrill, 1955 [1689], p. 48.
68 William A. Galston, 'Liberal virtues', *American Political Science Review*, 1988, vol. 82, p. 1287.
69 John Locke, *Two Treatises*, II, section 111.
70 Ken Masugi, 'Another peek at Aristotle and Phyllis', p. 283.
71 E.g. Aristotle, *Nicomachean Ethics*, 1179b 7–18.
72 Aristotle, *Politics*, 1295a 2

Index

For Product Safety Concerns and Information please contact our EU
representative GPSR@taylorandfrancis.com
Taylor & Francis Verlag GmbH, Kaufingerstraße 24, 80331 München, Germany